The Oldie

Annual 2021

Introduction

By *Harry Mount*, Editor, The Oldie

In her marvellous piece in these pages, the greatest living Australian, Dame Edna Everage, describes a book of wise thoughts she discovered in her mother's matinée jacket the night she burnt her things. 'There are no such things as crow's feet,' Dame Edna's mother wrote. 'Just the dried-up beds of old smiles.'

Well, there are plenty of smiles in this glorious *Oldie* annual, edited by the peerless Liz Anderson.

Here you'll find the greatest hits of *The Oldie* since it was founded by the great Richard Ingrams in 1992. Richard himself writes a characteristically iconoclastic rant against red kites. Beloved by many, kites are loathed by Ingrams, who's keenly looking forward to his first kite cull.

When Richard set up *The Oldie*, he brought with him old friends from his *Private Eye* diaries, including the late Auberon Waugh – appearing here in his original Rage column, bemoaning the great gulf of knowledge that separates oldies from youngies. Bron would have been comforted by this annual, which is full of figures that planet-brained oldies are devoted to.

Like Ian Lavender, who celebrates the 50th anniversary of *Dad's Army* by recalling his heavenly times as Private Pike. He adored his seven fellow cast members: 'My seven new teachers each summer, and eventually seven new friends. The down side of having these seven new older friends was that I was going to lose them early in my life. I was not long out of teens and they were my dream oldies.' Handkerchief, please!

One of the mournful occupational hazards of being *The Oldie*'s editor is employing talented writers who are mature in years – and then shuffle off their mortal coil to meet the final deadline. Among our much-missed columnists here is Wilfred De'Ath, who died in 2020, aged 82. The old rogue writes in his customarily grand way about the poor time-keeping and bad taste in interior décor of his heroic, long-suffering doctors.

Other *Oldie* stars between these covers are Edward Enfield (1929-2019) and our patron saint and deputy editor, Jeremy Lewis (1942-2017). We were privileged, too, to print regular *Oldie* contributor John Julius Norwich in his last ever article, about his friend Paddy Leigh Fermor, in 2018, only weeks before his death.

Enough mourning, though! In this ever more serious, ever more censorious age, the joy of *The Oldie* is in its laughs, free of any woke sensibilities. Alexander Chancellor, our much-missed editor from 2014 to his death in 2017, had the most memorable of laughs himself – and was gifted in commissioning amusing articles. It was Alexander who asked Craig Brown, Britain's funniest journalist, to write about Tintin, the world's most famous journalist, in 2016 – one of our most popular cover stories, incidentally.

Talking of funny people, Nicholas Parsons stars here, in his last interview, in 2017, where he revealed he was baffled by the mystery of *Just A Minute*'s success: 'The essence of comedy is that you pause for effect, you repeat for emphasis and you deviate for surprise. Yet these three things are exactly what you can't do in *Just A Minute*!'

The laughs just keep coming in these pages. Sir Les Patterson, Anne Robinson, Raymond Briggs, Beryl Bainbridge, Great Bores of Today, Gyles Brandreth… It's like some grand reunion of our greatest writers, some joining us from heaven, some happily still with us. Praise be!

Published by The Oldie magazine, Moray House, 23/31 Great Titchfield Street, London W1W 7PA www.theoldie.co.uk
Copyright © 2019 Oldie Publications Ltd. Printed by Wyndeham Roche Ltd
The Oldie would like to thank all the writers, illustrators and cartoonists whose work is reproduced in these pages
Editor: Liz Anderson **Design:** Lawrence Bogle **Cover:** Quentin Blake

Contents

1 **Introduction** by Harry Mount

4 **Sorry, Madam** by Angela Huth

5 **Off the rails** by James Michie

6 **Rage** by Auberon Waugh

7 **The marriage was breaking up: short story** by Alice Thomas Ellis

8 **Blast** compiled by Neil Shand

9 **Blog:** General Sir Peter Duffell

9 **How Boney snuffed it** by Tibor Csato

10 **Letter from Edna Everage**

11 **The French connection** by Patrick Marnham

12 **Robert Morley: a downright upright all-round man** by Christopher Matthew

14 **Stump Cross Roundabout** by Germaine Greer

15 **Food** by Jennifer Paterson

17 **Press** by Roy Greenslade

18 **Change for a tenor** by Robert Tear

20 **The life and death of a bookshop** by Bryan Forbes

21 **Looking for a result** by David Ransom

22 **Pin-ups** by Sir Les Patterson

23 **Video** by Larry Adler

23 **Down on the allotment** by Fiona Pitt-Kethley

I once met WH Auden by Oliver Stanley

26 **True blue: short story** by Paul Pickering

28 **Getting started** by Colin Clark

29 **What the young don't know** by Jeremy Paxman

31 **Pin-ups** by Gyles Brandreth

33 **Arthur and the Paignton Peach** by John Moynihan

34 **Thoughts on death** by Philip Callow

35 **I once met the Duke of Windsor** by Patrick Skene Catlin

36 **East of Islington** by Sam Taylor

37 **The ones that got away** by Charles Osborne

38 **Just the job** by Hugh O'Shaughnessy

39 **I once met Enid Blyton** by Terence Daum

40 **Hunters in the night** by Penelope Bennett

41 **Beauty and the freak show** by Joan Rhodes

42 **Shopping** by Alice Pitman

43 **Interview with Gene Wilder** by Mavis Nicholson

46 **Change your life. Do nothing** by Stephen Cottrell, Archbishop of York

47 **Brush up your put-downs** by Miles Kington

48 **Fred Whitsey on the garden at Hidcote** by Charles Elliott

48 **Michael Whitehall's tales of an actor's agent** by Hugh Massingberd

49 **Film** by Marcus Berkmann

50 **The joy of the axe** by Jennie Erdal

52 **Egypt's Old Cataract Hotel under threat** by Francis King

54 **I once met Lord Goodman** by Edward Mirzoeff

56 **Last chance saloon** by Des Wilson

57 **Perfect Puglia** by Patrick Reyntiens

58 **Cartoon** by Mike Williams

59 **Taking a trip** by Nina Bawden

59 **An Orthodox Voice** by John Michell

61 **Words: an Orcadian selection** by Diarmaid O Muirithe

63 **Michael Heath's Great Bores of Today** by Fant and Dick

64 **Labour of love** by Ken Cooper

66 **I once met the last king of Laos** by Jonathan Fryer

67 **Sport** by Frank Keating

67 **Not many dead**

67 **Tips for meanies** by Jane Thynne

68 **The world according to Edward Enfield**

69 **Life in the Pennines** by Geoffrey Moorhouse

69 **Rant** by Richard Ingrams

71 **Theatre** by Beryl Bainbridge

71 **Rant** by Mark Baker

72 **1963 and all that** by Stanley Price

73 **All tied up** by Raymond Briggs

74 **St Dorothy of New York?** by Stuart Reid

76 **I once met Ronnie Kray** by Duncan Campbell

78 **So well devised** by Douglas Hurd

80 **The sign of the cross** by Jane Gardam

81 **A jewel of a show** by Sara Wheeler

82 **I once met Bill Cotton** by Mel Hannaghan

82 **Genius crossword** by Antico

83 **Profitable Wonders** by James Le Fanu

84 **Waiting for the bird** by Ursula Holden

85 **Me and my doctors** by Wilfred De'Ath

86 **Gore and grief in Gdansk** by Simon Rae

88 **Superbyways: A Kindle convert** by Webster

89 **World's worst dumps: MediaCityUK** by Norman Deplume

90 **Dr Stuttaford's Surgery**

91 **Cookery** by Elisabeth Luard

91 **Pedants' Revolt**

92 **House Husbandry** by Giles Wood

93 **Granny Annexe** by Virginia Ironside

94 **Finding your final resting place** by Peter Stanford

96 **Music** by Richard Osborne

97 **Whiteboard jungle** by Kate Sawyer

98 **Unwrecked England: Luxulyan Valley Viaduct** by Candida Lycett Green

99 **Mind the Age Gap** by Lizzie Enfield

99 **Rant** by Stephen Heath

100 **Happy Birthday, Briggsy** by Russell Davies

102 **Edward Thomas's Adlestrop** by PJ Kavanagh

104 **Living Hell** by Jeremy Lewis

105 **Gardening** by David Wheeler

105 **Blog:** Liz Hodgkinson

106 **I'm with the uke band** by Trevor Grove

107 **Bird of the Month: the lapwing** by John McEwen

108 **Queen of the flies** by Patrick Bishop

110 **Tintin as saviour** by Craig Brown

112 **God** by Sister Teresa

112 **Learn Latin** by Harry Mount

113 **Restaurants** by James Pembroke

113 **Genius crossword solution**

113 **Classic read** by Matthew Parris

114 **Sixty seconds that hooked the nation** by Valerie Grove

116 **Getting Dressed: Prue Leith** by Brigid Keenan

117 **Short Cuts** by Anne Robinson

118 **The ruthless guide to parties** by Rachel Johnson

119 **Content on Como** by Henrietta Bredin

120 **Paddy the Great, king of Greece** by John Julius Norwich

122 **A Dad's Army feud? Who do you think you are kidding?** by Ian Lavender

124 **Grumpy Oldie Man** by Matthew Norman

125 **The Doctor's Surgery** by Theodore Dalrymple

125 **Kitchen Garden: apricots** by Simon Courtauld

GIVE A SUBSCRIPTION TO THE OLDIE

and get a FREE copy of our new Oldie Cartoon book worth £7.95

12 issues for £30 - a saving of £27 on the shop price

For overseas subscriptions, simply add £4 per sub anywhere in the world

CALL 0330 333 0195 NOW quoting 'Annual'

or visit https://subscribe.theoldie.co.uk/ and input code Annual

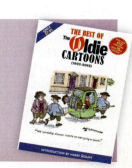

MARCH 1992

Sorry, Madam

Angela Huth seeks out an old-fashioned wash and set

'I can do you a scrunch,' said the nymphet in the pink nylon overall. She ran limp fingers through her own scrunch — hair that resembled the feeblest kind of scrambled eggs. 'Scrunching is all we do, like, for drying.'

She was approximately the 11th hairdresser to offer me a scrunch and to smile, with all the superiority of the untalented, at the very idea of doing anything more appropriate to my own curly hair.

'We don't straighten, we don't have no truck with rollers, all that,' she added. 'We're into the natural look.'

There was no point in explaining that the natural look, in my case, is manic Brillo. It's hair that needs discipline, I felt like confiding, but she wouldn't have been interested. After all, her scrunching ways are sought after by those whose ideal hair is a long tangled mess that needs flicking back every 45 seconds. Why should she bother about the tricky demands of the over-30s? Oldies like you shouldn't even bother to go to the hairdresser, I read in her skinny little mind.

Such humiliations were my own fault. When I came to live in Oxford 14 years ago I realised I could no longer travel to Sloane Street once a week to visit Patricia. I tried numerous local hairdressers, only to find that the art of coiffure does not exist outside London. Certainly there's no establishment in Oxford I could recommend, except to scrunch-lovers. Arrogant, slow, expensive, snooty, they concern themselves with trends rather than skills. I soon gave up in despair. The manic Brillo is now washed in the bath, my sister straightens the back if I'm going to a party and four times a year Patricia cuts it exactly as I want it, and, with a rare delicacy of tact, enters into a conspiracy with Loving Care, Dark Brown, to retain the colour I once was before two decades of blonde streaks.

Ah, Patricia. Our salon days began in 1957. I had just broken away from my mother's hairdresser in D H Evans, who would pin my 'quiff' into a kiss curl with two kirby-grips –- and was looking for someone with a touch more panache. Patricia, newly at Alan Spiers of Berkeley Square, with her conker-coloured hair

and chic little shirtwaisters, her lilting Welsh giggle and constant friendly smile, was just the person I was after. Like some of her other very early clients, including Maggie Smith, I followed her from salon to salon until at last, in 1966, she and her partner Aldo opened the immensely popular and welcoming Cadogan Club, recently moved to Lowndes Street.

Down the years, gazing at each other's reflections through kind mirrors, Patricia and I are able to believe the illusion that we haven't changed a jot. We've been through so much: the pure blonde, the streaks, the beehive, the Edwardian bun for glamorous nights, the extravagant hairpiece, the rollers, the blow dry, the sadness at the first twinkle of grey. And now the slightly shorter cut. 'Long swinging grey hair,' says Patricia, 'is something I try to guide against.'

Actually, her art is not to try too hard in her guiding, but to comply more or less with what her client wants. So among her old faithfuls the Lady Something who wishes to continue with her raven Sixties beehive is under no pressure to change.

Those of the frizzled grey perm are happily accommodated, while the anti-grey league are discreetly dazzled with a vast choice of burnished rinses. *Coups de vieilles* are treated with such kindness that they swing out of the salon almost waving their walking sticks.

Patricia says: 'Modern salons are very insecure, arrogant and unwelcoming, full of little Napoleons with absolutely no sense of humour. Most of them aren't remotely interested in anyone over 25.' In fact, some 25 per cent of her clients are under 25, another 25 per cent are real oldies. Of these, the very distinguished writer Frances Partridge is the most senior at the age of 92.

But the Cadogan Club is far from a geriatric parlour. The majority of clients are middle-aged oldies, including actresses, editors, politicians, visitors such as Jackie Onassis and Lee Radziwill. And these days there are even men, who no longer slink downstairs. Sir Nicholas Henderson, Michael Heseltine, Robert Kee and John Wells are all regulars. Some of them have minor flings elsewhere, only to return.

Recently, tempted by a much publicised trendy hairdresser, I myself sneaked off to a terrifying salon where androgynous clients and cutters were indistinguishable. When finally the Hair God deigned to pick over my hair, he did so with all the distaste of a chimp scouring the head of an enemy. I explained what I wanted. He had a better idea, he said, and gave me his Duchess of the Week Cut, which cost £72, and which took six months to grow out. Oldies can't take too much of that sort of thing. It sets them back.

Patricia heard, of course, and welcomed my return. I shan't be leaving her again. I mean, there are not many hair places where young and old can mix so easily together. Or where the willing patronne, in her supreme versatility, is as adept at scrunching (yes, she'll even do that, with a gritted smile, if asked) as she is at making her aging friends feel that there is still glamorous life in what remains of their crepuscular hair.

MARCH 1992

Off the rails

James Michie won't travel without sandwiches and a whistle

It began the moment I got my Senior Citizen's railcard — a series of haunting experiences on public transport which have left me a prematurely hunched and nervous traveller.

On the first occasion I was gazing out of the train near Didcot, recalling that this was the very stretch of landscape I had been passing 15 years before when I had hungoverly swallowed a large dollop of marmalade full of slivers of glass; how I had had to wrestle with the decision whether to get out at Reading and present myself at a hospital, or to chance it and keep my appointment in London; how the waiter had gravely offered to deduct the marmalade from the breakfast bill (oh, dear, dead days) . . . when phunk! and some other slivers of glass fell from the window between my feet and those of two newspaper-reading men opposite me. There was a pause and the papers were lowered. 'I say, that was a bullet, wasn't it?' remarked one. 'Definitely a bullet,' agreed the other.

There was a long, phlegmatically British pause. 'Ought we to report it to somebody or other?' 'Can't actually see a bullet,' said Basil Radford (by now we were all self-consciously playing parts in *The Lady Vanishes*). 'They'll only hang about for ages in Reading. Let's not make a fuss.' 'Good point,' conceded Naunton Wayne, and again the papers were raised. A second crucial decision about broken glass had been taken in my railway life.

Immediately afterwards I experienced a disturbing week on the Metropolitan Tube line. On Monday, in a packed carriage, I was holding my small son in my arms, caressing him clumsily on his fretful way to school, when a Scotch voice rang out: 'Look at the way he's playing with the wee laddie! It's a disgrrrace!' All heads turned, while I tried to juggle Edward into a more 'normal' position. 'There he goes — he's at it again! ' cried the terrible Old Person from Fife. I owed my escape from lynching to some large, motherly women who took my side.

> **'You know, it doesn't take very long to kill somebody with your hands. I could do that lot in about four minutes'**

The next day I was button-holed by a man in khaki shorts who, as if I were his ally, asked me at the top of his voice if I didn't agree that the carriage was filthy and that there were far too many black faces in it. I got out at the next station — the first time I had ever alighted at Royal Oak.

Friday was the climax. I was sitting minding my own business (never mind what it was) when I noticed that the middle-aged man next to me was gently leaning sideways to say something. He was conventionally dressed, his eyes were unglazed, there were no traces of foam around his lips, no suspicion of drink or drugs in the air. I got ready to inform him that I didn't have the time because I don't carry a watch. 'Do you see those people over there?' he asked, pointing to three unexceptional tourists in mackintoshes standing ten feet away. I said I did. 'Well, I could easily kill them all with my hands.' The nature of his message was so unexpected that I felt like the curate who has just seen his bishop park chewing gum on the altar-rail. 'Oh?' I vouchsafed. This clearly didn't satisfy him. 'You know, it doesn't take very long to kill somebody with your hands. I could do that lot in about four minutes.' I fled — Royal Oak again, damn it — searching for a parting shot, but the words that emerged from my mouth were grotesquely inane: 'The best of British luck, sir,' I said.

'I turned to share the transport — Oh, with whom... ?' (Wordsworth).

After that, I took to travelling self-protectively, as if I were dozing. The result, of course, was that I actually went on the Bakerloo line, just before Queen's Park, where the train terminated. When I woke up, I was alone in a stationary carriage, in a vast, silent, crepuscular shed, a sort of train dormitory.

'And when I found the door was shut, I tried to turn the handle, but — ' I could end here, with myself talking to myself and night deepening, but what in fact happened was that after half an hour I was released by a man who seemed more frightened of me than I was of him. From now on, I shall never travel without sandwiches, book, torch, whistle, miniature radio, blanket and 'Deaf and Dumb' lapel badge. Watch out for me.

'Yeah, you're right - there's something in your eye'

Rage

Auberon Waugh

If a single historical event launched *The Oldie* in the same way that the abduction of Helen from Sparta launched the Trojan war, then it was surely the death of Freddie Mercury. If he lives in history, it will be for this reason, that by establishing an unbridgeable gulf between the generations in Britain, his death created a new awareness and pride among older people which might yet rescue our collapsing national culture.

A young man's death from Aids is always a sad business, as it is indeed from soft drinks poisoning, or salmonella poisoning from eggs, or listeria from cheese or apoplexy for any reason. But Easter Monday's tribute to Freddie Mercury carried grief a stage further, like the former Hindu custom of suttee.

Over 72,000 were expected to cram into Wembley Stadium. An extra 200 medical staff were recruited, in case anybody fell ill from Aids or apoplexy or any other cause. The audience was expected to consume 20,000 hamburgers, 26,000 pints of lager and 64,000 soft drinks — in the course of a day. One can almost smell the poverty of the young people from these figures alone, even without a sight of their sad, shapeless clothing in cheap man-made fabrics, their ugly, worn canvas shoes, their uncoiffed hair ... but it is not material shortages which impress on these occasions, so much as the intellectual and cultural poverty.

A billion people in 80 countries watched this sad spectacle on television, while millions listened to it on their wirelesses. It was hailed in the *Standard* as the biggest memorial tribute in the history of the world. One thinks of all the men who have lived, from Alexander the Great and Joan of Arc through Shakespeare, Dr Johnson and Beethoven. What is it about this young man that justifies the biggest tribute in the history of the world?

The answer is that technology has given us vastly improved means of communication without giving us anything to say to each other. What was being celebrated on Easter Monday was nothing to do with an ugly and untalented, possibly unpleasant Persian singer from Zanzibar. It was a festival of international unanimity, celebrating an inability to communicate except in this debased and meaningless language.

There can no longer be any such thing as the Renaissance man, at ease in all the cultures of our fragmented society. Many young people were incredulous when told that we oldies had never heard of Freddie Mercury and his Queens, suspecting an affectation. When they discovered we were telling the truth, they were appalled, rather as we are when we learn they have never heard of Socrates or the Crusades.

Our mutual incomprehension grows. A half-page in the *Times* was recently taken up with an advertisement for Nigel Dempster's Diary. I have known Dempster for many years and am perfectly familiar with his Diary, but this turned out to be a mini-computer. The test promised 'an extensive data base. Comprehensive diary and time-management facilities. And a host of other useful utilities. Like dialling telephone numbers for you.'

I can just about understand the last claim — like those Swiss Army penknives which promise to remove stones from a horse's hoof — but am not sure what a time-management facility might be. Is this computer jargon for an alarm clock? As I read on, my wonder grew. 'Pre-emptive Multi-tasking (it's work-hungry). It drives dot-matrix, bubble-jet and laser printers ... The difference is you don't need computer skills to use it: icons, menus and question-and-answer boxes guide you through everything.'

My scepticism about the advantage of a computerised pocket diary derives from the fact that I seem to live a happy, comfortable life with an ordinary pocket diary, even if it does not dial telephone numbers for me or drive a dot-matrix. What advantage is there for those who live in the computer age using their diaries to dial telephone numbers? When I compare their microwave cooking, their soft drinks and lager beer, and hideous man-made fibre garments with food, wine and clothing as they were known to previous generations, I am happy in my ignorance. What other satisfactions are available to them? The women seem deliberately to make themselves as sexually unattractive as possible (possibly from fear of date-rape) and the men to cultivate a goofy babyishness (possibly to alleviate such fears).

Yet they seem happy in that condition, and would not change places with us. It saddens me that our cultures seem to have practically no points in common. Have they ever heard a nightingale?

Thou wast not born for death, immortal Bird!
No hungry generations tread thee down;
The voice I heard this passing night was heard
In ancient days by emperor and clown.

It is unlikely they will have read much Keats, I fear, because their education has deliberately concentrated on modern rubbish. John Patten, the new Education Minister, hopes they may yet be saved by a religious revival, teaching them the difference between good and evil. I doubt it's working. Saved from what and for what? If they are happy driving bubble-jets in plastic clothing, eating burgers, drinking soft drinks and listening to the noise of Freddie Mercury or whoever has succeeded him, why should we worry about them?

I hoped to find the answer in Bryan Appleyard's latest masterpiece. *Understanding the Present: Science and the Soul of Modern Man*. If anybody can explain the present, I feel Appleyard can. Yet in my case, I found he couldn't. His points of reference are too various. We all know different things. There is no common culture. We must each of us find our way through as best we can.

The marriage was breaking up

Short story by *Alice Thomas Ellis*

The marriage was breaking up – like a smart ship coming suddenly on submerged wreckage: wreckage too deep to see, but not deep enough to disregard.

They had married at a time when the prevailing mood was known as permissiveness, and had agreed that they must both feel free to have relationships with other people – as many and as often as they wished, but while Wyn had seen this merely as a means of keeping the options open, of avoiding unnecessary tensions and frustrations, Greta had taken it as a directive. At the reception she had kissed a wedding guest, on the mouth, standing behind a dish-laden trolley in full view of both sides of the family before the confetti had fallen from her hair.

The other guests had cried, 'You'll have to keep an eye on her, Wyn', but Wyn knew how much she loved him and felt no real apprehension. She was tall and fair and friendly; and while Wyn knew she was not particularly bright, he didn't mind in the least, because he was quite aware that he wasn't either. He was successful, but he was not what is known as an intellectual. Many of their friends were, but that didn't matter. Wyn and Greta were beautiful and smart, and when the children arrived, they were too, and they all got on together exceedingly well – Wyn and Greta and the children – and Wyn bought his wife glorious clothes and a lot of expensive things because he loved her and was proud of her.

Greta didn't flaunt and Wyn didn't sulk, and because it was all so open the lovers felt no need either to skulk or preen, and the smart ship sailed smoothly along, full in the light, exciting little remark. They were, it was widely felt, an ideal couple.

Then one day Wyn had an affair of his own. She was rather like Greta, but older, and she worked with Wyn and was nearly as good at her job as he was. Wyn was always the first to know when Greta had found a new fancy, but for some reason he didn't tell her about his affair, though, of course, someone else did. Greta's best friend, who was small and dark, remarked with wistful spite that she thought it was wonderful – how free their marriage was, and how strong.

Greta appeared to go mad. She went to Wyn's place of work and scratched the woman. For weeks she kept turning up at odd moments when Wyn was busy with clients, to sniff his clothes and look in cupboards. Her jaw took on a hard new line and she watched him sideways, through narrowed eyes.

This put a complete end to Wyn's affair. The woman did not leave her job, but now they seldom even spoke. He didn't mind much – his affections had not been deeply engaged and Greta was loving him so intensely that he would have been too tired to bother with another woman anyway. Life went back to normal and they both grew older, like everyone else. The children were big enough to leave home now, and Greta was less busy in the house. She got bored. Potential lovers were still fairly numerous, but not as numerous as they had been, so she had an affair with one of the intellectuals who previously hadn't attracted her at all.

She read *Effie Briest* and started on *Swann's Way*. One day at dinner she observed that she did not care for Capability Brown, that his great sweeps of turf and trees were ersatz, a lie, an imitation of nature, and his ha-has far more class-conscious and repressive than an honest wall would have been.

To his profound amazement Wyn realised that she had thought this out for herself, although none of the dinner guests believed it. They naturally assumed that she must be having an affair, and those who already knew thought they heard in her words the echo of the intellectual.

For the first time the word 'cuckold' took on meaning and importance for Wyn. It did not upset him unduly, but it was there, sitting in his mind like a fat bird, regarding him unblinkingly and demanding that he take a point of view. He stood back and looked at his wife and himself, and he decided on divorce. He said she could have the house and all its contents, and the car and the cats, and even the children, should they return and she want them. He suggested she should travel and take a course at the Open University. He said he would pay for anything she needed.

Greta went mad again. She scratched the intellectual, and attempted suicide. She appeared one night, stark naked under her fur coat, in Wyn's place of work, where he had once more retired. And when he refused her she went back to the house and cut up the leather Chesterfield with her Sabatier knives. Then she wrote him anonymous letters and told all his clients that he was a pervert. She even told the children that he wasn't their father.

Wyn began to look old but he remained quite immovable; consistently reasonable and courteous. He told Greta that she must forget him and settle down again with the someone (or someones) who would love her and look after her and make her happy.

And those with the sense to comprehend knew that the marriage was now quite over, and that Wyn no longer loved Greta, because he really did not wish to see her ever again and he truly and honestly wished her well.

Blast
40 Modern Irritations

To some, it's oafs who insist on using golf umbrellas on crowded city pavements. To almost everybody, it's Graham Taylor, the England soccer manager. These are the annoyances that really get our dandruff up, as Sam Goldwyn used to say.
Compiled by Neil Shand

1 Sportsmen who cry.
2 Call out and standing charges.
3 'At least you don't have to worry about Aids.'
4 Radio Four bishops called Jim.
5 'You are invading my space.'
6 Bus stops with an exclusion zone that prevents buses stopping any closer than 20 yards away.
7 'To be honest with you.'
8 Celebrities who are running out of closets to come out of.
9 Nigel Kennedy (pic right).
10 The time sponsored by Accurist.
11 Shrink-wrapping on video cassettes, toothbrushes and supermarket cheeses.
12 Pony-tails, except on ponies.
13 Dustbin liners that are too small for the dustbin.
14 'He's in a meeting.'
15 'Baby on Board' stickers.
16 'The code for so-and-so has been changed.'
17 Films on TV with the News in the middle.
18 'Got any spare change?'
19 English subtitles at Covent Garden when it's the ENO that needs them.
20 'Punters', as in 'Don't worry, the punters will love it.'
21 The Sign of Peace.
22 'Take care.'
23 The oldie habit of telling you how well you look. One never hears 20-year-olds saying to each other, 'You look very well.'
24 New Men. Especially New Men who are trying to 'get in touch with their feelings' on the Life pages of the *London Evening Standard*.
25 The 'Phone Book' which replaced 'A-D' etc.
26 Clothing sales where the only overcoats are 46 L or 38 R.
27 InterCity guards who can't stay off the public address system.
28 People getting away with more than five items at a five-items-or-less supermarket checkout; unless it's oneself, in which case the grievance becomes miserable checkout cashiers who won't even let you have just one piddling little item more at the five-item checkout.
29 People who say 'cheers' when they mean 'thank you'.
30 'We must have lunch some time.'
31 Mr Major's 5p coin.
32 Renting a video that hasn't been rewound.
33 Dry cleaners who can't get the stains out.
34 Men who say, 'that's a bit sexist' when you hadn't even noticed.
35 Not enough butter in a baked potato.
36 Twinned towns.
37 'Pop music is the classical music of the future.'
38 'How are you spelling that?'
39 Wednesday afternoon closing in libraries.
40 Silly lists in magazines.

SEPTEMBER 1992

Remembering V-J Day and dinner with 5 Gurkha VCs

BLOG
GENERAL SIR PETER DUFFELL, 2020

75 years ago, on August 15, 1945, it was V-J Day, the day Japan surrendered and war came to an end.

Sixty years ago, in 1960, I was commissioned into the 2nd Gurkha Rifles and I served with those indomitable soldiers throughout much of my Army career.

For over 200 years the Gurkha soldier has campaigned for the British Crown. Nowhere was his gallant service more in evidence than in the Burma campaign.

In 1995, the anniversary of the Japanese surrender was marked with a parade in London. A large column of veterans, including five of the six surviving Gurkha holders of the Victoria Cross won in the Burma campaign, paraded past the Queen in the Mall. During their visit to England, I accompanied these valiant Gurkhas to visit the President of the Gurkha Brigade Association, the late Field Marshal Lord Bramall, at his home in Surrey.

It was a memorable occasion. Following copious drinks in the Field Marshal's garden, we all set off for a popular Indian restaurant in Farnham. It was a happy, garrulous and drink-fuelled gathering that began to attract attention from a packed restaurant. The Field Marshal stood up, called for silence in the way that only Field Marshals can and announced to the diners: 'Ladies and gentlemen, I want to apologise for the noise, but you need to know that you are dining tonight with five holders of the Victoria Cross.'

Immediately, and as one, the whole restaurant rose to its feet and greeted the Gurkhas with prolonged cheering. It was an entirely spontaneous response and it moved us all most greatly.

How Boney snuffed it

There is a musical by Caryl Brahms called *Cindyella*. In one scene Cindyella complains that her beloved aunt is ill. The neighbour says: 'Why don't you get a doctor?'

   C: I got a doctor and he saw auntie.
   N: Oh, and what did he say?
   C: Well, he listened to her chest. Then he examined her. Then he took snuff. And then he said 'Hmmm'.

This doctor was modelled on me. And this is, or was, how I came to take snuff. I was waiting for a book in the British Museum library. An elderly asthmatic priest and another man were waiting ahead of me. Waiting. Waiting. Waiting. More waiting. They both took snuff. Waiting.

The priest asked, 'What's yours?' The other man: 'Macuba.' Waiting. Waiting. The other man: 'What's yours.' The priest: 'Prince's Special.' Waiting. The priest: 'What do you do?' The other man: 'I am writing the life of Lafayette.' The priest (blanching): 'B-b-but so am I!'

I do not know the priest's name but the other man was called Michael de la Bédoyère and his book was published. I did not write the life of Lafayette, but I thought it was a good idea to take snuff in libraries where you weren't allowed to smoke.

One day while travelling in France I made a historical discovery. I went to one of those small town museums – the kind of place where they exhibit anything older than 50 years, from enema syringes to fireplaces. This place had Napoleon's uniform complete with boots and white kid waistcoat. I became interested in the waistcoat because I thought I would like to have one too. I was the only visitor and the kindly but bored curator opened the glass case and showed it to me. Then I noticed that the left waistpocket had a double lining. The inner lining was of chamois leather. The curator said it was the duty of Napoleon's faithful Mamelouk to sew a new chamois into the left pocket daily, because that was where Napoleon kept his snuff. He had of course a handsome collection of valuable boxes but he lived much of his time on horseback. And let me tell you that taking snuff from a box on horseback is second only to taking snuff on a moving motorcycle. The odds are that when you open your snuffbox, the snuff will get into your eyes or the horse will shy when he gets a whiff of it (or the motorcycle will run away from underneath you). To keep the snuff loose in an accessible pocket, and take only the pinch you need, is brilliantly practical. The museum curator knew that much.

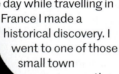

What had not occurred to him (nor anyone else before me that I know of) was that the snuff pocket provided the most natural and plausible of all explanations for Napoleon's historical (and allegedly histrionic) gesture of keeping his right hand on his heart.

The two other known explanations are not nearly so plausible. One is that Napoleon, like so many great men, was a small man and was taught by the famous actor Talma how to look dignified. The gesture was therefore Talma's invention. The other explanation is that the pains in his stomach were the early precursor of the cancer from which he was to die and this was why he habitually held his hand on his stomach. The French call indigestion *mal de coeur*, which is an appropriate expression if your heart is in your stomach, which Napoleon's was not. Furthermore, Napoleon didn't die of any kind of cancer. He died of medical neglect of chronic amoebic dysentery. The specimen was for a long time in the Museum of the Royal College of Surgeons in London but diplomatically vanished after I called attention to it in a letter to the *Lancet*.

No, I believe that fiddling with his snuff is by far the most plausible explanation of the imperial pose.

TIBOR CSATO

Edna Everage

HELLO POSSUMS,
'Why the Dickens is Dame Edna writing a column for *The Oldie*, I can hear my readers ask. I suppose it is part of my new Accessibility Initiative. Folk have put me on an ivory pedestal lately, and I need to get back in touch with real people and real issues. What better place to do that than on the pages of *The Oldie*, a publication, which, let's face it, could be the last thing a lot of people read before meeting their Maker? If Heaven has a waiting-room, like the ones I have loitered in on Harley Street, seeking psychiatric advice for my troublesome children, then its coffee tables are bound to be littered with back issues of this delightful publication.

I am a Renaissance woman, I'm afraid, although even other famous Renaissance women in history – Boadicea, Mary Queen of Scots and Jane Fonda, to name a few – never wrote a famous column in an adult publication. 'Is there nothing Dame Edna can't do, for heaven's sake?' I hear you say. Dame Nature gives everyone a little droplet of talent, like the tomato sauce our parents used to put on the side of our scrummy dinners when we were kiddies. In my case, I think Dame Nature banged the bottom of the sauce bottle a bit hard over my life's portion.

One other point: I'm not writing this for money. Years ago in Australia, I did write a column for Rupert Murdoch at a period in my life when funds were low. At the time, I was pumping a fortune into my husband's prostate. I had known Mr Murdoch since he was a kiddie in Melbourne. Little 'Roo' – sallow, prematurely balding little scallywag that he was – used to deliver our morning paper, whizzing past our lovely home in Moonee Ponds on his bike, and chucking a tightly rolled copy of the *Argus* over our front fence. He had to give the paper a nasty twist, like a Chinese burn, so that it 'flew' properly and often the scrunched-up front-page pictures looked more like originals by Francis Bacon, though I didn't realise it then. (Later Francis became a pal and he was working on a flattering portrait of my bridesmaid Madge shortly before he found the road too weary and the hill too steep to climb.)

Anyway, we never realised that little ragamuffin 'Roo' would print papers one day, but that sort of miracle can still happen in Australia – I am an Australian incidentally.

I'm sorry our superlative teams didn't win everything in Barcelona. Woe betide any athlete – or comedian or opera singer for that matter – who lets us down in the international arena. Several of our Olympic 'also rans' skulked home to headlines like 'Yugo Descendant Bungles Shotput' or 'Niece Of Dago Can't Swim For Toffee' or 'Son Of Greaseball Lousy Jumper'. Thank heavens I am a pure-blooded, 100% Australian!

Mind you, Possums, the press can be quite strict if you're royalty. Look what's going on now! 'Will the royal family retire?' sources close to a lot of thoughtful newspapers are asking.

Speaking as Australian royalty, I can now divulge, exclusively for *Oldie* readers, that a few years ago I nearly retired to write a thoughtful book and devote myself to unselfish and anonymous social work like John Profumo and Jeffrey Archer. But when the media heard I was retiring from public life there was a panic-stricken howl. You see, Possums, I'm big business to a lot of people. If it wasn't for me, squillions of people would be made redundant: Swiss bankers, dressmakers, helicopter pilots, glamour spectacle-makers, tax advisers, New Zealand bridesmaids, you name it! Wherever I go and whatever I do the economy picks up. The Minister for Australian Overseas Promotions expressed it in a candid if crude fax: 'Take your bum off the throne, Edna, and the arse will fall out of Australian tourism.' (What he said was actually much cruder than this but I've cleaned it up for *Oldie* readers.) Of course I stayed, and the rest is history.

Anyway, where would the press be if they got their way and banished my royal friends? They would only have me to write about and, incredible as it may seem, even I am not a totally inexhaustible topic. They would be left with the Geldofs, the Jaggers, Gazza and poor old Frank Bough! Rather unacceptable, don't you think?

Incidentally, readers, 'unacceptable' next to 'basically' is my favourite word at the moment. It's the only word in the English language that you can use to describe both a self-adhesive plastic hook on the back of a toilet door that keeps falling off, and the bombing of Dresden. What a wonderful, expressive language we have, don't we?

Lastly, my thought for *Oldie* readers. This comes from a little book of wise jottings I found in the pocket of one of my mother's matinée jackets the night we burnt her things. It is full of gems which I know my readers will treasure. Here's one for this week:

'There are no such things as crow's feet, just the dried-up beds of old smiles.'

Isn't that gorgeous, Possums!
A joyous heart always,
EDNA

The French connection

It wasn't a triumphal finish to the rally, as *Patrick Marnham* relates

Paris. Vroom!! Vroom!! The French word '*raid*' means both 'a hit-and-run attack' and 'a long-distance motor rally'. The French do love their *raids* and they have just completed a new one, Paris-Moscow-Peking. It was a complete sporting and social disaster. But that will not discourage the local Monsieur Toads.

The original French '*raid*' in the modern series was the Paris-Dakar which grew to rival the Tour de France in popularity. It became such a success that, by 1991, 300 lunatics in cars, motor bikes and lorries (yes, they also race lorries!) were crashing across the Sahara desert, inflicting multiple injuries on themselves, on each other and on the local population, always described as 'spectators'.

The drivers were pursued by a vast media caravan of gung-ho, pot-bellied television crews and by refrigerated trucks carrying chilled pâté de foie gras, jars of cornichons and crates of champagne. Through famine districts, regions of drought, war zones and across the fragile grazing lands of the Sahelian nomads, they raced for 13 years, until they eventually made themselves so unpopular that in 1992 even the most thick-skinned rally drivers grew tired of being showered with stones by 'enthusiastic Saharan spectators', and the destination was changed to Cape Town.

There is, however, one disadvantage to racing across Africa, which is that few of the spectators are ever going to buy most of the goods which the competing vehicles are advertising. Now, and for the foreseeable future, there is only a limited demand for Elf petrol or Michelin tyres or Rothman's cigarettes in Chad or Namibia.

At this point enter the Japanese. The Japanese, in the form of the Mitsubishi Corporation, have their eye not on Africa but on Eastern Europe, on the whole of the former Soviet Union and on China. Mitsubishi Corporation already employs 40 head office staff in Moscow and 60 in Peking. Hundreds of millions of potential new customers! Business, business!! And since much of central Asia is as barren and under-developed as Africa, it is perfect territory for a '*raid*'.

So, in 1990, Mitsubishi announced the first 'Raid Paris-Moscow-Peking'. The event had to be cancelled due to the massacre in Tiananmen Square. In 1991, the Japanese tried again. Again the rally had to be cancelled, 12 days before the start, this time because of the attempted coup against Mr Gorbachev.

Yukihiko Sato, of Mitsubishi, is a persistent man. And so is Monsieur Toad, alias René Metge, a veteran of the Paris-Dakar. Described in the press handout as 'a remarkable pair, fired by the same ideal, to link East and West, governments and people in a common adventure,' they struck it third time lucky.

On 1st September, 15 motorcyclists, 20 racing lorries and 93 car drivers set off from the Trocadero in Paris on a 16,000 kilometre journey to Brussels, Warsaw, Moscow and points east. They were led by

> **The drivers were pursued by a vast media caravan of gung-ho, pot-bellied television crews**

Mitsubishi's official team of five, and by Citroën, who have already installed a factory in China and who launched their ZX model by filming the car being driven along the Great Wall. In place of the hard sell it was left to Monsieur Toad to yap on about 'the dream of a lifetime', 'mysterious and magical China', 'Just imagine, dawn breaks and it's Red Square!' etc, etc, all faithfully reproduced by the motoring correspondents of France, tanked up on free cornichons and Château Lafite.

Across the Russian Steppes through Kazakhstan, Turkmenistan, Uzbekistan and Kirgiziya, then along Marco Polo's Silk Route and through the Gobi Desert to the Great Wall they trundled. Very little was left to chance on this particular 'great adventure'. The drivers were backed up by an air lift of transport planes ferrying in spare parts and fuel. The usual caravan of pâté de foie gras, charcoal for the barbecues, frozen filet mignon and champagne naturally followed on behind.

In a sane world, the whole lot would have been turned back at the Polish border and advised to drive round in circles on a closed racing track until they felt better. And strangely enough that, to some extent, is what happened. Forbidden any contact with the populations of Central Asia and China, and surrounded by a total force of 70,000 soldiers and policemen, the rally drivers had to consult their press handouts to find out when they were passing 'below the Celestial Mountains' or 'through the Canyon of Eagles' or 'the Black Desert of Karakum'. They were reduced to flaunting their Camel cigarette T-shirts at the occasional nomad and tuning into their satellite-dish television shows every evening.

Finally to the triumphal entry into Peking where the winner was looking forward to being greeted by cheering crowds after his four-week ordeal! It was not to be. Instead the Peking authorities directed the competitors into an area set aside for tourists below the Great Wall, which is dominated by (*quelle horreur!*) a Kentucky Fried Chicken concession and where an enormous army of municipal refuse workers, dressed up in historical costumes, chased them around making sure that they did not drop so much as a single cornichon.

Above them, armed guards prevented the drivers and media persons from mingling with local citizens and prevented the population of Peking from watching the triumphant parade of Mitsubishis and Citroëns. 'Mysterious China' indeed. No public announcement was made about the arrival of the rally and Tiananmen Square was closed.

The welcoming ceremony with the mayor of Peking was constantly interrupted by fist fights between the TV crews and the guards trying to keep them at a respectful distance. The rally was won by a Citroën. But since nobody remembered to mark the car's name in Chinese characters, this important detail passed unnoticed by the few Chinese who knew what was going on.

And the lesson of all this to Mr Toad? 'We will organise another Paris-Moscow-Peking as soon as possible!' Vroom!! Vroom!!

A downright upright all-round man

Christopher Matthew remembers Robert Morley, not perhaps the world's greatest driver, but one of its finest actors – and nicest men

'Are you doing anything for lunch on Sunday?' It was the early summer of 1961 and Sheridan Morley and I were playing small parts in an OUDS production of *The Shoemaker's Holiday* in Wadham College Garden. I had no serious plans for lunch, or indeed anything else much that weekend. 'I thought we might go to Fairmans,' he said.

We travelled down on the Greenline bus. Robert met us in Henley in a maroon Jaguar. As we turned off the main road at the top of Henley Hill, the front wheels mounted the bank and we continued for some distance at a 30-degree angle before lurching back on to the hard surface and continuing on our way. No comment was made. Neither of them appeared to have noticed. Robert was never at his best behind the wheel. We once bumped for several hundred yards along a pavement in Windsor. On another occasion he reversed into a lamppost. 'It was travelling far too fast,' he commented. 'And on the wrong side of the road.'

The day passed in a haze of pleasure. We swam and then had lunch on the lawn. Robert had been deeply impressed by a glossy advertisement he'd once come across for Martell brandy which showed a French family lunching in the sunshine in front of a château. He always hoped it might be possible to achieve a similarly elegant effect in Berkshire.

As we were leaving after tea to catch the bus back to Oxford, Robert said to me, 'Do come and see us again. You may not always want to see us, but we'd always like to see you.'

Looking back, I feel I may have taken him and Joanie up on their offer with rather more enthusiasm than he had anticipated. If so, neither gave the slightest hint of it.

Robert was never happier than when the house – and in summer, the pool – was full of people: family, friends, friends of family… He had an infinite capacity for being amused, and the least one could do in return for his and Joanie's hospitality was tell him a good story. Theatrical gossip was always welcome, but no more so than any other sort. He had an insatiable curiosity about other people's lives and was forever getting into conversation with total strangers in the hope that they might tell him something odd or funny or touching. And very often they did. He was unfailingly courteous to anyone who accosted him in the street, and I never once saw him refuse an autograph. Indeed I was usually the one who was expected to provide the pen. Travelling with Robert was not unlike travelling with royalty, and over the years I acquired a deep sympathy, and respect, for ladies-in-waiting.

Despite a carefully nurtured air of nonchalance, he was an enormously industrious man and couldn't abide indolence and indecision in others: 'Do stop fussing, darling, and try and get on a bit.' He made a great deal of money during his life and never came to terms with the principle of saving. His sister Margaret once asked him how much he put aside for 'spending money'. 'I don't know any other sort of money,' he told her.

His reputation as a trencherman was well deserved. He was always on for an outing and once in the car would spend ages thumbing through the *Good Food Guide* in search of some sensational new restaurant. A keen pudding man, he felt very let down by people who cast an eye over the trolley and then said, 'Just coffee for me.'

And of course he loved being on the racecourse. He liked racing people. Assuming that one who had spent a lifetime on the turf must know a thing or two, I once turned to him at Newmarket for a word of wisdom. 'I normally tend to study the people round the horse rather than the horse itself,' he explained. 'If they have a shifty look. I'm inclined to think they know something I don't. Large groups I generally discount on the grounds that they are probably only on a jolly day's outing. What more can I tell you?'

In all the years I knew him, I can't remember ever being bored with Robert. Whatever the current scandal, you could guarantee his views on the subject would always be completely original. He once arrived for lunch on a day when the papers were bursting with outrage about the theft of some rare osprey eggs from a secret nest in the Highlands. 'I'm so glad, aren't you?' he said. 'Such nasty birds. I once had an aunt who wore osprey feathers. I never much cared for her, or the feathers.'

Perhaps the most surprising thing about him was his shyness. To conceal his nerves he would often be talking as he entered the room – sometimes even before. In 1977, he invited me to join him on a short jaunt which included an engagement at a country hotel in Yorkshire where celebrities would join the diners over liqueurs and coffee, tell stories and engage them in light conversation. The customers that evening were obviously delighted to discover that he was just as they had imagined him: flamboyant, theatrical, larger than life. Few if any could have guessed how nervous he was. But he was soon into his stride, with a story about Mrs Agnes Pope. 'I was an ugly, sad, lonely child and she was the only friend I had. She lived in Courtfield Gardens and believed that all diseases in the world emanated from the nose. As a result, the use of handkerchiefs was strictly forbidden in her house, which is why I have sniffed ever since. When she was very old and ill someone came to visit her and blew his nose. Mrs Pope thought it must be the last trump and gave up the ghost.'

He told them about his childhood and his early days in the profession, about Marie Tempest and Louis B Mayer and John Barrymore and Bernard Shaw – 'the only saint I ever met' – and his beloved mother-in-law Gladys Cooper. For over an hour the stories tumbled out, sometimes sad, often touching, always funny. 'Is this the sort of thing you want, dears?' he asked the audience at the end of the story about Greta Garbo. 'Would you like to ask me some questions perhaps?'

'I have a question,' said a man in the front row. 'Why are your fly buttons undone?'

'I had rather hoped,' Robert replied, calmly adjusting his dress, 'that it added to the general air of informality.'

What did he think of Yorkshire? 'The important thing,' he replied, 'is what Yorkshire thinks of me.'

What were his favourite luxuries? 'Not having to be directed by Peter Brook. A really good new sponge. A chocolate Bath Oliver, followed almost immediately by another.'

What did he think of Malcolm Muggeridge? 'It's inconceivable that he would not bore God.'

Acting for the cinema? 'I've never really learnt how to do it.' And in the theatre? 'I'm the extreme example of the egomaniac. Occasionally I will attempt a token resemblance to a character by putting on a wig, but I nearly always play myself.'

How did he get on with young directors? 'I usually give them a week to find out if they know more than I do; and if not, I take over myself.'

Did he enjoy entertaining people? 'As long as I'm entertaining myself. I love hearing my own opinions, even if I don't actually agree with them.'

What did he think of people who live abroad to avoid British taxes? 'I was born a pauper,' said Robert, 'and I shall almost certainly die a pauper. If a man is fool enough to want to go and live in Jersey or the Isle of Man and take it all with him, then in my opinion he deserves everything he gets there.'

'Mr Morley, you claim to be a socialist…' One sensed that this was the moment he'd been waiting for all evening. There was nothing Robert relished more than the opportunity to lower his head and snort and stamp and make spirited passes at any smug Tory unwise enough to show him the red mantilla. But then suddenly the anger subsided and the fire went out of the eyes to be replaced by mocking self-doubt.

'Darlings, I'm just a well-travelled actor, with muddled ideas like everyone else.'

The following day we drove to Newcastle where he was due to speak at the Royal Institute of British Architects' (Northumbria Branch) annual dinner. It was a boisterous, beery occasion and in the middle of a Norma Shearer story he suddenly lost his patience with them and launched into a blistering attack on architects, planners, one-way streets, shopping centres, tower blocks, office blocks and the whole ghastly muddles of modern city life. 'This is the best country in the world,' he shouted at the astonished gathering. 'Why must you ruin it with your hideous buildings and your terrible schemes?'

He sat down to applause that was polite rather than heart-felt, and turned to me and pulled a face. 'Have I gone too far this time?' he asked. Then added, 'Actually, I've got a bit of a cold coming on.'

OCTOBER 1993

Germaine Greer

Stump Cross Roundabout

Where am I? I open the plastic drapes. No clues there. Streets. If it's Tuesday they must be Seattle streets, but is it Tuesday? Wednesday would be San Francisco, Friday Cincinnati. When you're eight hours behind it's hard to decide what day is which, whether what you're eating is breakfast or supper. Because you're tired all the time you have no idea when you should sleep, and you're tired all the time because you keep going up and down in aeroplanes, because you're never allowed to stop talking, and because you're never allowed to take any exercise. And what have you done to deserve such condign punishment? You have been a success.

Can't breathe, either. None of the windows seems to open. Whatever I eat seems to be the wrong thing. I want my own cooking, my own bed with its cotton sheets, my red cat. I think I saw a pet shop on the boulevard. Maybe I could rent a cat. No self-respecting cat would endure the limousine I spend most of my time in; like a sarcophagus on wheels it carries me from one chore to another, more dead than alive. I hate the limousine with its strange carpet-deodorant smell. I don't wanna be here. I wanna go home.

Because writers who get put through this mill have a reputation for cutting up rough, everything has been done to placate me. I have an historic room in an historic American hotel. The management has given me a present of fruit which seems not so much historic as prehistoric. Fossil fruit would have more taste than my wooden pear, my large red apple that seems to have grown a skin of shrink plastic, and my strange bunch of funny little maroon grapes that look like haemorrhoids. I ate the black plum, which turned out to be stuffed with yellow cotton wool. Oh, and the fig. The fig was good. Now what shall I do? At 4am there's a limit to what you can do. I am so hungry that I try to eat the apple, but my new porcelain teeth cannot pierce its polyurethane skin. I consult the 24-hour guest room dining menu and order a bottle of Tattinger plus guacamole and tortilla chips. The Filipino who brings them looks dead on his feet. Maybe I don't have it so bad after all.

The way it goes is, you write a book, the book does well, you owe them. Well, that's how they see it. You may think you have supplied the army of publicists, stationers, office suppliers, book-binders, paper manufacturers, loggers, agents, restaurateurs and what-all with the primary produce without which they would be compelled to earn a living by the sweat of their own brows alone; they think that without them you could utter all the text you want and it would waste its sweetness on the desert air. They reckon you owe them for providing you with the opportunity to foist your fantasies upon the world at large. I guess I feel guilty because the economics of publishing in the 1990s are such that new writers have less possibility than ever of finding a publisher, and we successful writers can command more in the way of advances than seems justifiable by any criterion.

True to the paradigm of the female who is grateful for the opportunity to be exploited, I can't find a good excuse for refusing to do promotion. It doesn't work to argue that your own book doesn't need promotion. As a known writer who commands an audience you owe it to the unknown writers to massage the image makers so that they have enough in the hand to try one or two in the bush.

Once it is clear that you have the potential to lay a series of golden eggs, you will be required to do so, in defiance of the law of diminishing returns. You may die before you finish your next book, after all, so it makes sense to get as much as possible out of you right now. The difference between the text that you originally uttered (that is now the book) and the stuff that squirts out of you under the pressure of promotion is that the text was costly and this second generation crap comes free.

As the successful author deposits her mounds of recycled product, she attracts a horde of lesser parasites, who nibble and forage about her with appalling assiduity, converting her fermenting out-put to their nutrient in-put. The most rapacious of these dung-beetles are the print journalists who gorge themselves for hours at a time, accumulating stores of product that they feel entirely justified in treating with the loftiest contempt. After all, she who puts out for less than a dime can hardly expect to be treated with common consideration, let alone respect.

Another kind of dung beetle carries a tape recorder and works for steam radio; the most brazen of these claim to be working for non-profit networks. All of them, the radio talkshows, the phone-ins, the TV news and the TV talkshows make the unfortunate author sign a release that gives them the right to use her contribution for any purpose whatsoever, not only to sell it to anyone who might like to use it, but also to edit it in any way they think fit and to include in their own promotional material. Some even ask the author to make little advertisements to use in their fundraising activities. When you're already sitting there excreting away, it is no easy matter to get off the pot.

Boy, do I feel sorry for myself. I cast

myself across the enormous bed I am too tired to sleep in and fiddle with the remote control for the vast TV set. Ping turns it on, click, someone is telling me how to get out of the hotel in case of fire, click, Bette Davis, click, Bette Midler, click, a television evangelist, foaming slightly at the mouth, click, Michael Jackson, click, click, hey! Back click. Happiness invades my wrung-out soul. On one of the hundreds of cable channels I have found the late-night re-broadcast of the ball game. Not American football, that clockwork clashing of head-banging space invaders mindlessly carrying out their coaches numbered sequences. Baseball. The best game that human beings ever learned to play. The most exciting, the least brutal, the bravest, the most expert, just the nicest spectator sport there ever could be. Kids can play it, old men can play it, and poor peasant boys from central America can become megastars by playing it. The ball park is not plastered with advertising and the fans are not hooligans.

Rounders you will say. Or softball. A girl's version of cricket. But no, baseball is the game cricket should have turned into. Heresy, I know, but even if professional cricketers fielded as well as professional baseballers do, if they moved as fast, if they took the risks that base-runners do, cricket would still be a pallid one-dimensional version of baseball.

To be sure bowlers practise the same kind of entrapment of the batsmen that pitchers do, but the pitchers have so much greater a range of resources, of sliding balls, breaking balls, curve balls, slide the change up and the change down, the blooper, the split finger fast ball, the knuckleball and others that I haven't learnt to identify yet. The batting side doesn't simply protect its wicket and add on run after run. As the bases begin to load, the game builds up the potential for an explosion until the runners are thwarted by the one-two double play or borne in on the wave of a king hit out of the park. In a good game, when the pitchers have the play screwed down tight, no hits, no runs, no errors, the pressure to score becomes unbearable and the longing for a shut-out almost as bad.

Watching the ball game I thank my stars for America, for its innocence, though murderous at times, for its generosity of spirit. I notice that the winning pitcher in this game was born with only one hand.

FOOD
JENNIFER PATERSON

I have been to two requiems this week. The first was for the dearly beloved mother of the five McCoy brothers who run the Tontine hotel and restaurant at Staddlebridge, Yorkshire, which I wrote about in the summer. It took place at the modern Catholic cathedral in Middlesbrough, a building hideous beyond belief, a wigwam of pale wood with a ghastly mural meaning nothing behind the altar. However the service and singing were full of gusto and general love, followed by a terrific wake back at the Tontine. Great log fires and groaning tables, dogs and splendid children running hither and thither, lovely children who actually talk to you with animation rather than grunting. A worthy, joyous party for the great Mary Clare McCoy.

The other requiem was at the London Oratory, a magnificent old fashioned tridentine mass sung most beautifully by the choir, full black and gold vestments, no addresses, then a mini-wake over the road at the Rembrandt. Give me a good requiem any day rather than these peculiar memorial services which are more like rather bad cabaret shows.

From there I went on to a lunch given by Dan Farson at the French Pub in Dean Street. A very jolly affair in all but the food, which was filthy. I was very disappointed as I had heard good things of this little restaurant. Let us hope that this was just a bad day or that something had gone terribly wrong in the kitchen.

My latest find is a shortbread from a small family firm where everything is done by hand. The taste and texture are a sort of crumble heaven. Apart from the traditional shortbread there are chocolate chip ones, stem ginger shapes, and they are working on a roasted peanut variety, when they can find the perfect peanut. The firm is run by Anthony Laing, whose grandfather invented the digestive biscuit, so he is a dyed in the wool biscuit maker. The label is 'Shortbread House' and they can be found in the big department stores, the Conran shops and good delicatessens. Expensive but sheer delight.

Fine great mackerel are plentiful at the moment, and are also one of the cheapest fish going. Try them instead of salmon for a poor man's gravad lax.

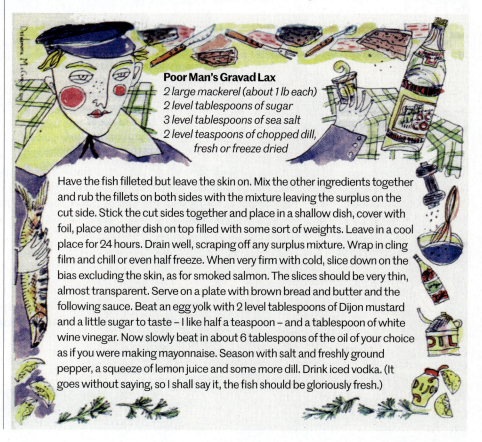

Poor Man's Gravad Lax
2 large mackerel (about 1 lb each)
2 level tablespoons of sugar
3 level tablespoons of sea salt
2 level teaspoons of chopped dill, fresh or freeze dried

Have the fish filleted but leave the skin on. Mix the other ingredients together and rub the fillets on both sides with the mixture leaving the surplus on the cut side. Stick the cut sides together and place in a shallow dish, cover with foil, place another dish on top filled with some sort of weights. Leave in a cool place for 24 hours. Drain well, scraping off any surplus mixture. Wrap in cling film and chill or even half freeze. When very firm with cold, slice down on the bias excluding the skin, as for smoked salmon. The slices should be very thin, almost transparent. Serve on a plate with brown bread and butter and the following sauce. Beat an egg yolk with 2 level tablespoons of Dijon mustard and a little sugar to taste – I like half a teaspoon – and a tablespoon of white wine vinegar. Now slowly beat in about 6 tablespoons of the oil of your choice as if you were making mayonnaise. Season with salt and freshly ground pepper, a squeeze of lemon juice and some more dill. Drink iced vodka. (It goes without saying, so I shall say it, the fish should be gloriously fresh.)

The *Assure*: Life-saving wristband
Comprehensive protection in your home, garden & beyond.

UK manufactured with customer service from our offices near Cambridge.

How would you get help if you couldn't make a phone call?
The *Assure*® gives you peace of mind

SOS Alerts – Buttons pressed by user; for sudden pain, shortness of breath, security concern, etc.

Fall Alerts – for severe falls when the wearer is unable to move or unconscious.

I'm OK Checks *EXCLUSIVE to Acticheck*
The easy way to confirm you are up in the morning and OK before bed.

Oldie special 10% off code: **XP-TOM**

Customer reviews
★★★★½ 4.7 out of 5
This has been an absolutely fantastic buy - our parents are happy to wear them and we all feel much more secure. Gives me peace of mind for me and my family.
Belinda from Truro, July 2020

"GoAnywhere" smartphone app included for *free*.

"One squeeze calls for help"

Comfortable and simple to use, the *Assure*® is waterproof and does not need charging; so you get continuous protection for a full year.

acticheck

To order or find out more call:
0345 25 75 080 or www.acticheck.com

From under £2.50/week

100% MONEY BACK 30 DAYS GUARANTEE

Help us Support the Royal Naval Officer Family

The Royal Navy Officers' Charity has provided valuable support and financial assistance to RN and RM Officers (both serving and retired), their spouses and dependants, at home and overseas for almost 300 years.

The RNOC greatly improves the quality of life for many beneficiaries through the range and diversity of grants awarded. In order to continue this valuable support, which includes assistance to those on low incomes, care home fees, reducing debt and transition to employment, we rely on your generosity via welcome donations and legacies.

Amid the current challenges of COVID 19, the RNOC also provides a sympathetic ear and an essential signposting service in addition to supporting its wide range of beneficiaries.

**Help us making a lasting impact.
All support goes to those who need it most.**

You can leave a legacy or make a secure online donation at **www.rnoc.org.uk**

Call 020 7402 5231, email rnoc@arno.org.uk
or write to 70 Porchester Terrace, London W2 3TP
for more information.

Registered charity no 207405

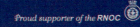

JANUARY 1995

Press
Roy Greenslade

Editors adore columnists. They are a symbol of their potency. They boast about the ones they publish. I have the most; I have the best; I have the most outspoken; I have the most famous; I have the ones who are read by the greatest number of people; I have the ones who are read by the people who count. The proprietary nature of the bragging is significant. Columnists may imagine themselves free spirits, but the editors feel they own them for the duration of their stay. And there is a big turn-over. It's like a football transfer market, with the editors playing manager, plotting to buy up new columnists from rivals by offering big money and better deals.

The latest merry-go-round is proof. Richard Littlejohn is leaving the *Sun* for the *Daily Mail*. Andrew Neil, apart from writing a column for the *Sunday Times*, is to write another for the *Mail*. Suzanne Moore, award-winning columnist at the *Guardian*, has accepted a reputed £70,000 to take her skills to the *Independent*. Nigella Lawson, who delighted us weekly on the *London Evening Standard*, has transferred her talents to the *Times*. Darcus Howe, television's glowering devil's advocate, has taken her place. Columnists are highly prized, highly paid, highly hyped and highly envied.

Many of them have lucrative freelance contracts, with deals that mere reporters would die for. While current financial constraints have meant that wages in most offices have decreased in real terms, pay for columnists has taken off. Needless to say, most writers are reticent to talk about their earnings, and managements are too embarrassed. But editors offer more than money to win their stars. One columnist's contract includes Concorde trips to the States; another can have a new car every year; another gets a new computer whenever he wishes, along with a secretary to input his golden words. It's the equivalent of satisfying the Hollywood star's desire for a newly decorated trailer to start every new film.

Of course, columnists have a long and honourable tradition in newspapers. We do tend to remember them. I grew up reading the cantankerous Cassandra in the *Daily Mirror*. My first national newspaper job was to send Bernard Levin's *Daily Mail* column to the print room. It was, in the jargon of sub-editing, just a matter of ticking it down. I can recall only one error. He misattributed a quotation from Newbolt to Tennyson. Such poetic matters are no longer a concern in modern tabloids. Though it is fashionable to say that Levin's best days are behind him, I still enjoy reading his *Times* column, both for its style and content.

Any straw poll tends to show that another grand old man, the *Daily Mail*'s Keith Waterhouse, is the columnists' columnist. It doesn't matter that we know what he will probably say about any given subject, nor that it will probably be in the mouths of Sharon and Tracy or a

> **Such is the lure of being a columnist, more and more people entering journalism think that is the point of the exercise**

Clogthorpe councillor. Part of the art of the humorous columnist is to create, over time, a familiar world peopled with characters who illuminate a point of view with which the regular reader identifies. That was also the essence of Beachcomber and is the strength of Peter Simple.

But I'm afraid I have wandered, for I come not to praise. There is too little to admire in the columns in modern

Crossdresser

newspapers. Too many editors have come to believe that creating columnists is easy. Anyone on television enjoying their 15 minutes of fame will be able to write a regular column. I hear the cry from the editor's desk: bring me that clever disc jockey, Chris Tarrant; get that comedy chappie, Paul Merton; doesn't that chat show fella, Kilroy-Silk, write as well? And what about that Jonathan Ross my daughter likes? More likely, an editor is looking for a woman. A new, young woman; an angry woman; a controversial woman. Oh yes, and hopefully a pretty woman. Poor Mariella Frostrup, who adorns the pages of the *Sunday Times*, is the classic example of the television blonde translated unfairly from screen to print. It isn't her fault. I understand she was persuaded that the transfer would be easy and she was properly reluctant when asked. Her first instinct was correct.

Whatever people might think, writing a column is far from easy. As Littlejohn often says, everyone has one column in them, maybe two. After that, unless you have something to say and the facility to say it interestingly, it will always be an uphill task. And if it's tough for the writer, you can be sure it will be even more so for the reader.

Such is the lure of being a columnist, more and more young people entering journalism think it is the whole point of the exercise. Why spend time on a cold doorstep when you could be at home tapping out a column? Why spend weeks on a story that might not make the paper when you can guarantee your picture above 800 words every week? Why try, in other words, when everything can come so easily, especially if you already have a name made famous by a mother or father in the same business?

Is it not blindingly obvious to everyone, editors, readers and columnists, that there are too many columns? And is it not clear that many columnists are not up to it? Has anyone been uplifted by reading the egocentric nonsense of Vanessa Feltz in the *Daily Mirror*? Whatever did the *Sun* think it was doing by taking Anne Diamond away from the *Mirror*? Her columns are a definition of triteness. Why does the *Daily Express* bother with Esther Rantzen? They are, in a sense, all victims of editors who think a column is a marketing tool and that having lots of 'famous' columnists is a guarantee of sales success. Have they not realised that the reverse might be nearer the truth?

Change for a tenor

Robert Tear on the trials of age and opera

As I stride towards my dotage, noting on my way that these joints which once helped me to skip like a spring lamb are now squealing in protest at the sight of stairs, and those eyes which could decipher the tail of a quaver through flickering candlelight cannot now decide whether print is too near them or too far off, I'm nudged to question whether there are any epiphanies, or even one, in this swift passage to new nappies and cheap caskets.

The physical side is all disaster. This is plain. Forking a little deeper on the philosophical side I do see a glimmer of light. This turns quickly into a walking epiphany that whispers into my ear: 'Have you considered that you seem to have more time for life, that you have less haste in your loins, that when singing a difficult aria you don't rush it, you consider from a distance, then you sing? Old age should bring a certain wisdom with it, an ability to see from a different perspective, a new dimension.'

So it is out. There is a blessing and I am a singer. Alas, as seems to be the case with all things, every cloud has its grey lining, there is no unadulterated pleasure, no perfection without a little alloy.

This is made dazzlingly clear to me when I work with conductors and producers (or stage directors as they now prefer to be called). From always being the youngest in any company, I am now inevitably and suddenly the oldest. There was no transition – it happened overnight, and whereas I perhaps have achieved a modicum of wisdom, sitting as I do in my eternal dimension, the young souls I work with are simply not old enough to sit chatting with me on my bench and to gaze wistfully at the setting sun. I have to endure from each new talent, that not only have they spotted all life's problems, but they also have new and radical solutions.

I worked with a young conductor the other day who was performing his first Beethoven Ninth. He came up to me and explained that if these bars were phrased like that and those like this then the whole piece would be seen afresh, blindingly new. As he was talking to me I could hear gross laughter in a passing cloud and saw a white mane being tossed about in helpless mirth. At the performance the work sounded disturbingly familiar.

Directors, too, are the strangest bunch. They come with most of the psychological problems known to science. First there are those so anally retentive that a pin couldn't be inserted even in early June. These same have a problem with control. I'm reminded of an opera I was performing in Austria, a kind of lamb's tale from Salzburg. I'm playing a shepherd, the rehearsal period is two months. At the first rehearsal I'm presented with a woolly, skittering, slippy-hooved creature just approaching adolescence whom I'm supposed to carry about my neck. She is heavy. In my innocence I mention the fact that in 56 days this madonna of the bleat will be a monster sheep. The director pronounces with deadly seriousness: 'It vill not grow.' How comforting, I thought.

Then come those who need to exorcise their childhood fears, their misogyny, their terror of cupboards or the masterpieces of musical literature, most

> **Directors are the strangest bunch. They come with most of the psychological problems known to science**

on the dartboard of the *Ring*, it must be said. They vindicate their infantilism by calling their antics the 'theatre of the absurd'. They also think their labour quite original, forgetting that the '*Merde!*' of Alfred Jarry had happened about a hundred years earlier and that Beckett in his sad, empty way had already sucked the cardboard orange dry.

I have been told through Goebbels's pupils, 'Do not countermant mein orders,' and was once informed that if I should bring out my handkerchief again, 'I vill leaf by ze next plane.' I did and he stayed.

I recall, too, the Austrian conductor Josef Kripps saying to me (when I was almost a baby, and he should have known better): 'I can nefer forgif you for vat you dit to our vimmin in ze war.' I refused to accept the national guilt on this one.

Now before you think me a completely cantankerous old curmudgeon I must say that at this moment I'm working with the kindest, wisest, most gifted director. I'm convinced he made up the eternal bench in one tea-break and has been sitting on it waiting for me to arrive. His name is Peter Sellars. One three-hour session in such visionary company is enough to convince me that not only is the job I do worthwhile after all, but that epiphanies are out and about and wearing boots to kick their way into my consciousness should I become wilfully hubristic.

ADVERTISING FEATURE

Why have a stairlift when you can have a *real* lift?

A Stiltz Homelift will help you continue living in the home you love.

Elegant, practical and discreet. A Stiltz Homelift will transform your home and your life.

AS SEEN ON TV

STAIRLIFT? NO THANKS!

A Stiltz Homelift is an ideal and affordable alternative to a stairlift. You can now safely travel between the floors in your home while keeping your stairs the way they have always been.

NEAT & DISCREET

A Stiltz Homelift can be installed into almost any room in your home. A Stiltz is uniquely compact with the smallest model taking up just over half a square metre – now that IS discreet. The homelift plugs directly into a standard domestic socket and uses less power than boiling a kettle. The homelifts run on self-supporting rails so there is no need to drill into walls and the motor is fully self-contained within the lift car. Neat.

YOUR FOREVER HOME

While some Stiltz customers have an immediate need for a homelift, others are looking to future-proof their existing home for when the stairs do eventually become a challenge.

Don't go through the unnecessary expense and emotional upheaval of moving house or the disruption of adapting your home for downstairs living. Save money instead; live comfortably and independently in the home you love for as long as you want, with a Stiltz Homelift.

"We've had our lift for 2 years and were so impressed with how it was fitted from our hallway to our landing in what at first appeared to be an impossible space. And in such a short time."

Mr. Eames

PEACE OF MIND

Stiltz are proud to hold the highly-regarded Which? Trusted Trader status meaning they are a reputable, established and trustworthy company. Stiltz customers love them too, rating them 'Great' on Trustpilot. They use their own teams of expert installers, so you can choose a Stiltz Homelift with complete peace of mind, knowing you and your home are in a safe pair of hands.

"Excellent product installed by polite and very competent tradesmen. Fits perfectly into my home. Made a huge difference to my ability to live independently".

Mark via Trustpilot

TEST DRIVE A HOMELIFT

When you're ready, a Stiltz Homelifts consultant will conduct a FREE, no obligation survey in your home. There may also be the opportunity to meet with an existing Stiltz customer local to where you live to see a homelift and 'test drive' it for yourself!

So, why not give your lifestyle a lift with Stiltz. Call FREE today.

Rated 'Great'

The UK's No.1 Homelift

- **Urgent install service**
- **Ready to take your call now**
- Cost-effective
- Small footprint
- Freestanding design - no wall needed
- Wheelchair model available
- Manufactured, installed and fully guaranteed by Stiltz
- 3-floor travel available

For a FREE brochure or no obligation survey
Call FREE on 0808 271 9901
or visit www.stiltz.co.uk

The homelift company

Queen's Award for International Trade Winner 2020

The life and death of a bookshop

Bryan Forbes explains why he ran a bookshop for 38 years, and why he doesn't any more

It was a small village store to begin with, and I was just a regular customer, the best customer I suspect and the one who kept it afloat. It was owned by a somewhat eccentric lady, Peggy Pegler, the daughter of a once-famous publisher. In addition to being an insatiable collector of books, I had always been a frustrated bookseller from the time when, immediately after the war, I struck up a friendship with the late, and remarkable, Tony Godwin who, almost single-handed, dragged bookselling into the 20th century. Better Books in Charing Cross Road was a trail-blazing shop, for Tony was a true innovator, slightly mad, a passionate man, who only lived for books. As our friendship developed he let me serve in the shop as a happy, if unpaid, assistant during my frequent 'resting' periods between acting jobs.

Fate intervened when Mrs Pegler was involved in a car accident, sustaining injuries which eventually killed her. First she asked if I would like to become her partner, an offer I readily accepted. Then, following her death, the executors approached me to purchase the remaining 50 per cent. I took over the lease, but when I examined the books I found that the business was virtually insolvent. The annual turnover was a pitiful £8,000, and the small, eclectic stock mirrored Peggy's taste rather than appealing to the general reader.

So began the long, expensive task of making the enterprise viable. Because I was often away filming I needed to find somebody of like enthusiasm to operate the shop in my absence, and this proved difficult. I went through four managers before finding a young man named Patric Glasheen as dedicated as I was, and who has remained with me for the past 28 years. I provided the money but it was Patric's unsurpassed knowledge of and love for books that, over the years, built up our clientele.

We vastly increased the stock, refitted the shop, and made of it a small oasis of calm, where no customer was ever pressurised and no enquiry too difficult to satisfy. I made many mistakes which I had to subsidise out of my film earnings, but gradually we began to turn the corner, occasionally even making a small profit. I was content with that.

At that time my landlord was the Prudential, a company that had always advertised itself as the champion of the small man, but after 17 years as a model tenant I received a letter from the good old Pru telling me that the shop had been sold to a property speculator. Within weeks the new landlord hiked the rent by some 50 per cent and then, after a short lapse, served notice that I had a month to decide whether I would like to buy the freehold – at a quick profit to him, I discovered, of some £90,000. Fortunately I had an understanding bank manager and somehow managed to secure a mortgage for the £170,000 being demanded.

Today, after the recent demise of the Net Book Agreement, it is worth describing the economics of bookselling as they pertain to the small independent. When I first operated the shop the maximum publisher's discount was 33.33 per cent. Gradually, over a period of years, this crept up to the strange figure 36.63 per cent and most independents, according to surveys, were lucky if they ended up with 3 per cent net profit at the end of the year. To return unsold books was a chancy business entailing that one first got authority from the publisher's reps, and then waited for the sales manager to okay it – a process that more often than not took three months before a credit note was passed. This despite the fact that booksellers were only given 30 days credit or else risked being put 'on stop'. Under licence we were permitted to hold a sale once a year.

Over the years Patric and I managed to edge the turnover towards the £150,000 mark, which proved virtually the break-even point, covering the overheads some years and allowing of a modest 'book profit.' For nine months of the year we trod water with the aid of an overdraft, only October to December provided the fat, bringing in nearly half of the yearly turnover.

We introduced computerisation, allowing us to satisfy single customer orders of any British book in print within 48 hours, and this side of the business increased every year, for it was a service that customers valued. The shop became the village pump and we served coffee, maintained a comprehensive stock of fiction and non-fiction, together with the widest range of children's books, held signing sessions, gave some shelf space to decent secondhand titles, allowed local artists to display their wares and gave special discounts to local schools and charities. We were fortunate in that the American school, Tassis, was nearby and became a major customer. During the Christmas period we stayed open late for the convenience of commuters who wished to browse at their leisure and we gift-wrapped for free.

But none of this, none of our constantly revised efforts, proved enough when the

FEBRUARY 1996

Net Book Agreement folded overnight, for the cream went to the multiples (it does not take much skill or effort to move bestsellers). The shopping parade itself which, when I first moved into the district 30 or more years ago, provided every daily need and was a living entity, was gradually whittled away as rents and the onerous business rate forced small traders out of business.

Instead of the widest choice we now have four estate agents, three wine shops and two cleaners. Even service with a smile and, that rarity, free parking are not enough to seduce people away from the superstores and malls, so the passing trade now passes us by. I am all for widening the readership of books, illiteracy being what it sadly is, and happy for anybody to get a bargain. But whereas the wine stores, petrol stations and tobacconists can legally sell books, the independent bookseller cannot sell alcohol, petrol or the weed, and there's the rub.

I would gladly have soldiered on had I and others like me been granted the sort of discounts offered to the big multiples, but the downturn was too immediate and dramatic. I held on to see whether the Christmas season would bring about a revival of my fortunes, but it was not to be – the turnover went down by 26 per cent and sounded the death knell.

I don't regret one moment of the 38 years I devoted to the shop, for it was always a release valve. I never lost the thrill of opening up the parcels of new books, or of being able to recommend and sell a first novel I had discovered and enjoyed, to stock a young poet, to guide a teenager towards one of the great, now neglected, books of the 20th century as well as the older classics.

The function of a dedicated bookseller goes beyond making a sale and it must start with a real love of the printed page. We are not selling our wares as just another commodity, like pet food or frozen hamburgers, we are selling pleasures less transitory, pleasures that can be returned to time and time again and handed on to future generations. Somebody once wrote that 'A man is known by the company his mind keeps' and if in some small way, in a small community, The Bookshop, Virginia Water, encouraged a few more to discover the worth of books in the increasingly arid world of the multimedia and tabloid instant-dross, then all is not lost.

Looking for a result
David Ransom

Before Rupert Murdoch destroys the sports coverage on what we have now come to know as terrestrial television I have been watching as much as I can. I have vowed that I will never subscribe to a Murdoch enterprise of any kind, including his newspapers and particularly his television channels, and whilst I will miss the pleasure of seeing sportsmen and women in action I will miss even more the wondrous use of cliché and hyperbole which characterises so much of TV sports coverage. In our house we have developed a game called 'Best of order – Game on!' in which you are not allowed to talk while watching a sports programme, unless you use a cliché. Anyone falling foul of this rule has to pay a forfeit, usually making the tea, or fetching more logs. We have also developed a system of points which, if a transgression from the straight and narrow occurs, can be used to offset a forfeit.

> In our house we have developed a game called 'Best of order – Game on!' in which you are not allowed to talk while watching a sports programme, unless you use a cliché

The highest points are awarded to someone who anticipates a phrase used by the commentator. For example, watching a recent *Match of the Day*, I predicted Alan Hansen would lean back in his chair and, flashing his Celtic eyes at his pencil, cast angrily on the table before him, say to Jimmy Hill: 'I cannae agree wi' that!' And blow me, he did! I owe this bullseye to Mike Yarwood, who said the art of impersonation is to think of a catch-phrase which perfectly encapsulates an individual, but which, because of the very way in which it exposes their character, the person would never have uttered. As an example, he cited his impersonation of Harold Wilson, in which he used the phrase 'As I said at the Brighton conference...' Wilson never said those words, but we recognised them as epitomising a sort of copping-out shiftiness in the man. Hence its success.

Some sports are easy. Football wouldn't be the same without John Motson and Trevor Brooking, what with 'flat back four', 'midfield trio', 'competing in the air', 'holes in the defence' and 'slotting it home'. We had great fun at Christmas waiting for a seasonal cliché. It was Tony Gubba who couldn't resist it, when a goalkeeping blunder allowed Newcastle to score an easy goal. 'And Seaman makes it a Happy Christmas for Les Ferdinand,' said Gubba.

However, it is snooker, and its commentator Ted Lowe, which provide perhaps the greatest scope for easy points. Some time ago my stepson Christopher and I were watching the final of a tournament, and whilst his opponent was happily smashing balls into every pocket on the table, the camera lingered on the face of a dejected Steve Davies. 'And Steve Davies's face says it all,' muttered Christopher, to be followed seconds later by precisely that comment from dear old Ted. Oh, what joy!

The only problem with this fascination with cliché is that it can permeate all your viewing and listening. It just isn't fun guessing how many times the expression 'coming to terms with' will be trotted out on the occasion of some frightful death or disaster. These events also seem to have spawned another cliché – that of strewing bunches of flowers all over the place. Murder, sudden death and disaster are bad enough to contemplate without being told that 'the people of Ipswich are struggling to come to terms with the death of little Jimmy...' and then seeing pictures of tacky bunches of flowers littering a park or pavement.

So this funny old game has its drawbacks. But, at the end of the day, it could provide a happy trip down memory lane, when Murdoch has potted all the reds and finally cleared the table.

The Oldie Annual 2021 21

Sir Les Patterson

PIN-UPS

1. Michelle Roberts
To me brains are more important than looks and this talented lass fits the bill. I always read one of her raunchy poems at bedtime. A turn on.

2. Princess Anne
Just about my favourite royal, next to old Chazza. She likes a laugh and enjoys her freedom (like me).

3. Tamara Beckwith
A well connected little hornbag who can connect with me any time she likes.

4. Charlotte Rampling
Now that she's ditched that Frog she needs a real man, and I'm ready, willing and able.

5. Lavender Patten
Fellow RC, and real spunky little goer. My horny Honkers helpmate.

6. Mary, Lady Archer
Fragrant? I wouldn't say no to a closer sniff.

VIDEO
LARRY ADLER

The Cincinnati Kid

This one is about poker-playing. The main players, Steve McQueen and Edward G Robinson, have little to do except stare at each other earnestly in close-up, each trying to find out if the other is bluffing. There are some great characters in the cast, including Cab Calloway, without so much as a hi-de-hi, as one of the poker players, also Joan Blondell (how nice to see her again!) who illuminates the screen whenever she's on it. Although she plays the part of Lady Fingers, an expert at stud-poker, she never gets to play, acting as a substitute dealer to relieve Karl Malden. Malden is first-class as the dealer who is blackmailed into dealing crooked cards so that McQueen can win. McQueen catches on and almost chokes Malden to death to make sure he deals from an honest deck. McQueen feels he's good enough to beat Robinson, generally considered the champ, without the need for crooked dealing. Rip Turn, one of the most destructive names in showbusiness, is fine as the rich blackmailer. The best line comes at the end when Robinson, who has bluffed McQueen into conceding defeat, says, to McQueen, as he rises from the table after an all-night session: 'You're good, kid, you're really good. But just you remember, so long as I'm around, you'll always be second best. You may as well learn to live with it.'

It is a joy to watch peerless pros like these doing their stuff.

Where Eagles Dare

They're always trying to put one over on us reviewers. I remember Richard Baseheart, in *Moby Dick*, saying 'Call me, Ishmael,' as if he was leaving a message on an answering machine. I didn't fall for that one. If they remake the film, the speech will probably be 'Don't call us, Ishmael, we'll call you.'

Then there was a film, I forget the name, with a character named Lauren Adler. No, that was too obvious. Forget it.

Now along comes *Where Eagles Dare*. The film takes place in wartime Germany, the German name for 'eagle' is *Adler*, so there I am, daring as usual. The plot involves a British hit squad freeing a US general held captive by the Germans. And where is he being held prisoner? I thought you'd never ask. In Schloss Adler, that's where. The dialogue is loaded with 'Schloss Adlers' from then on. Somehow they make it sound like a personal insult. The Germans speak to each other sometimes in German, at other times in flawless English, depending on the mood of the director. We are told that the British hit-squad speaks fluent German, but they are never asked to prove it.

Richard Burton commands the rescue squad, not only looking old but has to put up with several cracks about how old he looks. An astonishingly youthful Clint Eastwood, who looks as if he's rehearsing for his Bar Mitzvah, is almost buried in the film – as is anybody who isn't Richard Burton. There are innumerable plot twists, so that literally every member of the hit-squad is, or could be, a German secret agent. (I had a German agent once, he wasn't worth the 10 per cent I paid him.) There are some females in the film but they don't amount to much. Although Mary Ure, as No 1 female, gets to do a lot of shooting.

I can't remember whether Burton, who at one moment *seems* a double agent, remains one or not. Leave it to me, I'll check and call you back later. (See first paragraph.)

Down on the allotment

I used to consider the idea of sitting down while gardening highly decadent. The only pause from toil allowed was a little rumination with one foot on the spade. Now I have young Alexander that's all changed. When he starts cooing and turning his wrists as if twiddling knobs, I know it's time for another draught from the maternal fount. I usually park my backside on a grassy verge and breastfeed like the woman in Giorgione's *Tempest*. If she had muddy leggings and bovver boots, I'd reckon she was taking a rest from tending her allotment.

Now I have a family. I'm beginning to feel the time has come for a little garden furniture, even picnics, maybe. I have sometimes wondered whether garden centres would consider delivering some naff plastic chairs to an allotment address. Somehow I doubt it. Garden centres believe we're all motorists. They are reluctant to deliver anything, or will only do so for an exorbitant fee. I once had to cycle several miles home with a three-foot fig tree on the back of my bike to avoid a £10 charge. The more literate passers-by quipped about 'Burnham Wood come to Dunsinane'.

Furniture should really be secondhand on an allotment. The Victorians coined the phrase 'poor but honest'. The allotmenteer is usually 'poor but enterprising'. If he can manufacture cold frames and compost containers, why not furniture? He of the Old Testament beard on the middle plot has built a marvellous contraption. Several pieces of bent iron support a mattress frame. He keeps an array of large, brightly coloured cushions in his shed. When his family arrives, the whole thing is turned into a swinging seat long enough to recline on. I lack that amount of ingenuity. For the moment I have invested in a secondhand deckchair for £4 and a 75p straw beach mat for the baby to sit on. I park him beneath the shade of a seeding broccoli plant.

It's funny, he won't eat the stuff cooked but quite likes nibbling the leaves in the raw state. I give him unsalted rice cakes and bread sticks to stop him stuffing his mouth with soil. The deckchair is principally for my husband so that he can enjoy the good old English pastime of watching the wife dig. He's not that keen on digging himself. I heard him muttering 'This is like effing Alcatraz!' the last time I persuaded him to do any. To be fair, he is currently suffering from seven blisters on the hands and demands that I write about them. Being an air force child, brought up in Singapore, he took a shine to my jungle knife. The last few feet of my allotment had become overgrown and James decided to panga it down manfully. And oh no, he wouldn't wear gloves. They're cissy. Unfortunately he has the delicate hands of a pawn-pushing grandmaster and couldn't take it. Now he has a spell of enforced idleness or glove-wearing. Back to the deckchair....

Fiona Pitt-Kethley

WH Auden

Oliver Stanley recalls an encounter with the poet and playwright

In 1951, Senator Fulbright invited me – together with several hundred others – to spend an academic year studying at a university in the United States. We were to imbibe the True American Way of Life, and take back the Good Word to a corrupt and decadent Europe. The *Queen Mary* carried us to the Promised Land. The Statue of Liberty loomed through the mist, and in Manhattan we tasted dry martinis, Budweisers, whisky sours and toasted BLTs. For those from rationed, dried egg, gin-and-orange England, this was a land of plenty. Automobiles and girls bulged astonishingly – 'falsies', as we soon discovered.

That semester, the Harvard Drama Society had decided to mount W H Auden's *The Dog Beneath the Skin*, to be played – how else? – as an outrageous pantomime. As I was, like the author, a Britisher, I was invited to direct. I bought a green eye-shade. Rehearsals began. Soon we were chorusing:

Stand aside now: the play is beginning
In the village of which we have spoken; called Pressan Ambo:
Here too corruption spreads its peculiar and emphatic odours
and Life lurks, evil, out of its epoch.

On the first night, the producer, director and heroine, Miss Iris Crewe of Honeypot Hall, complete with falsies, waited at the train station to meet and greet the author, who had condescended to receive applause and homage. Wystan Auden was a shambling, unkempt figure, saying little, every inch a 'foreign' poet. During the drive to Cambridge, he intimated he was thirsty: wouldn't it be lovely to stop at a saloon for a cocktail? We looked at our watches, but had to agree.

After two or three martinis, he livened up enormously. Cricket, he told us, was like bullfighting – a question of style. He was reading William Faulkner for the first time, and liked *Intolerance*. New York was best in early morning because of its clarity. Christopher Fry's *The Lady's Not for Burning* was beneath contempt. *The Rake's Progress*, on which he'd been working, was delicious, and Igor Stravinsky a darling. Down went the dry

martinis, as wit and wisdom flowed. We struggled to bring the conversation (monologue) round to *The Dog Beneath the Skin,* which he had written with Christopher Isherwood some 15 years earlier. It became apparent that the great poet's recollection of his oeuvre was fragile.

'What's it about?' he asked us.

'It's a pilgrim's progress through Life and Society,' we told him.

'Ah, yes.'

'Alan and Sir Francis – who has been hiding in the dog's skin – reject authority, learn about life and. finally, go off together to be a unit in the army of the other side…'

'What other side?'

'We hoped you'd tell us.'

Auden visibly scratched his memory and downed another dry martini in a single swallow. Miss Iris Crewe, who'd kept very quiet, suddenly asked him: 'Are you a Commie, Mister Auden?'

He looked at her as one would an alien creature, but replied evenly: 'I have become agnostic: I am learning sacred formulae for combating demons. For reuniting the divine element in man with its proper sphere.'

We gulped our drinks in uncomfortable silence. Unprompted, he expounded the sense of language necessary to a poet, and how that sense manifested itself. The notice 'Pleasure Vehicles Only', he found satisfying. We nodded but failed to understand. Soon it became apparent his eyes were closing. On his feet, slightly unsteady, our distinguished guest needed to be helped back into the Oldsmobile.

At the theatre, there was just time to welcome VIPs, including the British Consul-General and his good lady in pink. What on earth would they make of the play? Particularly the louche scene in the Ninevah Hotel, in which a diner chooses the third chorus girl from the right, pinches her thigh and orders her stewed in white wine, fingernails served separately as a savoury. Like all first nights, it didn't go smoothly. Iris Crewe forgot her lines, and the dog moved too slowly in his heavy costume. The words of the chorus were indistinguishable. From the wings I could see the author slumbering happily throughout, but he awoke at the end, and clapped heartily. Otherwise, applause was perfunctory, puzzled and weak. There was booing. No one could understand what was the 'other side' in whose army the two heroes were going to fight. They'd walked off, hand in hand. Were they just good friends? Or something more? Something unmentionable?

As pre-arranged, there were several loud cries of 'Author!' For a while, nothing happened, then Auden got up and shambled on stage. The theatre fell quiet as he sang in a cracked Oxford voice to the tune of *John Peel*:

The sun has arisen and it shines through the blind,
The lover must awaken and recall to mind,
Though the pillow be soft and the boy be kind,
Yet the man has to pay in the morning.

In the ensuing embarrassment, he wandered off; mercifully, the curtain fell. Later, at the first-night reception, he dozed throughout in an armchair. The Consul-General, his lady in pink and the other VIP guests departed immediately without so much as a thank you, so that cast and director were left to congratulate/commiserate together, aided by a generous supply of dry martini cocktails. In the morning, when we poured Auden on to the train, he finally muttered that Christopher or someone had written most of that crap, and we'd been crazy to bother with it.

ZANE: Zimbabwe A National Emergency

LIFE-SAVING AID TO IMPOVERISHED COMMUNITIES IN ZIMBABWE

ZANE supports some of the most destitute communities in Zimbabwe with:

- Food and medical aid to impoverished pensioners, including over 600 war veterans and their widows
- Pop-up classes for children in townships who otherwise would not attend school
- Creative therapy programmes for female victims of political violence and torture
- A clubfoot correction programme treating children from destitute families.

HELP US SAVE LIVES IN ZIMBABWE

John Simpson CBE
World Affairs Editor of the BBC

'I have seen a little bit of ZANE's work on the ground and from what I have seen it is very, very impressive... ZANE is one of those lovely organisations that make a little bit of money go a long, long way. ZANE is a good cause and the money is properly and well spent.'

For more information or to make a donation please visit
www.zane.uk.com

Registered with FUNDRAISING REGULATOR

Registered Charity No: 1112949

True blue

A short story by *Paul Pickering*

'I still think we should plump for the Dordogne, Gerald, don't you? Matisse may have said the sea was bluer on the coast than in any other part of the Mediterranean. But I bet he never came here,' said Muriel, and tetchily crammed another prawn into her mouth. Gerald was about to tell her that Port Vendres was a proper French fishing port, as down in the harbour a group of children rolled an oil drum into the water near where he had parked his 'Vagabond' mobile home.

Muriel had celebrated today by putting on blue eyeshadow for the first time in ten years and resembled a hamster that had tried to explore an ink bottle. Gerald stared out at the green-grey water of the harbour and at the sailors stacking and folding the pink and maroon nets by a neat line of alcoholics. The place smelt of fish, Disque Bleu, pastis and diesel. He glanced along the parade of restaurants and over the bay to the fish factory and the marina. True, this was not the most romantic of ports. But if they bought a place he might be able to afford a yacht. A modest boat. He had always wanted to sail his own little ship. When he confessed his ambition to Muriel she had laughed until she made a creaking noise, like an old hinge. 'You'll feel better about everything when your watercolour technique improves.' When a person said 'yacht', of course, it was easy to get the wrong idea. Gerald simply meant a vessel powered by the wind, and had only failed to join the bank's sailing club because Nottingham was not near to the sea, unless one counted Skegness. He did not mean the sleek white powerboat which had careered into the harbour and made a trawler sound its hooter. Motor yachts give way to starboard, he murmured to himself as the aggressive craft moored with a bump at a wharf next to the fish factory. 'I bet he's run out of fuel,' said his wife. 'That gin palace looks out of place here.'

Gerald went back to his mullet and his wife niggling at her surroundings between crustacea. He liked the town, he told himself, wondering what might be the best time to get her to view a little villa complex nearby, in a fort from which men were once transported to French colonies. He daydreamed and toyed with the buttons on his old cricket club blazer and almost did not notice the frisson of approval that ran round the hot pavement tables. When he glanced up he saw a wiry Frenchman the same age, height and colouring as himself, indeed he might have been a brother, except for a certain quiet joy in the man's every movement as he was seated, alone, by the waiter. Such men were often alone, thought Gerald. But then the Frenchman stood up again and Gerald saw the reason for the little commotion around the tables. A tall black woman, who must have been six-foot in her high heels, hurried to join the Frenchman after perusing the lobsters in the tank. She was the most beautiful creature Gerald had ever seen.

He had a problem with looking at beautiful women these days; he always felt he was being a dirty old man. 'Well, really,' Muriel said, as if to echo his feelings. The woman, a girl really, was probably 20, at the most 25, and wore a flimsy waistcoat and trousers, white high heels and nothing else. Gerald, and everyone, knew she had nothing but her perfume underneath. There was the indentation of her prominent nipples and the muscular curve of her buttocks and thighs. Gerald choked on a morsel of fish. 'He's bought her. He should be ashamed,' said Muriel.

But the Frenchman was not ashamed. When the girl got up and went to the ladies, which was on the first floor inside, the eyes of men and women followed her approvingly. Jokes were cracked, and there was a mock grabbing of a man's collar by one of the Catalan women, probably the wife of a fisherman. But everyone smiled at the Frenchman, who basked in the sunshine and the approval of his fellow diners until the young lady came back, fluttering her hands and rubbing her lips together before managing a morsel of crab. Her companion ordered champagne, and there was a small cheer around the restaurant as if for a newly married couple when the waiter pulled the cork. Gerald swallowed as he saw the girl lick the rim of the glass before taking a sip. 'I suppose it is the Spanish influence here near the border,' said Muriel. 'He should be ashamed of himself. He's three times her age and drinking all that wine and smoking all those cigarettes, he'll give himself a heart attack.' Gerald nodded, automatically. But he was staring at the girl. He hoped it was not just resentment, but he doubted very much if any 'hanky panky', as Muriel would call it, went on between the Frenchman and the girl. The Frenchman had hired her for the evening, to show off. That was it. A show-off.

The Frenchman eventually glanced at his watch and called for the bill. The couple rose and arm in arm, hip against hip they left the restaurant, and as they did so a ripple of polite applause went around the tables and was acknowledged by a backward wave by the Frenchman. The girl, momentarily, gazed at Gerald and smiled in a way that made him blush to his roots. 'I think we'll take coffee in the van, Gerald. The food is nice here but I would like to listen to some Mozart before retiring, wouldn't you?' It had not been until this trip that he realised just how much he hated Mozart. And watercolours. 'Yes, dear,' he said, waving for the bill and trying to catch a glimpse of the couple. When the bill arrived he saw the black girl and the Frenchman on the wharf near the fish factory, boarding the white yacht.

Later, Gerald was unable to sleep, and it was not the heat. He tossed and sweated in the small double bunk of the camper until finally he got up and dressed. 'You've given yourself an acid stomach with all that wine,' began his wife. 'Where on earth are you going?' He was tying his yachting shoes. 'Oh, just for a walk,' he replied.

'I'd be careful if I were you. You know what sailors are,' she said, turning over.

It was half past three, but some of the bars were still open and he very nearly stopped for a brandy. Yet something drove him on past the fishing boats and the moored yachts to the darkness of the fish wharf surrounded by black, oily water. At the end was the illuminated silhouette of the motor yacht and a light coming from the portholes. He had to know the truth.

Gerald crept nearer to the boat, nearly tripping over the moorings, and worked his way to the portholes where he peered into one of the ample cabins and saw a hint of flesh on a white bed and then the Frenchman...Gerald felt a flush of dismay, and then a match flared and he realised, a little fearfully, he was not the only spectator. At least three other men were crouched in the darkness amid the warm stench of fish and urine. But it did not matter. He turned back to the porthole. The Frenchman and the dark girl were locked in a... It was too true. He stood up, feeling giddy, just as the deck lights of the yacht came on.

He ran along the greasy dock of the fish factory as fast as his legs could carry him. But a man caught him easily. An Arab sailor in his twenties, who had a cigarette in the corner of his mouth. 'Boss wish you have this. Blue movie. Everyone get one.' The man then headed back to the yacht.

Gerald sat in the mobile home for a long time staring at the video tape. In the end he put it in the video television, a feature of the Vagabond, and witnessed the Frenchman ravish the black girl, again and again, with the sound down. He watched with the loneliness of a non-believer at a long and beautiful church service. When the video came to an end he sighed, went out and sadly threw it into the harbour. He then slipped into bed beside Muriel, who was dressed in a nylon nightie and whose neck smelled of Boots bite ointment. At breakfast he saw the white yacht cast off and speed out into the channel as Muriel put her hand gently on his. 'If this is really where you want to buy somewhere, dear... It's not so bad. We all need our dreams.' But Gerald shook his head, in relief.

'No, dear. The Dordogne it is. I'll drive. You know where you are with the Dordogne. Truly.'

Getting started

'Goodbye' (as in 'Get lost'), said the great lady literary agent, but *Colin Clark*'s timidity paid off when she got his first book into print

It all started when I appeared on a BBC documentary about my father, Kenneth. The day after the programme was broadcast, a very friendly chap called me and said he was the editor of the *Evening Standard*. He had seen the film and wanted to send someone round to do an interview. 'What about?' I asked. 'Anything you like,' he said, so next day a nice, motherly lady turned up on my doorstep and we had a chat.

It wasn't a great success – unplanned things rarely are: I learnt that when I was a television producer – but as she was leaving I decided to ask her advice. 'Many years ago,' I said, 'I kept a diary.' The lady reporter groaned, niceness and motherliness both vanishing at the speed of light. 'I wanted to ask you if you thought it was worth publishing.' My new friend fled for the door. 'What is your diary about?' she asked over her shoulder. 'It's about the four months which I spent making a film with Marilyn Monroe.' She paused, her face a pleasant mixture of conflicting emotions. In the end, honesty won. 'You better get an agent,' she said and she gave me a name.

The agent in question, a lady, was not in the habit of returning telephone calls from strangers, but I persisted and one day, to her surprise and mine, I got straight through. 'My-name-is-Colin-Clark-and-I've-got-a-diary-about-Marilyn-Monroe,' I said before she could disconnect.

Silence. Well at least that was better than the dialling tone. 'I kept a journal while I worked for Laurence Olivier on *The Prince and the Showgirl*,' I went on. I heard a sigh. Better humour him, I suppose. 'And where is this diary now?'

'It is in an old notebook in my bottom drawer.'

'Type it up and send it in and I will have someone read it.'

Click. The literary greats of this world do not waste time with 'Goodbye' or any of that nonsense.

So I got my journal transcribed, at considerable expense, by a very patient lady in Ealing, and a month later I delivered it personally to the great agent's office. I couldn't say I got much of a welcome from the receptionist, in fact I remember vowing never to go back there again, but at least I knew that my precious manuscript had arrived.

Another month went by, and then the agent actually called me. 'Someone here tells me your diary reminds them of P G Wodehouse. I have never read P G Wodehouse, but I am prepared to see what I can do.'

'Thanks very much,' I said, but she had already hung up. Two more months then, late one night, an old friend rang up.

'I was sitting next to the head of a publishing company at dinner this evening,' she said, 'and I asked him to recommend a book. He said he couldn't recommend anything at this moment but that he had just bought the rights to a brilliant diary by someone called Colin Clark and I should wait for that. I said I knew Colin Clark but he doubted if it was the same one. So I am just ringing to check.'

The next morning I called 'my' agent. 'Yes, I have shown it to a few people,' she said. 'You'd better come in to my office straight away and sign some papers before I go any further. Then we will see.' It was pouring with rain, but I jumped into the car and 30 minutes later I presented myself to the snooty receptionist once more. 'Wait here,' and I stood in the lobby, dripping and steaming, for what seemed like an hour.

'Come in.' She was talking on the phone. There was a chair in front of her desk but she did not ask me to sit down, nor to remove my coat. 'I have got someone in my office,' she said into the receiver, 'but they will not be staying long. I'll call you straight back.' To me: 'Sign these. You needn't read them. It's a perfectly standard contract authorising us to represent you.' 'But a friend of mine said a publisher had made an offer.' 'I can't do anything until you sign these. I will be in touch in a week or so. Goodbye [as in 'Get lost'],' and I stumbled out.

What a spineless twit, I hear you say. Why didn't I insist on knowing what was going on? Well, dear *Oldie* reader, I must tell you that my agent (and she was 'my' agent now) is a remarkably handsome woman, with a very strong character and a powerful mind. My public school upbringing absolutely forbids me from standing up to such a person in any circumstances whatsoever, so I left without a word. But I suppose my timidity paid off. I did get a very generous offer in the end, from another publisher, as it happened.

And so far I have delivered three books to them, all arranged by that same agent, whom I now revere.

I suppose the only moral is that getting your first book into print is not for the faint-hearted, or the vain.

'I still think we should re-word it'

What the young don't know

...quite a lot, admits *Jeremy Paxman*. But don't feel so smug – how many of you oldies can identify Schrödinger or explain Planck's Constant?

I suspect I've been asked to write this piece because the Editor thinks it will enable *Oldie* readers to feel smug. As a dedicated viewer of *University Challenge*, he claims frequently to be astonished by the fact that so many of the contestants don't know things which he had thought were common knowledge, like who had the fourth highest batting average in the 1949 England cricket tour of South Africa.

As the students look blank, the Editor sits at home, like all *Oldie* readers, thwacking the arm of his Parker Knoll Recliner, screaming at the television, 'It's Crapp, Crapp, Crapp, you fools.' We cannot all aspire to the Editor's ability to recognise the euphonious Gloucestershire left-hander, J F Crapp. But I suspect he is accurate in his vision of people across the nation hurling their cups of Ovaltine at the television screen with cries of 'What on earth do they teach young people nowadays?'

I share the irritation about some of the questions one is expected to ask. Why an ability to recall the canon of Fat Boy Slim is thought by the producers to be evidence of intellectual achievement is a mystery. It probably has something to do with the fact that the programme was commissioned by the BBC's 'Youth' department. Whoever's responsible, it's hardly the students' fault that they can answer the questions.

I confess that sometimes I, too, am astonished by what they don't know.

The other week we had a music round entirely made up of three of the best-known hymns in Christendom. No one was able to identify the starter question, and when the bonus questions were eventually allocated, they all fell to Keble College, Oxford. This being an institution built in memory of the founder of the Oxford Movement, you might have expected the Keble students to make a clean sweep. Instead of which, the best and the brightest the college could produce sat dumbly as one hymn after another echoed around the studio. They might as well have been a collection of Aztec prayer chants.

What do we conclude from these astonishing lapses? Are all students nowadays irredeemably ignorant? I'm sorry to disappoint. But it has been a sad fact of the British educational system for decades that in order to qualify for university you need only to be able to appear plausible to a bunch of lecturers who know little or nothing outside their specialised field. The idea of the general education which produced the well-rounded mind was smothered when A-levels were invented. We should have to admit, too, that, as the number of universities has expanded, the level of intellectual achievement has gone down. How could it be otherwise, when the proportion of the school age population going on to tertiary education has risen almost tenfold?

Although all the student teams on *University Challenge* have had to qualify by passing an entry exam, the chasm between the highest-scoring qualifiers and the lowest is vast. In the early stages of the competition, there are bound to be embarrassments. There is nothing worse than sitting there asking question after question as one team fails to provide a single correct answer. But there does come a point – when the scores are 200 against minus 10 – when the thing acquires the awful fascination of a car crash. Yet even among the better teams there can be astonishing lacunae. How, do you think, can they not know the date of the Battle of Crécy, or Tennyson's first name?

But all knowledge exists in a cultural context. Even Pythagoras, Einstein, Mozart or Goethe must, very occasionally, have exclaimed, 'Well, I never knew that!' And since no one can be expected to know everything, the question is merely which things some of them do know.

Clearly, times have changed. The average contestant seems to know a lot less about classical mythology that you might have expected 40 years ago. But they know a great deal more about science. They may have no idea who Sisyphus was, but they can probably identify Schrödinger.

Before you hurl your mug at the television, remember two things. Firstly, that (with one or two exceptions – that 'perpetual student' really does exist and is even now signing up for a tenth degree somewhere or other) they are all a lot younger than you.

It's all very well attacking them for not knowing something you fondly imagine you might have known at the age of 20. But how many armchair critics, with the luxury of another 20, 30 or 40 years, can explain Planck's Constant? They ought to be able to do so. Knowledge, as much as wisdom, accumulates over the years.

And secondly, it's a damn sight easier watching at home shouting out the answers than it is sitting in a tense television studio knowing that if you get it wrong half the Student Union will refuse to share their pork scratchings with you. One team, from another Oxford college, fielded a Catholic priest who, while he seemed to know almost everything about Josephine Baker, was unable to identify the *Magnificat*. Nerves can do that to you.

No, I think I am going to disappoint *The Oldie*'s, distinguished Editor. Armchair criticism of the 'Bah, students nowadays know nothing' variety is as valid as a capon's comments on why the cockerel failed to get the hens laying.

Social Distancing in comfort

WE ARE ALL DIFFERENT AND SO ARE OUR SCOOTERS

Portable, folding mobility scooters good for your wellbeing, helping you to stay active!

We are the only lightweight scooter company in the UK that researches the global market to provide the best portable scooters for you to test and try out at one of our two large, well stocked showrooms.

With so many mobility scooters on the market, choosing the right one for you can be a hard decision.

So we make it our mission to help you find that scooter which best suits your needs and lifestyle and to make life even easier we can bring a selection to your home.

That's right, a **FREE NO OBLIGATION** demonstration at the place you feel most comfortable.

 LIGHTWEIGHT SCOOTERS

Call one of our friendly team today!

0333 414 1881

or visit **lightweightscooters.co.uk**

FREE Home Demonstration
Try at your leisure with NO Obligation

Our Portable range gives you/offers

Electric or manual folding	Up to 14m travelling	Up to 32st weight capacity	Tackle uneven ground	Lightest in the world	Good manoeuvrability	Suspension seating	Automatic safety braking system	Lightweight Lithium Battery	Flight Friendly	Portable Scooters

Gyles Brandreth's PIN-UPS

1. Brigitte Bardot
I know other contributors to this series have chosen the likes of Harold Macmillan and J B Priestley as their pin-ups. I am afraid posters of Che Guevara and W H Auden have never adorned my walls. My idea of a proper pin-up is a picture of a truly fanciable woman – and, for my money, you still can't beat BB in her prime.

2. Jane Asher
Jane Asher was the first undeniably beautiful girl to sleep in my bed. Maddeningly, I was elsewhere at the time. The story of how she came to find her way to my room at Oxford in 1968 is as long as, unhappily, it is innocent. Thirty-two years later she introduced me to her personal trainer, so our bodies are still in touch, and still at one remove.

3. Michele Brown
I married Michele Brown in 1973. Her physical beauty is matched only by her intelligence, integrity and finely honed sense of the ridiculous.

4. Hillary Clinton
In the 1980s my fellow Conservatives were lusting over Margaret Thatcher. I admired her, but can't pretend ever to have fancied her. My feelings about Hillary Clinton, on the other hand, are rather alarmingly complicated.

5. Marlene Dietrich
Marlene was the first international diva with whom I can claim intimate contact. In the 1960s, outside the Golders Green Hippodrome, I helped her off the roof of her limousine (dressed in a miniskirt, she had been signing autographs for adoring fans) and, for a fleeting moment, found myself holding her left thigh.

6. Melinda Messenger
Last year I interviewed Melinda Messenger, the *Sun*'s 'Page 3 Girl for the Thrillennium', and found her to be lovely in every respect. At the end of our encounter, she wrinkled up her nose and said, 'Shall I get my kit off, Gyles?' Now, that's my idea of a pin-up.

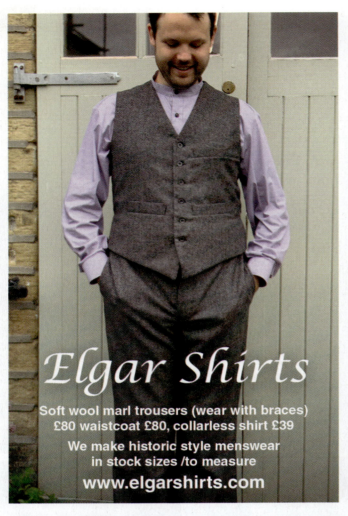

Elgar Shirts

Soft wool marl trousers (wear with braces)
£80, waistcoat £80, collarless shirt £39

We make historic style menswear
in stock sizes / to measure

www.elgarshirts.com

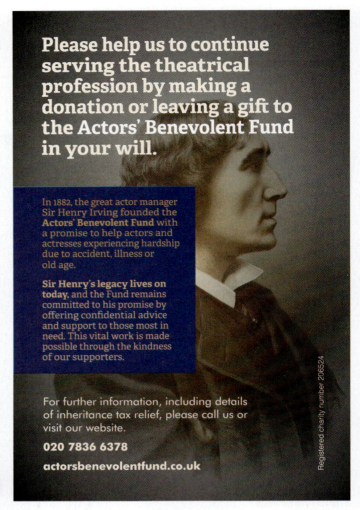

Please help us to continue serving the theatrical profession by making a donation or leaving a gift to the Actors' Benevolent Fund in your will.

In 1882, the great actor manager Sir Henry Irving founded the **Actors' Benevolent Fund** with a promise to help actors and actresses experiencing hardship due to accident, illness or old age.

Sir Henry's legacy lives on today, and the Fund remains committed to his promise by offering confidential advice and support to those most in need. This vital work is made possible through the kindness of our supporters.

For further information, including details of inheritance tax relief, please call us or visit our website.

020 7836 6378

actorsbenevolentfund.co.uk

Registered charity number 206524

FERNSBY HALL TAPESTRIES

Tapestry kits produced by Diana Fernsby from the original paintings of Catriona Hall. Kits from £55.

Email: kits@fernsbyhall.com   **Tel:** 01279 777795   www.fernsbyhall.com

Arthur and the Paignton Peach

John Moynihan watched the young Sue Barker learn her tennis the hard way

'New balls, please...' Wimbledon is with us again, with the serene, unflappable, blonde television presenter Sue Barker dishing out daily results and facts from the All-England Club with the assurance and professionalism of Doris Day on a film set.

The nation will sit back and marvel at Sue's ability to inform – no angst, no nerves, and an occasional touch of humour. It wasn't quite the same back in February 1975, when a shivering teenage Devonian girl turned up to practise on a freezing morning by the sea, on a court attached to a luxury Torquay hotel.

It was obvious that the 'Paignton Peach', as she was nicknamed, could barely hold her early morning cup of tea because of the presence of her dictatorial coach, Arthur Roberts – always 'Mr Roberts' to Sue.

Roberts was putting his new bunny through her paces before an Under-21 tournament, watching every stroke made on court with the malice of a gazing cobra. Even this reporter began to feel uneasy as Sue, looking ever more terrified, responded to a shower of instructions – 'Yes, Mr Roberts ... Right, Mr Roberts.'

Not that Sue Barker could claim to be a total novice in those far-off days. Since coming under Roberts's coaching wing after leaving a convent school in Paignton, she had improved her game to the extent of beating the Russian girl, Olga Morozova, in an Australian Open.

Great stuff – but the fastidious Mr Roberts was not the kind of coach to sink to his knees and bestow wallowing congratulations: when she arrived back, it was up at dawn – and don't be late.

Roberts already had a large appreciation society within the British game, having launched the careers of Mike Sangster and the future Wimbledon champion, Angela Mortimer. Now he had Sue as a member of his 'stable'. No one ever dared say 'squad' – Roberts hated squads, and refused Sue permission to attend squad training abroad.

It was easy to see why the former Queen's Club ball boy exerted such an influence on his pupils. He reminded me of a drill corporal at Aldershot. 'Guts,

A very young Sue Barker with her scary coach, Arthur Roberts, in 1971

tennis has always been about guts,' he barked at me at the courtside as Sue knocked the ball about with her British team colleague Linda Mottram.

'Guts' was an expression which Sue went on to use frequently about her own performances, especially when she had thrown games away. 'I didn't guts it out enough. Mr Roberts used to say: "Guts it out for yourself on court if you're not going to guts it out for us. That's what you need – a bit of pride and concentration."'

Roberts was part of the old tennis school, reared on the amateur code, and although Sue Barker went on to make a modest fortune, he deplored the rise of mammon within the game. 'I have always been suspicious about people with too much money,' he told me. 'The lovely thing about tennis is that you can't buy it. The alley cats tend to be the most dedicated – they don't fade in and out.'

Roberts was rigidly in favour of caution, and his latest 'alley cat', a retired brewer's daughter, had by no means risen to the heights of the game when we met that morning. 'Sue has still to prove herself. So far, she has poked her little nose into the game – she's got to keep on her feet, keep going, and do it over and over again. It's going to be tough for her. She came along on that tour in Australia – but you've got to play a lot of bad tennis to become a good tennis player.'

Inwardly, Roberts did have a great respect for the Paignton Peach's game: 'There isn't a better forehand in the game than Sue – she's got a big, fat forehand – but you've also got to have the brain to handle it. She's got to cultivate her backhand.'

It was hard work all the way, but, despite successes in the Wightman Cup and other tournaments, Sue Barker only won one Grand Slam title – the French Open on 13 June 1976 in Paris: 'Mr Roberts wouldn't have spoken to me had I lost to Renata Tomanova – it was a thrilling feeling.' Having beaten Martina Navratilova, Billie-Jean King and Virginia Wade in previous encounters, Barker rose to number 4 in the world rankings and went on to earn an overall $878,701 in prize money before leaving the game.

One of her major regrets was not reaching the Wimbledon ladies' final in 1977 – she lost in the semi-final to Betty Stove when she should have won. Many commentators thought she would have beaten Virginia Wade in the final.

Now she has become a bit of Mr Roberts herself, drilling out television quotes from shy, perspiring athletes – 'Come on, guts it out.'

Thoughts on death

The evidence for it is all around us, says *Philip Callow*, but even at my age I persist in thinking that death is something that happens to other people

If I tell myself, as I sometimes do, that thoughts of death have occupied my mind with some regularity over the past n years, I know I am only stating the obvious. In 1989 my wife suffered an awful blow, losing her daughter to meningitis in her 21st year. Since then we have tended her grave more or less fortnightly.

There is something monstrous about a young person cut down on the very threshold of life. Kneeling at the graveside cutting grass, planting snowdrop bulbs, I ask myself how this can be. Why should I be spared, my days numbered, and this vibrant girl be in her grave?

Thirty years ago, in the throes of a complete breakdown, I contemplated ending it all as the only way out. But even the worthless life that mine then seemed to be was stronger than death. The inexorable law of life is that we must live, even when we are utterly without hope. 'One day,' my doctor told me, 'you'll look at the world with new eyes.' And so it turned out to be. The force which drives us as it drives the sun and the stars is almost impossible to withstand.

So, of course, is death, and that is the paradox. Death approaches like a force embedded deep in the earth. In fact, life and death seem to be speaking the same language, so dependent are they on each other. Winter gives birth to spring: a seed falls to the ground and from its little death a flame of growth spurts up.

I subscribe to no conventional religion, I have no belief in a personal God, yet the grand majesty of old hymns can inspire me. If I find it hard to believe in oblivion waiting for us at the end of existence, it is because there are no full stops in nature. Somehow we are part of something endlessly flowing. And for me the laughable thing is this: even now, in spite of my age and the evidence of death all around me, I can't imagine being dead. Death is something that happens to other people. Of course if I had a chronic illness it would be different. When we are young we feel immortal, and that is perfectly natural, but to feel it at my age is absurd. Yet I do. I wonder if this inability to accept the inevitable is more common than we realise.

I cannot imagine an afterlife, but nor can I deny its possibility in some form we cannot possibly grasp, mired as we are in our senses and unable to comprehend anything beyond the scope of the life we know. What if my spirit shoots off into space after death and joins billions of others? There is room for us all out there. What if it swoops into a newborn baby at the moment of birth, as more than one religion believes? The vitality which determines our existence cannot be measured or explained by science, coming as it does from a Fourth Dimension, which a Christian would call the Holy Ghost. If my spirit wanders forth to seek another incarnation after my body has expired, why not? But to my wife this is anathema. Once is enough! she cries.

I am indifferent to the fate of my body when it dies. After all, it is only a carcass. But as I am 15 years older than my wife and will no doubt predecease her, she rightly argues that I should make choices as to what kind of funeral I should have and how it might be conducted. That is right and proper, and I have settled for burial.

I have written a number of biographies, four of them about men who died comparatively young. A biographer is, of course, in the business of obituaries. The plot is given in advance, as it is for all of us: the same journey from birth to death. Van Gogh, in one of those letters to his brother Theo in which he speaks so entrancingly from the heart, wonders if we are taken to a star by death, 'just as we climb on a train to Tarascon'. Maybe, he goes on, diseases are our fast transport. 'Dying of old age in our sleep, we arrive on foot.'

A writer's devious nature is not easy to live with, and after my death, I should like to return as a ghost in order to reward my wife in some way for her forbearance, if the lords of death will allow me. I hope when my time comes I will summon up some courage. I am comforted by the thought of Walt Whitman, lying paralysed for years, who could even joke on good days about his slipping hold on life, telling his young Boswell, 'As Miss Nipper says in *Dombey and Son*, I don't know whether I am temporary or a permanency: I don't know whether I am to stay or move on.'

I once met...

The Duke of Windsor

Patrick Skene Catlin recalls going Over the Hill in Nassau with the Governor of the Bahamas

The Duke, as usual by teatime, was drunk. Not very drunk, but sufficiently soft in the head to have driven his Cadillac convertible along the fairways of Nassau's premier golf club. This was before electric buggies. Evidently he was not in the mood for long walks between shots; and, after all, he was the Governor. He was still HRH the Duke of Windsor, and I was an 18-year-old Pilot Officer, still easily impressed. He had given me a friendly wave as he drove his car past me on the 16th fairway.

He finished his game quickly and was well ahead of me in the bar. In the early stages of drinking, he had a charmingly whimsical, some said boyish, slightly tilted smile. Free for the afternoon from the Duchess's surveillance, he was able to indulge in playful informality. 'Hope you didn't mind my playing through,' he said. 'What'll you have?'

It was gratifying to be recognised by someone so senior, and astonishing to be offered a drink.

We were both in civilian clothes, but they did not disguise the disparity of ranks – I in a white shirt and khaki trousers, he in a lime-green shirt and doeskin slacks of Schiaparelli shocking pink. After more than one drink, he became quite chatty, asking some of the questions that strangers ask in casual bar-room encounters: what's your name? Where are you from? What do you do? 'A navigator, eh?' he commented. 'That must be jolly interesting. Astronomy and mathematics and so on. Training on Mitchells?' 'No, sir. Ferrying.' 'Ah! Trips to Egypt and India. I envy you.'

Since Churchill had ordered the Duke to assume the governorship, he was confined to the Bahamas. The Prime Minister was determined to prevent the ex-King from attempting to negotiate peace with Germany to help his friends there to fight more effectively against Communism.

'Come on,' he now said to me. 'Let's go for a ride.' Coming from him, the suggestion seemed very much like an order. 'You've been Over the Hill, I suppose.' 'Not yet,' I admitted, as suavely as possible. Over the Hill was a district, I had heard, that airmen and others sometimes daringly visited after dark. It was the black ghetto, noted for furtive all-night revelry in shebeens and shanties. Over the Hill was where the colony hid poverty, where the haves, for fun, went slumming with the have-nots. In this respect, the ghetto was like Harlem in the distant past.

I knew that the Duke of Windsor had the reputation of a fun-lover, a bit of a sport. He enhanced this reputation by encouraging Blind Blake, Nassau's foremost calypso singer, to perform as a sort of court jester at parties, even in Government House, accompanying himself on guitar and singing *Love Alone,* his popular new song:

Love, love alone,
Caused King Edward to leave the throne.
I know King Edward was noble and great,
But his love caused him to abdicate.
He got the money and he got the talk
And the fancy walk that would suit New York...

The Duke always led the laughter and applause.

But now I looked at my watch. Wasn't 4.45 rather early for this expedition? Part-way down the far side of the hill, I was surprised when the Duke produced an Army cap with the scarlet band of superior rank and jammed it jauntily on his well-groomed fair head. He turned off the main road, along a narrow, unpaved road with a row of dilapidated wooden shacks on each side, and announced his arrival with long blasts on the horn – baaaahp! baaaahp! baaaahp!

I must have looked alarmed. 'It's all right,' he assured me. 'They know me. I come here often.' Several front doors opened promptly, as if his signal had been expected. Small boys, one by one and in twos and threes, ran out and gathered in the road near the car. There were about 15 of them, ranging in age from, say, 8 to 12. They were dressed in cotton shirts and shorts that looked faded by many launderings, and they were all carrying rifles – that is to say, homemade facsimiles and sticks that represented rifles.

The Duke stood up in the car, a short, upright, slim figure of paradoxical dignity, the authoritative cap transcending the gaudy green shirt and pink slacks. The expression on his face was stern. Without any preliminaries, he commanded the boys, in a high-pitched yet military shout, to 'Fall in!' They duly obeyed, forming fairly straight ranks.

Then the Duke proceeded to drill them in accordance with the protocol of the Brigade of Guards. When he ordered them to 'Slo-ope ... arms!' they propped their toy rifles on their tiny shoulders very nearly in unison. When he yelled, 'By the left, qui-ick... march!' they quickly marched, and the order 'A-bout ... turn!' soon got them back again.

When at last he stood them at ease and then easy, the boys were more like boys as they scrambled for the silver coins that their commander scattered in front of them.

How His Excellency laughed! I thought then that he was an awful fool, but I was grateful to him, and I am still, for demonstrating so vividly that warfare, or at least his part in it, was absurd.

East of Islington

Sam Taylor makes her remodelled outhouse 'authentic' with echt sooty brickwork

In common with the rest of London, the residents of East of Islington were having the builders in. Roof extensions, brutal glass cubes precariously attached to the rear of tiny terraces, patios, gazebos, whirlpool baths, the air was suddenly awash with the whirr of pneumatic drills and cement mixers.

And our household was no exception. For the price of a small family car, we had decided to 'remodel' our collapsing outside loo into what the designer had artistically called a 'garden room'.

'It'll add thousands to the price, sweeties,' he explained while simultaneously presenting his bill. And so it did, but not, unfortunately, to the value of the property. Because no sooner had the designer left for the airport – for what he referred to as a creativity-collecting trip to Morocco – than the man from the council arrived.

Armed with his clipboard, he didn't like what he saw. 'I don't like what I'm seeing,' he gasped, staring at our newly erected brickwork. 'I don't like what I'm seeing at all.'

It seemed there had been a change of thinking at council HQ and we were about to be among its first benefactors. Apparently it was a problem with soot, or lack of it. In order to preserve the olde worlde charm of East of Islington's slummy terraces, the council had decided that soot was to be reapplied to all new buildings. 'We need things to look authentic,' he elaborated. 'As if the original occupants had never left.'

The clean air act was out, and 'washing' the entire building in soot was in. Helpfully, he suggested we contact a local sweep for soot-purchasing tips. Meanwhile, he would be back later in the week to inspect what he called a 'sample soot patch'. Other than that, we were on our own. 'No soot, no building,' were his final words on the matter.

It took the local chimney sweep several minutes to compose himself. As instructed, I had called in search of soot. Would it be possible to buy some, I wondered? And if so, how much? 'What do you think I do with it, love?' he mused, when he finally stopped laughing. 'Bring it home and keep it in the sitting room?'

Besides his lack of stock, there was another problem. 'Soot isn't what it used to be,' he confided. 'Smokeless fuel,' he sighed. 'It's just not black enough.' What we needed, he explained, was a substitute. Charcoal maybe. 'Perhaps you could try the fire brigade?' he chortled. 'They often have a good blaze on their hands.' Clearly we were facing a national soot crisis. There simply wasn't enough to go round, and certainly not round a building.

Slab, the builder, sucked his teeth. Slab lived in a gleaming clean cul-de-sac. To him, the idea of dirty brickwork was unthinkable. 'Nutters,' was all he could contribute when I pleaded for guidance. It fell to Mini Slab, his trusty assistant, to come up with possible soot stand-ins.

'Manure,' he suggested. 'From pit ponies. Or perhaps cigarette ash.' As the former seemed themselves to be as much an historical rarity as soot itself, it was agreed that Mini Slab would bring in the contents of that evening's ashtrays from his local. It's darts night,' he explained. 'I should get a good sackful.'

Squid ink, liquid eye-liner and plain old dirt were all added to the soot stand-in list. The next day the new brickwork was covered in fake soot tester patches, but nothing seemed authentic enough. Time was running out. The man from the council was due and our building was still too clean.

Finally, it was Willy's Walker who gave us the solution. 'Consult this,' he said, and handed over an aged *Blue Peter* annual. And there, in black and white, was the answer. Alongside a very fetching picture of Valerie Singleton was a cereal box model of a chimney.

'Stick powdered black poster paint on the surface to give it that authentic soot-covered look,' read the instructions.

With no time to lose, Slab and Mini Slab did exactly what Valerie Singleton dictated. The man from the council was impressed. 'Very authentic,' he nodded, sagely. 'This is just the kind of traditional workmanship the council are keen on.'

'Yeah,' said Slab the builder. 'Next week we're building Tracey Island from Fairy Liquid Bottles.'

The ones that got away

It's Nellie Melba 0, Laurence Olivier 3, says champion name-dropper *Charles Osborne*

Time for some more name-dropping. What about Clara Schumann, the famous 19th-century pianist, and wife of the composer Robert Schumann? No, of course I didn't know her. Come off it, she died in 1896. But she was also a distinguished piano teacher, and one of her last surviving pupils, Irene Fletcher, who was by then in her eighties, was teaching piano in Brisbane in the 1940s. I went to Irene for lessons because I wanted to be able to say I was a pupil of a pupil of Clara Schumann. However, Irene turned out to be an enthusiastic member of the Australian Communist Party, much more interested in promoting communism than in improving the piano technique of her pupils.

The famous Australian soprano Dame Nellie Melba is someone else I never met – she died when I was three – but 15 years later I lodged in Melbourne for a few weeks with a retired Scottish nurse, a Sister Hopkinson, who had come to Australia as nurse-companion to Dame Nellie. The arrangement, Sister Hopkinson told me, had been that, if she wished to leave Melba's employ, her fare back to Europe would be paid by the diva. After a year, Sister Hopkinson could stand no more of her employer's tantrums, and gave Melba notice of her intention to quit. When the time came for her to leave, Dame Nellie handed her an envelope containing one week's wages. 'Where's my fare back to England?' Sister Hopkinson asked. 'Jesus Christ walked on the fucking water, and so can you,' replied Melba. That was why, 15 years later, Sister Hopkinson was still in Australia, taking in lodgers.

At that time, I was a young actor – a profession I gave up at the age of 30 because, although I was keeping in work, I'd got bored with it. But in the 1940s and '50s, at first in Australia and then in England, I earned my living from acting.

I worked with some famous names – Michael Redgrave, Richard Todd, Leslie Henson – and encountered others, ranging from Laurence Olivier to Marilyn Monroe. I rubbed shoulders with Olivier on three occasions. The first was when he

What about Ronald Reagan? Well, I did once share an elevator with him at the embassy in London

and Vivien Leigh came to Australia in 1948 with an Old Vic company. When they got to Brisbane, where they appeared in *School for Scandal* at Her Majesty's Theatre, I was a few hundred yards away at the Guild Café Theatre, playing the young poet Marchbanks in Bernard Shaw's *Candida*. Olivier gave me his autograph on a copy of my *Candida* programme, which I still possess.

My second encounter with Olivier was nearly ten years later, when I was filming at Pinewood Studios in Geordie, with Bill Travers, Virginia McKenna and Alastair Sim. I had a one-line part as a newspaperman. On the set next door, Olivier was filming his Richard III, and whenever we had a break in shooting I would rush next door to catch a glimpse of the great man at work. Once, I found him in his Richard costume and make-up, staring gloomily at a group of actors as a scene was being set up. He looked as though he were in the depths of despair.

The third occasion was in 1966, at a reception at the Arts Council in London. My right arm was in a sling after a motor accident, and I was standing by a window when Olivier approached me. 'What have you done to yourself?' he asked. I told him, and he made sympathetic noises. 'I have a great deal of experience of this sort of thing,' he said. 'I'm always breaking an arm or a wrist or an ankle or something. It's because I'm such a physical actor.' 'You certainly are,' I murmured fatuously. He looked reflectively at me, with that Mahlerian *Weltschmerz* I recognised from his Heathcliff, his Darcy, his Hamlet. 'I would like, really, to be a cerebral actor, but I haven't got the equipment,' he said. To my exasperation and relief, someone came up to us at that moment and led Olivier away.

I had occasion, once, to send a script to Laurence Olivier. Having just been reading about Cocteau addressing an envelope to Proust in verse (*'Cent-deux Boulevard Haussman, Oust!/Tirez, facteur, chez Marcel Proust'*), I thought I'd try something similar. The Oliviers were living in Eaton Square, so I addressed my package thus:

O postman, deliver this parcel, I pray,
To the Eaton Square flat of Olivier.
You'll find him there or, if not he,
Please hand it instead to Miss Vivien Leigh.

(The package was delivered safely.)

In 1957 a friend of mine was filming in *A King in New York* with Charlie Chaplin. My sole purpose in visiting the set was to meet Chaplin, and I took with me a photograph from an earlier film, *Limelight*, which showed Chaplin as an old clown staring in quiet desperation into his mirror in a dressing-room. I did manage to meet him, and asked him to autograph the photo. He smiled as he handed it back to me, but put my quite expensive ballpoint pen in his pocket as he walked away. I felt pleased that we had something of each other's.

What about Ronald Reagan? Well, I did once share an elevator with him at the American Embassy in London, but we didn't exchange a word. I'm afraid that the photo of me in New York, walking down Fifth Avenue with President Reagan, is a fake. It's not Ronnie, it's a life-size cut-out, and my friend Ken Thomson and I paid five dollars to be photographed with it. Enough for now.

Just the job

Hugh O'Shaughnessy is enjoying the company and conversation of an altogether better class of builders

We were talking abut Tom Stoppard, my builder and I, and I ventured that I did not understand how a Czech whose native language was not English could have such mastery of our tongue. 'Well,' says Chris, 'look at Joseph Conrad.' My exemplary builder used to be a publisher.

I went downstairs and the carpenter Tommy and his Polish helper Marcin were at work repairing the chaos wreaked on our house when RWE Thames Water flooded us last November. Tommy had just finished a new architrave and we fell to chatting about the dreadful situation in Colombia, where three Irishmen are in prison. I'd just come back from there. Tommy and I had met a few days previously. 'Mr O'Shaughnessy,' said John the engineer on the doorstep, with a gleam in his eye which indicated to me that he'd been looking forward to this moment for a week or more, 'meet Mr O'Shaughnessy.'

Like me, Tommy had been born in Britain and, also like me, he'd been taken across the water at a young age. He'd kept his Dublin accent: I hadn't kept the lovely Cork one I had when I was six. But we were obviously cousins. We O'Shaughnessys share an ancestral line which goes back to AD 358 and to Daithi, who lies under a small monolith in the middle of a field in County Roscommon. They buried him after he died tragically while crossing the Alps in a bid to overthrow the Roman Empire. Our common family roots didn't exist just in my imagination. 'He's very good-looking,' whispered my lady wife with a distant look in her eyes. 'All our family are. Don't you remember?' I replied a little testily.

The O'Shaughnessy spell – his, not mine – became more powerful still after my lady wife offered him a bottle of modest claret for a little job he'd done on the side for us. 'No thanks, I'm teetotal,' said Tommy. 'I fell off a roof in Germany and decided I'd not take another drop.' After 42 years of married life she is inexplicably still prey to all the common misapprehensions about booze and the Irish and she was very impressed.

A couple of days previously I'd been chatting to Marcin from Poznan about his country's prospects after its accession to the European Union at mid-year. 'It's going to be great,' he said enthusiastically.

Last week Monique came to help with the painting. Black-haired and mini-skirted, she explained to me with all the aplomb of a great actress who was temporarily resting how she helped out Chris when there weren't any murals to get on with.

Her family connections were South American. We swapped reminiscences about the Buenos Aires of yesteryear. Mr Jones is coming to replace the floor tiles that the water monopoly destroyed. I gather he once ran a night-club and I am looking forward to his views on the world from the vantage-point of a bouncer.

The whole reconstruction process has been a valuable revelation for one who has spent a working life worrying about humdrum things like the effects of the 'war on drugs' on the jungles of Colombia and the success or otherwise of the government of President Lula in Brazil. Our flooding brought me into contact with intelligent, well-informed and skilled people working in small businesses whom I never would otherwise have met. It also gave me the impression that intelligent, well-informed and skilled people don't often work in large companies, whose gifts for mismanagement are outstanding.

Example: the German-owned Thames Water giant (managing director the richly rewarded William Alexander), which doesn't know where its water mains are, so doesn't know where to tell the men to use their pneumatic drills.

Example: Subterra, a part of some misnamed company called Enterprise, the Thames Water subcontractor who actually broke the water main and caused the flood. They claim to 'minimise excavation and disruption' but they omit to add that they also promote them. They drive their vans around Islington like psychopaths and spit at you when you complain.

Example: EDF, the French company which sells electricity to Londoners yet confesses openly to working with Balfour Beatty, the firm which is charged with bringing us the Hatfield train disaster.

We are all condemned to do business with the big incompetents. But I shall do my best to avoid them in future. The small business people are more reliable and more fun.

And if you want a good carpenter, remember the name of O'Shaughnessy,

I once met...

MARCH 2005

Enid Blyton

Terence Daum was an avid reader of her books and decided to get on his bike to meet her

I was ten and the school holidays were becoming monotonous. I had re-read all my *Famous Five* books. Now, like George and the others, I wanted an adventure. So I decided to call on the author of the *Famous Five* – Enid Blyton.

The week before, I had been taken on a coach trip to Beaconsfield, where the prolific children's writer lived in Penn Road. After visiting the model village – the object of the trip – I had persuaded my aunt and uncle to stroll along Penn Road in search of Green Hedges, the author's home. And suddenly, there it was, exactly as pictured in Enid Blyton's own magazine that most of the pupils in my class read avidly. I stood at the gate and gaped, willing her to come out. She didn't.

A short time before this, a poem I'd submitted had won first prize and had been published in *Sunny Stories*. I'd called it *Enid Blyton's Party* and incorporated in it the names of many of the characters from her books. On the strength of this, I reasoned that she would be pleased to see me. We could chat about my poem, and then about *The Adventurous Four, Bumpy and his Bus, Mr Galliano's Circus* and all the folk of the *Magic Faraway Tree*. Perhaps she'd give me a hint as to what the Famous Five would be up to next. That would be something to tell the kids at school. How envious they'd all be.

I set off on my Raleigh upright bicycle to follow the route that the Smith's Luxury Coach tour had taken the previous week. It was a long haul. But I was fortified by the reception I imagined I'd be given when I got to Beaconsfield.

'So you're the child who wrote that amusing poem – well done! And you've cycled all the way from Reading to see me? You must stay to tea!' Enid Blyton was bound to say, clapping her hands delightedly – adding, like a cosy character from her books, and with lots of exclamation marks, 'Oooooooooh! What tremendous fun we'll have! There will be four kinds of jam! Lemonade! Ice cream! And three different cakes!'

At last, hot, weary but triumphant, I reached her home in Penn Road. I carefully padlocked my bike to the slender trunk of one of the Green Hedges and, with a feeling of utmost excitement, walked up the drive to ring the bell.

But instead of Eeny Blyton, as she was affectionately known in my class, a maid opened the door. This threw me. I was suddenly tongue-tied.

'Er...excuse me, I...um...don't feel well,' I heard myself mumbling, in panic. 'Could I have a drink of water, please?'

Before the maid could respond, almost before I had taken in the large Chinese vase placed just ahead at the turn of the staircase, the writer herself appeared from a room on the left. The frizzy hair was unmistakable. She was wearing a New Look frock and had scarlet fingernails.

'What does this child want?' she asked, as if I were not there.

'He says he feels unwell, ma'am.'

Enid Blyton turned a concerned gaze towards me. 'Do you need a doctor? There's a doctor across the road.'

'No, no,' I stammered, 'I'll be all right if I drink some water. I just... feel sick!' 'Well, you mustn't be sick here!' she exclaimed firmly. 'Show him into the garden,' she told the maid.

I sprawled on the lawn, frustratedly staring at the back of the house. This wasn't the way I'd planned it. Out came the maid with a tumbler, a jug of water and a few boiled sweets on a tray. This was when, to my later shame, I recovered my composure and conversational skills.

'By the way,' I said chattily, as if suddenly discovering something.

'Wasn't that lady Eeny Blyton... the authoress?'

The maid gave me a shrewd look that turned into a smile. How many other star-struck children had pulled this one?

'Indeed it was,' she replied. 'She sent you these sweets to have with the water and said do stay – in the garden – and don't leave until you feel better. Goodbye!' Not long afterwards I slunk away, unchained my bike and dawdled dejectedly down to Slough to catch the stopping train home.

I had met my literary idol, but where was the evidence? I had no autograph. No photograph signed 'To Terry, from Enid Blyton'. No 'Happy Snap' taken together. Only my word. And that wasn't enough for the kids at Grovelands School.

'Anyone could say that,' they scoffed after the holidays, when I recounted my true-life Enid Blyton adventure. 'Bet you're only making it up.'

> 'Well, you mustn't be sick here!' Blyton exclaimed firmly. 'Show him into the garden,' she told the maid

The Oldie Annual 2021 **39**

Hunters in the night

Penelope Bennett braves the rainforests of Kensington in search of bats – will she find any? And what else lurks out there in the dark…?

It's 8.15 pm and we (35 of us) are about to set off on a Bat Watching Walk in London's Holland Park. 'We' consist of women, men and children plus our bat-expert leader. It's been raining all day and has only just stopped so we're bedecked in mackintoshes, hats and sturdy shoes.

After passing the laid-out flowerbeds, we enter the interior of the park which is wooded, dripping and now filling with dusk. We shuffle along, one behind the other, talking quietly. Our leader carries a bat detector machine which is about the size of a transistor radio and has a red light. Some adults and children also have detectors (what an infinitely more rewarding present for a child than a mobile phone) which, as it becomes darker, make us resemble a swarm of red glow-worms.

Having no idea where we now are or where we're being led, we stop beside a pond covered with what appears to be bright green bouclé knitting. The detectors are pointed towards the sky and they've started emitting faint clicking tapping noises. Our chattering stops. All heads are tilted upwards. The bats were here but now they've gone, flying at a speed faster than our eyes can follow.

On we walk, ever hopeful. Deeper and deeper we go, penetrating the heart of London W8's rainforest. The trees grow more closely together.

The path has become steeper and narrower. We walk in single file, members of an expedition, mackintoshes swishing, shoes slithering. Leaves drip big drops; the trees' soaked bark looks naked and muscular. The earth exudes an intimate, damp, truffle-ish scent.

As we continue, we learn more bat facts; here, in hollow trees and woodpecker holes, bats roost. During the day they sleep hanging upside down, or clean their faces with their thumbs. Now they are searching for food. Each kind of bat has its own call in the form of a high-pitched squeak too high for most people to hear. When these squeaks collide with an insect they bounce back as an echo which the bat hears and so discovers its prey. This is the mysterious echo location, enabling them to find minute insects in pitch darkness. Usually they catch insects in their mouths, but they also use their wings, scooping up

> **Some adults and children have bat detectors which, as it becomes darker, make us resemble a swarm of red glow worms**

anything from tiny gnats to large beetles. In one night a pipistrelle bat can eat 3,000 insects. A healthy adult pipistrelle weighs about 5 or 6 grams – the weight of a small walnut.

A frog perches on its haunches in the middle of the path, imagining it is camouflaged. Soft-pawed black rabbits (discarded pets) hop silently over wet leaves. Above us, in their nests, squirrels are probably asleep, wrapped warmly in their own tails.

In their nurseries, baby bats, born in the summer, will be clustering close together; sometimes baby-less bat aunts snuggle up, adding additional warmth. There may be old bats here, too; some live until they're 30 years old. Kensington High Street is only a few hundred yards away.

The detectors suddenly start clicking excitedly. We stop, all 35 chins raised towards the sky, resembling a troupe of penguins. A cheer goes up, enough to frighten the bravest of bats.

'There's one! And another!' I gaze intently at the sky and see a flash of something but suspect it's the onset of astigmatism rather than a bat.

'This is a unique experience,' one person whispers to another. It is indeed. And the fact that I haven't seen any bats doesn't really matter.

The walk is over. It is time to disband. Suddenly, hidden loudspeakers announce, 'All visitors must leave the park. The gates are about to close.' But we can't find even one gate and the rest of the expeditionary force has mysteriously disappeared. Nothing quite looks as it did when we entered in daylight. It could just as well be a different park. Eventually we find a gate. It's locked. Helped by the Belvedere Restaurant's concierge, we finally discover a gate that is open. But where are we, and where is my car?

Through a high hedge wafts the smell of soup – an odd thing for a hedge to smell of. On we walk through unrecognisable, empty streets.

At last we spot a Guard Dog Patrol van. A large, black Alsatian with wolf-like eyes and a growl to match approaches me. I make an immediate confession to its handler that I'm frightened of dogs so would he please restrain his and could he tell us where we are? Then suddenly I recognise the street and see my car.

Beauty and the freak show

Joan Rhodes used to perform as a strong woman. She tore a telephone book in half and bent iron bars with her teeth, and once dropped Bob Hope on his head…

The Hackney Empire was slowly dying by the time I got there for the first time in 1949. I had been very strong as a child, and after I'd left home at the age of 14 I saw a strong man performing outside the National Portrait Gallery, offered to take the hat round, and – to his and my surprise – bent one of his six-inch nails in half. After working as a dancer in Spain, I answered an ad for 'Freaks Wanted'. 'You don't look like a freak,' I was told when I went for an interview, so I tore up the interviewer's phone book and carried him round the office – and got the job.

At the Empire I was in a show called *Would You Believe It?* in which the 'Wonders of the World' could be seen – among them two giants, one seven feet three inches and the other over nine feet tall, having a mock boxing match with a dwarf as the referee. Then there was Elroy, the 'Armless Wonder' – he really didn't have any arms, yet there on stage, before your very eyes, he painted Rolf Harris-style pictures. He shot at a target, threaded needles, and had the best footwriting I ever saw. He was a lovely man. Once he caught me coming downstairs, put his leg round my waist and said, 'You're a pretty thing.' He liked to sit on a stool in the pub, order a pint, take out his purse and pick up his pint with his mittened foot, which had been beautifully manicured by his faithful help, George, a tiny, busy man who arranged everything for him and hardly ever spoke – at least within my hearing.

Mushie the 'Forest-Bred Lion', who ate steaks off a lady's forehead, was also on the bill. Every night, when his cage was drawn away, poor old Mushie was left standing, chained and centre-stage. He used to face the auditorium and pee against the backcloth. He was presented to audiences by Captain Jack Harvey, dressed like a great white hunter, who had been in the jungle since the days before Mushie was born. The Captain wore the most amazing red ochre make-up. Getting the girl to lie down, and the meat on her chest, was a race between the Lion and Harvey.

Then there was Pelletier and Partner, the World's Only Dog's Dancing Partner, and Johnny Vree, billed as a Dutch porter, who threw what appeared to be a large golliwog (this was before they became understandably unacceptable) around the stage and then tried to get it back in its box. At the end of the act, the golliwog would remove its mask, revealing a beautiful girl, six feet tall and very slender. Reco and May were a comedy wire act: he did amazing things on a slack wire, dressed as a clown, while she shouted encouragement and caught him when he fell off (all beautifully rehearsed). Bob Andrews, billed as 'Genial Generalities', was the compère. He knew every gag in the business: they hadn't been spoiled by repetition on TV, so every one seemed new.

Whoever arrived first at the theatre would run through the music. We used to perform twice nightly, at 6.30 and again at 8.40. By six most artists were arranging the props for their own acts – your lighting plot had been given out, and the stage manager informed of your needs while the band tuned up and the artists warmed up. I liked a dark backcloth, with maybe a lilac or a rose pink swag, a small table, and four chairs. I would invite the four strongest men to come on stage. For a moment I wondered whether anyone would take up my offer, but then they rushed up to help. I must have had good legs in those days! Known as the 'Mighty Mannequin', I used to tear telephone directories in half and bend iron bars with my teeth. King Farouk used to send me tiger lilies, and asked me if I would break his bed in two – to which I replied 'Not tonight, Josephine!'

I was usually in the second half of the show, so I had time to peak through a crack in the curtains and watch the people come in

> I tore up the 'Freak Show' interviewer's phone book and carried him around the office - and got the job

OCTOBER 2006

Joan Rhodes: strong woman

and the theatre coming alive, all bright with coloured lights, plenty of gold leaf and lots of red velvet. Having paid their half-crowns, the public were ready to enjoy themselves. Smart usherettes sold two-penny programmes, there was the rustle of chocolate boxes being opened, a tap of the baton, and the show was on.

The public were very loyal, and if they liked you, they let you know. If they didn't, they sat on their hands. A whole family would see a two-hour show for a pound, wandering off afterwards to eat fish and chips from yesterday's newspaper.

Then came the big names from America: Johnny Ray, Bob Hope, the Deep River Boys and countless others whose names I can't recall – though I do remember dropping Bob Hope on his head. They all demanded so much money that only half the bill was 'variety', and the 'star' would stay on stage for a whole hour. Prices went up to pay the stars, and TV was on its way.

Variety acts only lasted between 12 and 15 minutes, and if the old man didn't care for an act he could pop out to the bar for a pint – but acts that lasted a whole hour were a very different matter.

So let's have some good variety back again – though it will be hard to find good acts at first, since the best are now Continental.

SHOPPING
ALICE PITMAN

We take it for granted these days that when we go shopping we will be treated with surliness, contempt or rudeness by the staff. Surliness tends to come from bored adolescents who supply cheap labour to the supermarkets and chain stores that dominate the land. Contempt comes from the more upmarket establishments whose staff scan us robotically: 'Second-hand car. Scruffy clothes. No disposable income. Ignore.' And rudeness is pretty universal in all shops these days. But nothing in my experience quite prepared me for the reaction I encountered while on a recent holiday in Venice. It may be the most beautiful city on earth, but it is also a city of indescribably bad-tempered shopkeepers.

They are so rude that for some holiday sport my cousin Rebecca and I ran up a tally of the rudest. Top of the list were: the teenager who blatantly ignored me and carried on talking to her boyfriend as I stood with a basket full of shopping, then, after eventually serving me, refused to give me a bag from under the counter until I had managed to telepathically work out that to get one you had to pay an extra euro; the crow who ordered my 12-year-old son to leave her souvenir shop before he had even stepped over the threshold; the terrifying supermarket till lady who slammed every item down after scanning it, and then threw a courgette across the floor because we hadn't weighed it ourselves; the young man at the stall near the Rialto who, as I was about to choose one of his scarves, pushed me aside with the order that I do not touch. 'How rude!' I said, sounding like a Maggie Smith character in a Merchant Ivory film. 'I don't want your rotten pashmina if that's your attitude.' I stormed off, leaving my cousin to face the music. 'You can tell your English friend I think she is also very rude!' the man told her.

Never mind *'Don't Look Now'*, it ought to be 'Don't Effing Touch Now', for even the most tatty souvenir shop in Venice seems to abhor any physical contact with their precious stock. It is most off-putting having them hover over you, waiting to lash out lest an inquisitive paw reach out for something it fancies the look of. As well as contemptuous 'Do Not Touch' signs everywhere, some shops even had 'No charge for admission' signs. That's decent of them.

Perhaps their bad attitude towards customers (okay, tourists) is hardly surprising when you consider that for over five centuries Venice was one of the greatest trading empires of the world. It must be galling to think that after surviving plagues and wars, and the fall of Constantinople, they are now reduced to knocking out ghastly masks, plastic gondolas, Mussolini boxer shorts, and aprons showing Michaelangelo's depiction of David's goolies. The strangest things were the bottles of wine with a portrait of Hitler on the front. I know he was the Pope's old boss, but even so. Then there are the rip-off gondola rides, and it costs nearly 20 euros to sit with a gin and tonic in St Mark's Square. At those prices, it's no wonder Dirk Bogarde staggered around the place looking so miserable in that film. Of course, not all Venetian shopkeepers are rude. There was the very nice fellow who sold me a brass lion's head door-knocker for 25 euros (and mended the chain on my daughter's necklace for nothing). And the gentleman in the posh jewellery shop who allowed me to try on a very expensive ruby necklace even though he knew I couldn't afford it.

Getting back to Surbiton, Waitrose on my return was like being reunited with a friend. Foreign shops are all very well, but you know where you are at home. As we meandered up and down the aisles, the Aged P, 81, started telling me about an erotic dream she had had while I was away. 'Who with?' I asked. 'Matthew Parris,' she said, throwing a fish and chips meal for one in her trolley. 'We were having a picnic together. Just the two of us. It was lovely. We never stopped talking. At the end of the picnic, I cupped his face in my hands and said, "Oh, Matthew, why must you be a homosexual?"'

You hear all sorts down the supermarket

When a care home's not on your 'to-do' list

WOULD YOU LIKE TO REDUCE YOUR CARE COSTS? Try our new price comparison service & find out how much you could save **+ 25% OFF** your first week of care* **CALL US TODAY**

"Moving into a care home". What were your first thoughts on reading those words? Resignation, dread, the worry that it would mean having to sell your home?

If you're reading The Oldie, chances are you want to live well in your own home for as long as possible – research shows that nearly three quarters of us feel that way.

But what if illness, dementia or Parkinson's means living life your way isn't easy? Perhaps a care home might be a good idea after all?

THERE IS ANOTHER WAY, AND IT'S CALLED LIVE-IN CARE

It's an affordable alternative to moving into a care home. A care worker comes to live with you. And as you are still living there your home's value isn't taken into account as an asset.

A PERSONAL APPROACH TO ARRANGING LIVE-IN CARE.

Having someone coming to live in your house can be a big step. That's why Agincare takes so much care matching client to and live-in care worker- a process carried out by people, not a computer.

Agincare looks for hardworking people with a special blend of compassion, reliability and a great sense of humour. All the care staff are English- speaking and enhanced DBS (police) checked.

CARE TAILORED TO YOU

It can just be companionship, so you don't feel lonely. If you need support with medication, eating and drinking, your care worker is there to help. Or if housework is getting too much for you, they can take care of cooking, cleaning and laundry.

And Agincare is experienced in supporting people with dementia, MS, Parkinson's and cerebral palsy, and providing reassuring and sensitive palliative and end-of-life care.

CARING FOR SOMEONE WITH DEMENTIA

Agincare's live-in care workers use familiar possessions and daily routines to stimulate conversations and memories, helping to stem the progress of dementia and memory loss.

REGULATED & MANAGED CARE

Agincare's live-in care service is special because they fully manage it. Other live-in care services offer less protection and fewer guarantees for the same price.

Agincare employs and pays the care staff, which means they have a duty of care. For example, if your care worker is ill, Its Agincare's job to find someone to replace them.

Agincare is proud to be rated 'good' by the Care Quality Commision, give you a higher level of protection and peace of mind. And tehy are always at the the end of the phone if you need support.

HELPING YOU BACK ON YOUR FEET

If you're worried about recovering at home after illness, a hospital stay or fall, live-in care can give you intensive support to regain your independence and skills.

Agincare is fully regulated by the Care Quality Commission, giving you a higher level of protection and peace of mind. And they're always at the end of a phone should you need support.

CAROL'S STORY

"Maggie's changed my life. She's quite simply a lifeline, helping me keep my independence. She drives me wherever I want – hospital appointments, to the shops, trips to Cornwall... we've even been on a cruise!

"If I need something in the night, Maggie's there to help me. Live-in care has changed my life. As long as I can stay in my own home, that's the main thing."

THE SAFEST FORM OF CARE

During the coronavirus pandemic, live-in care from Agincare is one of the safest and most comfortable forms of care.

You can self-isolate in the comfort of your own home, alongside pets, in complete control over who enters your home.

A live-in care worker keeps you company, giving your family and friends peace of mind, knowing help in on hand 24/7.

Agincare
Live-in Care

Call Agincare now on **0808 273 2198** or go to

agincare.com/live-in-care

Gene Wilder

has been one of America's most admired comic actors ever since his first break 40 years ago in Mel Brooks's *The Producers*. He talks to *Mavis Nicholson* about heaven, hell, love, death and acting

MN: Very nice to meet you, I've read your books, seen a lot of your films, I feel I know you. Your eyes are so melancholy on the screen –
GW: [laughs] Yes.

MN: They suggested you needed to be loved.
GW: Yes, but I do have love now, I'm very happily married. After Gilda died [his first wife, the comedian Gilda Radner, died in 1989] I was fortunate enough to meet, what should I say, the great love of my life, that's a corny expression, but I've been married for 15 years now and I'm happier than I've ever been in my life.

MN: I know that's the truth. I remember reading that when you walk through the house, and you pass each other, you kiss.
GW: [laughs] Well that's true.

MN: Do you know what I think? Affection is the greatest indication of real love.

GW: I agree with you. I was brought up in a Jewish home, we didn't talk about God or religion but we kissed and hugged. I can't understand when I see a married couple and they never touch hands, they don't kiss... maybe it's not always a true barometer but I think I agree with you. How can you not show your affection to someone you love?

MN: Would it be accurate to say that your novel, *My French Whore*, is also a love

affair with acting?
GW: I think it happened partly unconsciously. I wrote it 38 years ago, as a screenplay. I put it aside and after I wrote my memoir, *Kiss Me Like a Stranger*, I didn't want to stop writing, so I looked at it again. I thought, well, it's not a good screenplay but it is a wonderful story so I started writing and it just flowed out.

MN: I found it intriguing because Paul Peachy, your main character, is a loser in a sense, isn't he? He loses his wife, he's timid, he's a coward for most of the First World War. But then when he pretends to be a spy he's suddenly a hero. I was wondering whether you were exploring the idea that there's a lot of potential lying dormant in all of us.
GW: I'll tell you how it happens. Paul Peachy was also an actor in an amateur theatre company in Milwaukee. So when he was lined up against a tree and about to be shot by the Germans in 1918, the actor in him comes out. In that sense it's autobiographical because I was very shy as a young man except when I was on stage.

MN: Too shy to be yourself, but bold as somebody else, which is what Peachy is, isn't it?
GW: Yes, I could be bold as a character in a play but in real life, without the play, I was sometimes terribly shy.

MN: You've said that acting is not a career you'd ever recommend to someone because it's such a hard – relentless almost – business.
GW: I am frequently asked by young people, how do I get into acting, what should I do? And I say, don't do it. Often the mother will come by and say 'Why did you say that to my daughter?' Because, the road to getting anywhere in acting is just filled with rejection. And if she can't take my rejection how is she going to do with all the rejections she is going to receive auditioning for a part, meeting a producer, then meeting a director who says 'No, no, she's all wrong'? You have to want it so badly that you don't care what they think because you know you're good and you know you're going to make it. But when you say make it, what's the 'it' that you want to make? Fame? Money? Or art? If all you want is to be famous, become a movie star, have your picture on the cover of a magazine, but if you haven't learnt your acting craft yet, then it's silly and it's not going to last very long.

MN: What did you want from acting? Would you have ever done it if it hadn't been for the trauma of your mother's illness?
GW: I saw my sister, she's four years older than me. I was 11 years old and she gave a dramatic recital in a small auditorium of about 200 people and the lights went down, the curtains opened and a spotlight hit my sister and you could hear a pin drop. All eyes were on her and I thought that that was probably about as close to actually being God as you could get. I think I wanted attention, I wanted someone to look at me. I wanted someone to listen to what I was saying. Our family was very loving but my mother was so ill that all the attention went to her – rightly so, but I still had this craving.

MN: What exactly happened with your mother?
GW: She had a disease called mitral stenosis. The mitral valve in her heart was blocked and so she was always in pain. A cardiologist brought my mother home after her first heart attack and said to me: 'Don't ever get angry with your mother because you might kill her.' The other thing he said was try to make her laugh.

MN: What a responsibility to put on your eight-year-old shoulders. Do you think you couldn't ever enjoy yourself, not really, until she died?
GW: My enjoyment came in spurts because I would feel so guilty. I felt what right do I have to be happy when she's suffering? It took me seven and a half years of psychotherapy to understand why. And as you can see, I'm now a healthy, sturdy young fellow!

MN: But you weren't right as rain, were you, because you went through a major threat to your life from cancer.
GW: Well that was in 1999 and I thought I had a kidney stone, a little pain in the back there, so I went to get tested, ultrasound and then tissue samples, and they said no, actually what you have is non-Hodgkin lymphoma. I had nine chemotherapy sessions and after four the tumour was all gone. The specialist said 'You're very healthy, Mr Wilder, and very chemo-responsive but it's going to come back.' I asked when? She said 'six months'. I asked her what'll I do? she said 'Stem cell transplant'.

MN: So you knew what you were in for?

GW: Oh yeah. Even though she told me all those things, the radiation and the heavy chemotherapy and all that, I wasn't frightened about that. I was afraid about what would happen to my wife if I died, because it took me so long to find her.

MN: So you're cured?
GW: I'm in complete remission, which is a little different. Two years ago I went to my doctor and I said 'I'm going on a book tour, and if they ask me can I say I'm cured?' He said, 'Don't say cured because that's an insurance word, actuarial tables and all that, just say you're in complete remission.' I asked what if they don't understand, and he said, 'Just tell them that if you outlive your doctor, then you're cured.' And I realised the best way to achieve that would be to get a gun and shoot my doctor!

MN: You were really facing up to possible death though, weren't you? Do you think that as you have got older that you are more brave about dying? I still don't believe I'm going to die!
GW: I'm brave about it in my head. When the time comes, none of us know what is going to happen, how brave we're going to be.

MN: Do you think there's an afterlife?
GW: No, I don't. But you know I once opened an umbrella inside the house when I was 11 or 12 years old and my father said 'Do you know you just opened an umbrella indoors?' I said 'Daddy, are you superstitious?' And he said 'Not at all, but why take a chance?' I heard Stephen Hawking on Larry King and Larry said 'May I ask you, do you believe there's a God?' And Hawking said 'If by God you mean the mathematical equation that accounts for all the galaxies and the black holes, then yes I do.' And I wouldn't say it quite like that, but I would say heaven is here, now, on earth and my heaven is now. I don't believe in the devil or heaven or hell except for the hell that we have on earth, like the Iraq war for instance.

MN: Yes, I was glad to see that you were against that.
GW: It's not a war anyway, it's a police action. You can make heaven in your head and your heart and when you find love then you find heaven.

MN: Well it's been heavenly talking to you. Thank you very much indeed.

Change your life. Do nothing

Far from the madding crowd: *The Bishop of Reading* stresses the crucial importance of simply sitting still and paying attention to yourself and the world

A couple of years ago I was due to lead an assembly at a Church of England comprehensive school that I visited regularly. This is a tough gig: 700 or 800 adolescents, crowded into a hall first thing on a Monday morning and forced to endure a hymn, a prayer, a worthy talk and, usually, a ticking off. On this occasion my anxiety levels were particularly high since I had not really prepared anything much to say. It was the beginning of Lent and I had a vague idea about encouraging them to take something up rather than give something up, but as I walked to the school I became all too aware that my situation was similar to driving in the fast lane of the motorway, with no petrol in the tank, and realising you've just gone past the services.

But these moments of panic can also be moments of prayer, moments when we are more open to the wiles of God. And it was almost as I got up to speak that a crazy idea was suddenly born within me. I stood up and found myself saying something like this:

'We live in a crazy, frantic world. Our world is full of movement and noise. Even this morning, in the few hours since you woke up, you have probably filled your time with the radio, the TV, the computer, the PlayStation; you've probably phoned someone and texted half a dozen others. As you got dressed, washed, showered, ate your breakfast and came to school, noise and busyness have accompanied your every move. I believe many of the world's problems are caused by our inability to sit still and to be quiet and to reflect. I believe that, in this season of Lent, we should try to give up being so frantic, and we should take on some moments of stillness.'

Then I stopped, as if I had lost my thread (actually, it felt as if the thread were being handed to me inch by inch, and even I was not aware what was at the end). And I said to them, 'Hey, you don't know what on earth I'm talking about, so let me give you a demonstration. Let me show you what I mean. This is what I'm suggesting you do, each day in Lent, for exactly one minute. It will change your life.'

I then picked up a chair, placed it in the centre of the stage, and slowly and carefully sat down upon it, with my feet slightly apart and with my back straight and with my hands resting gently on my knees. And, for a minute, I sat still. I didn't say anything, and I didn't do anything. I wasn't even consciously praying. I was just sitting there. And I breathed deeply, and I thought about my breathing. And when I reckoned the minute was over, I stood up.

But before I could say my next bit, there was a huge, spontaneous round of applause. Now, I had done lots of assemblies in that school. On many occasions I had slaved over what I would do or say to capture the imaginations of young people. But I had never had a response like this. In fact, in the days that followed, I was stopped in the street on several occasions by parents who told me that their child had come home and told them about the priest who took assembly and just sat on the stage in silence for a minute and then suggested they might do the same thing. Because, when the applause died down, that's what I'd said. I just suggested that sitting still, being silently attentive to things deep within ourselves and things beyond ourselves, would make a difference. You didn't need to call it prayer. You didn't need to call it anything, because it would be in these moments of sedulous stillness that God could be discovered.

Stephen Cottrell became Archbishop of York in July 2020

TEN TIPS FROM THE BISHOP

1. Don't make tea by dunking a tea bag in a mug. Buy proper tea. And warm the pot.

2. Throw away that electric razor and buy an old-fashioned shaving brush, some shaving cream and a razor blade and do it that way.

3. Keep to the speed limit.

4. Start learning the names of the flowers in the hedgerows.

5. Cook a risotto. It is quite the most time-consuming recipe I can think of.

6. Never say that you have an hour to kill. Rather, say you have an hour to revive, to bring to life, to ravish.

7. That email that is shouting for a response can wait until tomorrow. Or go and make a cup of tea. A considered reply will be better anyway.

8. Prune your collection of televisions. Have a happy hour where all televisions, computers and radios are switched off.

9. In conversation, don't always feel you have to be the first person to speak.

10. Practise the art of listening.

Taken from Do Nothing to Change Your Life: Discovering What Happens When You Stop © Stephen Cottrell. Reproduced by kind permission of the publishers (Church House Publishing, ebook £6.39)

Miles Kington

Brush up your put-downs

Vidal, Wilde and de la Rochefoucauld and the art of the well-turned phrase

I have read several pieces about Gore Vidal recently, all of which, oddly, have quoted the same remark of his: 'Whenever I see the success of a friend, something within me dies.' I may have misquoted the actual words, but the sentiment is clear enough: that the success of others is hard to bear. It is always quoted with a frisson of delight, as if malice had suddenly come back into fashion. But Gore Vidal was always well-known for his one-line poison darts. Was it not of Truman Capote's death that Gore Vidal said 'Good career move'? I think so, although, since then, I have quite often heard it said about many other people.

It is the combination of wit and malice which distinguishes Gore Vidal. It is said that, when he wrote his memoirs, he knew that his old enemy Norman Mailer would turn straight to the index to see if he was mentioned. So Vidal put in the index the following entry: 'Mailer, Norman. Hi, Norman.' And nothing else. I have not dared to check this, in case it's not true, but I do hope it is.

When I first read Gore Vidal's little remark about the success of others, I was immediately reminded of another writer that people don't read much any more either, namely the Duc de la Rochefoucauld and his *Maxims*. La Rochefoucauld was equally distrustful of human motivation but did not target individuals with his barbs – he aimed at all humanity. It's rather curious, when you stop to think, that they should have survived at all, his *Maxims*. They are not really literature. They are not particularly useful. They're not gossip, and they are almost 400 years old, and I, for one, had not referred to them for a long time, not until the Gore Vidal quote made me think that that was the sort of thing the old Duc would have said. Didn't he make some remark about how watching a friend drown was not a totally tragic experience?

Well, he may have done, but I have not unearthed it. The nearest to it is his remark that 'We all have strength enough to help us endure the misfortunes of others.' Excellent. He was also, it seems, responsible for the definition of hypocrisy as 'the tribute that vice pays to virtue', which I am sure I have previously seen assigned to Oscar Wilde.

> Didn't the old Duc make some remark about how watching a friend drown was not a totally tragic experience?

To give you a flavour of the man, here is a little fruity helping of some more of his *Maxims*:

'The love of justice in most men is no more than the fear of suffering injustice.'

'If we judge love by most of its effects, it resembles hatred more than friendship.'

'Old people love to give good advice, to console them for no longer being able to set a bad example.'

They are all quite thought-provoking, without exactly being the sort of thing you could easily slip into a conversation. They're all a bit bookish, a bit too well-tailored for that. I mean, if someone complained to you (as they do to me all the time) that their memory was starting to go, it would not sound all that casual if you responded immediately: 'Ah, we all complain of our memory fading, but nobody ever complains of their judgement starting to go.'

And if, in response to the curious look you got, you said: 'As the Duc de la Rochefoucauld said...', I am not sure it would make it any better.

I was once approached by a publisher who wanted me to translate a new set of the *Maxims*. I dithered. About two months later, the poor old publisher lost his job, so I never had to make the decision, but I think, on the whole, the right answer would have been No. They all smell too much of the midnight conversation and courtly cynical talk of ladies and gents who do not have enough to do.

And yet, I don't know, I don't know. They do sometimes have an amazing relevance to today. For instance, as you all know, we live in a culture of blame, where it is thought that sackings and resignations are a cure for everything, and the media are always calling for heads to roll. Compare this to La Rochefoucauld: 'The readiness to believe the worst without sufficient investigation reflects only our pride and laziness. We want to find the guilty parties, but we do not want to take the trouble to examine the crimes.'

Yes, quite good. At the same time, I can see no handy way of turning that into modern, living English. No, I think I would have been right to say No.

The quiet American
CHARLES ELLIOTT
The Garden at Hidcote
by Fred Whitsey
Frances Lincoln Publishers £20.00

Hidcote is one of those very few iconic gardens, like Sissinghurst, that every self-respecting hortophile must visit. To Americans especially, it represents a kind of pinnacle of English garden-making, their interest and admiration accounting for a large proportion of the 150,000 gawkers who now tramp through the grounds each year. That it was created by an American in the first place, albeit a strange, secretive and thoroughly internationalised American, merely adds a note of mystery to the mix.

In the words of Fred Whitsey, the veteran garden writer whose handsome new book on Hidcote contains a short biography of Lawrence Johnston, the man himself 'remains an enigma'. Few papers, letters or other documents survived him; he never married; though he had friends in the gardening community he appears to have had few close acquaintances. After a Henry Jamesian upbringing in Europe as the child of rich expatriate Americans, he chose to take British citizenship in 1892, and in 1907 bought a couple of hundred acres and a house on the northernmost end of the Cotswold scarp overlooking the Vale of Evesham. From then on, apart from service in the Northumberland Fusiliers in World War I (wounded, according to Whitsey, gassed and once left for dead), he devoted himself to Hidcote. He seems to have been a rather sad and lonely figure, mother-beset. But for all that he was clearly a skilled plantsman and a garden designer of real genius.

While there has been some debate in recent years about the exact nature of Johnston's original creation at Hidcote – the National Trust took it over in 1948 and a number of changes were apparently made in restoring it – he evidently based his plans on the Arts and Crafts principles current among garden designers in Edwardian times. This called for a good deal of formal hedging to divide garden 'rooms', geometrical beds and pools, walls, and carefully controlled planting. At the same time, it involved a strongly romantic feeling, which today at Hidcote, with its richly mature trees and shrubs, can be almost overwhelming.

Where Johnston went beyond the conventions, however, was in his fascination with rare and unusual species. Not all of these survive today, but the garden is still blessed with exceptional specimens, including a collection of old roses. So taken was Johnston with collecting rare plants that he not only bankrolled plant-hunting expeditions but actually went on a couple of them himself. One, with the great George Forrest to Yunnan, was a disaster; the two men fell out and Forrest, in fury, later wrote that he could not have found a worse travelling companion. 'Johnston is not a man, not even a bachelor, but a right good old spinster spoilt by being born male.'

Fred Whitsey has spent 60 years visiting Hidcote. His detailed descriptions are loving and accurate and, with Tony Lord's deeply evocative pictures, do justice to the place. I suspect that even the dour Mr Johnston would be cheered.

Formal hedging at Hidcote

Life with the thesps
HUGH MASSINGBERD
Shark Infested Waters:
Tales of an Actor's Agent
by Michael Whitehall
Timewell Press £16.99

I think it was Nigel Dempster – himself once dubbed 'the Greatest Living Englishman' by Auberon Waugh – who called Michael Whitehall, agent to such oldie pin-ups as John Le Mesurier, Edward Fox and John Wells, 'the funniest man in London'.

Whitehall was a wit from an early age (a school report complained of his 'bastic buffoonery') and honed his humour on the eccentricities of his family. To annoy his mother, a suburban snob who insisted upon her frock salesman husband parking his van in the next street, young Michael would pretend in public that he didn't have a father. One grandfather liked to dress up in his wife's clothes (even in his late seventies he was attired in 'a large feathered felt hat, a floral print dress and high heels… roaring with laughter and puffing away at his pipe'); the other was devoted to knitting.

Class and its attendant embarrassments are the basis of so much classic English comedy, and the 1950s, in which Whitehall grew up, was an especially fertile decade. The author's mother's aspirations for what she defined as the 'à la carte' way of life, as opposed to

> **'What are these eggs doing in my silver cigarette box?'**

the 'common', are excruciatingly exposed. There are effective set-pieces describing her attempts to impress a prep-school friend of her son's with silver dishes on the sideboard for breakfast (only to be sabotaged by her husband's enquiry, 'Why have you put my bacon in your jewellery box? And what are these eggs doing in my silver cigarette box?') and the agonies of making the right impression on visits to Ampleforth, her son's public school.

A career as an actor's agent was not what his mother had envisaged. 'Mucking about with actors won't get you anywhere, dear,' she said. 'Get yourself a proper job.' Unfortunately, his early efforts to do so in the fields of schoolmastering, the law, journalism and advertising were unsuccessful, though they yielded a rich seam of hilarity. In particular, his adventures as a prep-school master are worthy of Evelyn Waugh. I loved the description of the breathless septuagenarian sports master equipped with 'a hearing aid, which fell out of his ear every time he blew his whistle'.

For anyone interested in how 'showbiz' works, Whitehall proves an instructive, unstar-struck guide on such arcane techniques as 'unsettling' other agents' clients ('Well it's just that I'd heard, I'm sure wrongly, that she'd started drinking again'). But, happily, above all, this is a treasure-trove of entertaining anecdotes and affectionately observed personalities, like Kenneth More, Whitehall's colourful business partner Julian Belfrage (who wouldn't take Peter Bowles to lunch at the Turf Club because the actor was 'carrying a handbag') and David Tomlinson, who, frustrated by his agent not returning his calls, insinuated himself into an office on the other side of the road and waved at him through the window.

There is much sardonic fun about the vanities of the theatrical profession. Escorting the veteran star Dorothy Lamour in a taxi, Whitehall broached the delicate question of her 'playing age'. She replied firmly, 'I play 40', as the elderly cab-driver sniggered. Stage stories embrace everyone from Gielgud and Wolfit to Sinden and Leslie Phillips, but my favourite is the tale of the veteran stage-doorman who confided to the author: 'I saw 'em all, Michael. Vesta Tilley, Little Titch, Marie Lloyd, Harry Lauder, the lot. They were all fucking awful. Every one of 'em.'

FILM
MARCUS BERKMANN

When did you last see a western? More to the point, when did you last want to see a western? Call me an old cynic if you wish, but I suspect there comes a time in almost everyone's life – somewhere between the ages of 6 and 75, I'd guess – when you realise you have seen far more westerns than any sane person could wish to see, and can't even imagine seeing another one without screaming. Again, I'm guessing, but this may be why so few westerns do well at the box office nowadays. Cowpoke chewing matches... devilish Apaches hiding behind every rock... audience fleeing from cinemas in droves... They can't be unconnected. And yet every new generation of filmmakers is drawn to the genre, and so is every new generation of actors.

3.10 To Yuma (15) is a remake of a 1957 film, itself based on an early short story by Elmore Leonard, but it's hard to imagine that it would be here again if Russell Crowe hadn't fancied it. Here he's Ben Wade, a notorious murderer and robber of stagecoaches with a twinkle in his eye and an excellent hat. His latest crime is witnessed by Christian Bale, not so long ago the little boy in *Empire of the Sun,* and now the first call for any director who needs someone to look haunted and tortured and ready for more suffering. For one recent film he had to lose four stone, and for this one he appears to have lopped off a chunk of his foot. (Obviously it's a visual effect, but let's just say that you wouldn't put it past him.) Bale is a rancher, heavily in debt, threatened by cackling villains who want his land when the railroad comes through it, as it will very shortly. When Crowe is captured and must be taken to a nearby town to be put on the 3:10 to Yuma, where he will be imprisoned and possibly hanged, Bale volunteers to go along and guard him.

Russell Crowe has a twinkle in his eye and an excellent hat

The two stars are interestingly contrasted: charismatic Crowe, whom you can't help but like even though he's thoroughly bad, and gaunt, beardy Bale, whose belief in the power of decency echoes that of most heroes from golden-age westerns. Sometimes the dialogue feels like a meeting of two cinematic eras: the simple black-and-white morality of Forties' and Fifties' westerns, and the grimy, moral relativism of the Sixties and beyond. But then the whole film feels like this, taking an ancient genre and respecting its conventions, while also seeking to be as modern and up-to-date as possible. So the West looks as filthy and scary as it surely was, but even so, only rarely is anyone ever hit by a bullet, despite thousands being fired. The villains all have horrible yellow teeth, while Bale, impoverished to the point of hunger, clearly spends his last cents on toothbrushes and toothpaste. He also

Matt 'the Plank' Damon

runs pretty swiftly for a monopede (or should that be uniped?) Still, if you can disregard its occasional absurdities, it's a highly satisfying film, which suggests that there are new things to be done with the western – or at least, old things to be done in a new way.

Meanwhile, I finally caught up with *The Bourne Ultimatum* (12A), as if to show that, while *The Oldie* might not always be the first magazine to review the latest films, it can sometimes be the last. But, by crikey, it's good.

Some of the action sequences are so exciting they actually made me laugh with pleasure. The economy and speed of the storytelling are astonishing. And the hero's extraordinary inventiveness, his ability to think his way out of the least promising situation, remains just about believable because, in every other way, he is effectively an automaton. Who else could have played the part but blank-eyed Matt 'the Plank' Damon? Could he be the luckiest man alive?

The joy of the axe

Jennie Erdal describes the therapeutic effects – physical and spiritual – of a simple, elemental, outdoor activity

For over 30 years I have enjoyed a beautiful relationship with that most satisfying of implements: the axe. One of my childhood chores was to chop kindling for our kitchen stove, but it was such absorbing work that it never felt like a chore. I don't remember being shown how to hold the axe, or being told to take care. In those days children were allowed to do all kinds of things now deemed dangerous.

Once I had flown the nest, I graduated from a small hand-axe to the more versatile long-handled variety. Since we lived next to a small wood there was a plentiful supply of windblown branches and limbs. My three young children collected fallen branches and dragged them up the garden to be sawn. We built a sturdy sawhorse and levered the trunks onto it. I sawed them up with a bow saw, which is equally good on green and dry timber. I found that the rhythmic repetitive movements associated with sawing brought great benefits. Not only did they stimulate the brain and elevate the mood, but they created a deeply relaxed mental state similar to that achieved through meditation. Freshly cut wood is about 25 per cent water, but the sun and wind dry it for free. You can deal with any lump of wood with the same tools that would have been used a hundred years ago: an axe, a splitting maul, a sledgehammer, plus a wedge or two. A maul, with its broad, wedge-shaped blade, is by far the best kind of axe for splitting logs. If it gets stuck in the wood, its base is square enough and tough enough to be hit with a sledge, giving it a huge advantage over a normal axe, which is essentially a chopping tool. No self-respecting axe-woman will ever drive one axe with another axe, or worse, attempt to drive a wedge with the broad end of an axe.

Cherry wood has the scent of mild pipe tobacco, oak has a vanilla bouquet...

Different woods respond in different ways. Ash and sycamore, being straight-grained, are amongst the easiest to slice; wych elm, with its cross-grain, among the most resistant. Beech is one of the hardest woods, yet it cuts like butter, whereas yew, though evergreen and classed as a soft wood, can grow in on itself and present difficult knots. You learn to grade the force to suit the type and heft of wood you're cutting.

An axe is a personal thing: you have to find the weight and the balance that suit you best. But once you develop a natural swing, the axe itself does most of the work. It's surprising how easily you can establish a rhythm, and how long you can keep going without tiring.

Aim is important and takes time to perfect. Only the blade should make contact with the log; if you bash the handle on the log it can easily break and send the shock all the way up your arm. Stand with your legs apart and place the blade on the log in front of you, in much the same way as a golfer tees up. Then pull the axe to one side, up and over in an arc, at the top of which the axe will start to fall by itself. At this stage you have to concentrate on guiding it into the log, not just with your eye, but with your shoulders and biceps.

Splitting logs delights all the senses. There is a magnificent range of colours between sapwoods (the most recently formed) and heartwoods (the dense inner part of the tree). In yew, for example, the sapwood is almost pure white in contrast to the dark ginger of the heartwood, with pink, red and even purple streaks. The aromatic quality of freshly cut wood is wonderful. Apple and pear smell of their fruits, while cherry wood has the scent of mild pipe tobacco. Oak has a vanilla bouquet, ash is as sweet as honey, and pine has that back-to-school smell of sharpened pencils.

Age is no barrier to splitting logs, providing you are reasonably fit. You don't even need to live in the countryside – tree surgeons are happy to deliver their spoils to town or country.

The whole process is enjoyable from start to finish – prolonged outdoor activity followed by muscle tiredness in front of a blazing log fire.
Bliss.

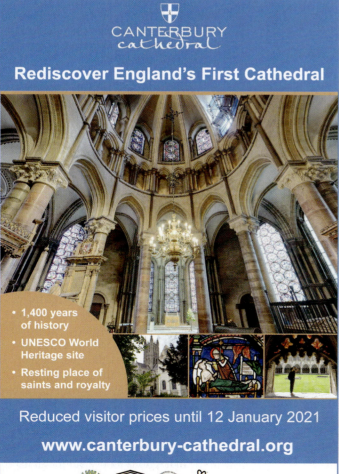
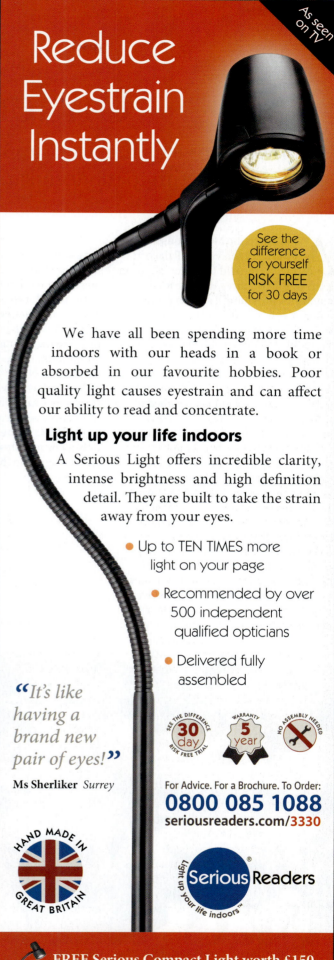

Under threat

Francis King visits the historic Old Cataract Hotel in Egypt before it falls victim to modernisation. Can its charms survive?

Along with the Mena House in Cairo and the Winter Palace in Luxor, the Old Cataract in Aswan is one of Egypt's three historic hotels, as famous for providing a setting for the film of Agatha Christie's *Death on the Nile* as for entertaining Winston Churchill. After a refurbishment more than 30 years ago, this venerable establishment is now about to undergo a further one. Hearing this, I decided that if at my advanced age I ever wished to make another visit, I had better go at once.

I first heard of the beauty and glamour of the Old Cataract in the late Forties when a friend told me that the happiest time of her life had been when she and her husband had spent their honeymoon there just before the First World War. The Aswan that she described was totally different from the Aswan with which I have become familiar. In those days only a few came for archaeological marvels – most were impelled by the search for health or pleasure.

The winter climate, sunny with the purest and driest of air, was regarded as ideal for sufferers from 'weak chests', 'nerves' and other fashionable ailments of the day. For those robust enough to participate, there were endless diversions: riding, gymkhanas, horseracing, tennis, bridge, billiards, badminton, balls, concerts, amateur theatricals. Never a dull moment, my friend said. On my own stays in Aswan there have, sadly, been many dull moments, as well as many exciting ones.

At that time the railway station was only a few minutes walk away. When the train chugged in, hotel staff in scarlet

> **I dread what renovation will do to a hotel that, for all its imperfections, I have come so much to love**

uniforms and fezzes collected the luggage for immediate transfer to rooms. Today on the site of the station there stands a bank where I was cheated out of a fortunately modest sum of money by the old trick of substituting, in the copious bundle of soiled notes handed to me, two 50s in piasters instead of in Egyptian pounds.

Things at the Old Cataract are now in most ways markedly different from what they were during my friend's visit. The present owners, the French chain Sofitel, are clearly at pains to maintain the establishment's century-old reputation for exclusivity, but although I witnessed a burly security guard refusing entry to a middle-aged English couple as they pleaded to be allowed to pass through the main gate merely to 'take a quick look round', from morning to night coaches constantly drew up outside the hotel entrance to unload tourist parties or to carry them off.

Undoubtedly the planned renovation is badly needed. My sparsely furnished, ill-lit, high-ceilinged room provided a marvellous balcony view of the Nile from the granite bluff, brilliant with bougainvillea, from which the hotel, a Moorish fantasy dreamed up by Thomas Cook and the world-famous engineer of the first Aswan Dam, Sir William Willcocks, dominates everything around it except the crudely hideous bulk of its junior sibling, the New Cataract. But many of its antiquated amenities refused either to function properly or at all.

Of the many architectural glories of the hotel, the supreme one is the '1902 Restaurant', with its soaring black-and-white arches and high dome. When, on our first night, the head waiter had at long last deigned to notice us, the light was so dim that my myopic eyes had difficulty in reading the menu. He then explained that the dimness was deliberate: that was how it would have been back in 1902, when the restaurant was first opened. My friend had spoken of the marvellous food – but for all its

OPPOSITE: The Old Cataract Hotel in Aswan on the Nile River
ABOVE: Bette Davis, Peter Ustinov (centre) and David Niven in a scene from 'Death on the Nile', 1978

showiness, it now proved far less enjoyable than the simple but delicious fare available at a small restaurant that we discovered nearby.

Three things were perfection: the building itself; its immaculate gardens; and the view, from the terrace and the path beneath it, of the Nile, over which the sails of feluccas fluttered like white butterflies in their zigzag comings and goings. Being an early riser, I used to walk along that path every morning to sit in a sunken area, King Fouad's Corner, to watch the river slowly respond to the first touch of dawn. This involved a steep descent. On my first morning, an ancient gardener rushed forward to help me, grabbing my hand. Then, as I thanked him, he tilted his head to one side, gave a coaxing smile to reveal broken and blackened teeth and extended a palm. I reached for one of the notes, each worth 50p, that I kept for tips in the breast pocket of my jacket. Every morning subsequently he was there waiting to help me, and every morning I yet again reached into my pocket. The Egyptians are the friendliest and sweetest of people. Their tragedy is that for most of them gratuitous kindness is something they cannot afford when dealing with foreigners whom, judged by their own pitiful standards, they naturally regard as millionaires.

I dread what renovation will do to a hotel that, for all its present imperfections, I have come so much to love. But if I live long enough, I shall certainly return, partly out of morbid curiosity to see what horrors modernisation has inflicted, but chiefly to sit once again in King Fouad's Corner as the dawn begins miraculously to quicken the previously dead waters beneath me to urgent, glittering life.

Lord Goodman

Edward Mirzoeff recalls a time when the big man was lost for words

'I am the finest after-dinner speaker in the land. There is no need for me to write anything down in advance. And certainly no need for you, young man, to tell me what to do or how to do it.' With jowls quivering, the intimidating bulk that was Lord Goodman swept my protests aside. It was the summer of 1974. The BBC had invited the celebrated solicitor, reputed to be of infinite subtlety, wisdom and behind-the-scenes political influence, to give the annual Richard Dimbleby Lecture. I was the producer.

A year before, Sir Robert Mark, Commissioner of the Metropolitan Police, had given a coruscatingly delivered lecture he called 'Minority Verdict'. Beforehand, with the help of a young barrister called Lennie Hoffmann (now Lord Hoffmann, a senior Law Lord), he had composed draft after draft. For months he rewrote, revised and rehearsed. After all, the lecture was 50 minutes long at prime time on BBC1 – and it was live.

Lord Goodman proposed to dispense with all that and go it alone. I told my head of department that Goodman was adamant – a prepared script was not necessary. He warned Brian Cowgill, controller of BBC1 who, in turn, referred up the ladder to the managing director, Huw Wheldon.

From on high the answer came down. If the great man says he is happiest speaking off the cuff, so be it. But I didn't like it. I went back to Goodman's over-upholstered flat in Portman Place. When he lumbered in I explained that standing in a studio before a cold audience and five large television cameras was not like telling some jolly tales after a good dinner; that 50 minutes was a remarkably long time to fill; that a live broadcast was a tense business, even for television professionals.

Goodman shrugged away my fears. Had he not told me already that no speaker was more experienced or more in demand? There would be no scripts, no rewrites, no rehearsals, no editorial preparation. I had a horrible sinking feeling.

> **There would be no scripts, no rewrites, no rehearsals, no editorial preparation – I had a horrible sinking feeling**

On Tuesday 22nd October 1974 Lord Goodman turned up at Television Centre. The most recent of his numerous appointments was chairman of the Housing Corporation, so he would talk about housing. He began confidently enough with a plea for government to deal with the horrors of squalid homes. He called for a passionate approach to help build more houses, control the price of land, inject a sense of urgency into the planning process. But soon he started running out of things to say. He lurched from the cost of Concorde to the value of gala performances at Covent Garden, but when he began to describe the inadequate size of BBC dressing-rooms, I knew all was lost. 'He's blown it – the bugger's blown it!' I heard 'Ginger' Cowgill's down-to-earth Clitheroe voice shouting behind me.

Somehow Goodman got to the end. The applause was desultory, the party afterwards unusually subdued. In the *Daily Telegraph* Christopher Booker called the performance 'lamentable'. I never saw Lord Goodman again.

Alzheimer's Research UK
Make breakthroughs possible

One of the biggest joys in life is spending time with your loved ones, making memories together. So, it can be heartbreaking when a disease takes it all away – your loved one's memories, their knowledge of family and friends, the very essence of what makes them, them.

But dementia is not an inevitable part of ageing.

Alzheimer's Research UK investigates the brain diseases that cause memory loss and other symptoms of dementia, like personality changes and becoming unable to carry out daily tasks. Our scientists have already discovered so much and, with more support now and in the future, research will find a cure.

Writing a Will is one of the most important things you can do to make sure your loved ones are taken care of as you'd wish in the years to come. A gift in your Will can also help to end the fear, harm and heartbreak of dementia.

For families
For memories
For cures
Please keep us in mind

Request your guide for useful information on:
- What to consider if you or a loved one have dementia
- Making or updating your Will
- Lasting Powers of Attorney
- Managing future care costs
- Including a gift in your Will to Alzheimer's Research UK

Get your FREE Will Writing Guide today.

Visit **alzheimersresearchuk.org/gifts-in-wills-guide**
Email **giftsinwills@alzheimersresearchuk.org**
Call **01223 896606**

Registered charity numbers:
1077089 and **SC042474**

Last chance saloon

Des Wilson puts on his poker face for a visit to the World Series in Las Vegas

Like everyone else I was told as a kid that 'it matters not who won or lost, but how you play the game.' It's nonsense, of course. Any worthwhile competitor will tell you that the only thing that matters is winning. That is why as a keen games player I count my life as a failure – never hit a century, never played a round of golf in scratch, never ran in the London Marathon, and now at 67 it's too late. Well ... nearly too late. There is still poker, a game I've loved since, at 16, I played it with the older reporters in the newsroom of my local paper.

So, when I read about the World Series of Poker, I think, hey, poker is a game I can still play. This I can still win. Maybe it's not too late to be a champion after all. This is why I am in Las Vegas, about to compete in the world seniors' event.

The World Series has, since it began in the 1970s, become the Olympic Games of poker. It consists of 55 events spread over six weeks, culminating in the 'main event' to decide who is world champion. Anyone can play: you just have to come up with the 'buy-in'. For this you receive chips, and the winner is the one who ends up with the lot. He or she then receives a gold bracelet as well as a lot of money. The sums involved are enormous: for the 'main event' the 'buy-in' is $10,000 and last year the winner from a field of over 6,500 picked up a cool $10 million. The seniors event this year has attracted 2,218 players and there is a first prize of about $350,000.

Normally the place is packed with hardened professionals battling it out with the 'young guns' of the game – kids in their twenties in baseball caps and jeans, cut off from Planet Earth by iPods. Many of them have already made millions on line. They are fearless and ferociously aggressive and terrify their elders. Fortunately, they are banned from the seniors' event...

We seniors turn up with our walking sticks or in wheelchairs, limping, wheezing, and complaining there are not enough toilets. There are elderly cowboys in Stetsons and ex-soldiers and sailors with caps proudly proclaiming the name

of their battalion or ship – some look as if they could have been at the Alamo. There's a 91-year-old – but also a man at my table who looks so young he has to produce his ID to prove he's qualified (it turns out he was 50 this very day and his wife has paid his $1,000 entry fee as a present).

The atmosphere is extraordinary. Don't tell me the old can't still get excited about a game – I would say we're far more excited than the young guns ever get. But then there's a reason for this: they always have tomorrow, but this could be our last chance to be a winner, to be a champion.

Most of us know we won't be coming back. Assuming we're still around in a year's time, it's doubtful we'll have the money. Chasing this dream has cost everyone in the room $1,000. We can

> **Many of the 'young guns' have already made millions on line. They are fearless and ferociously aggressive and terrify their elders**

defend this to ourselves and our families once; everyone has to do what they have to do. But more than once ... I doubt it.

So when they call out 'shuffle up and deal', there is an intensity that is difficult to describe. We peer at our cards. (I have a small dilemma: I have these expensive dark glasses to prevent my opponents seeing my eyes so they can't detect either confidence or fear. The problem is I can't see through them. Black and red cards merge into one colour. Chips all look the same. I eventually discard them.) The standard is high and why should it not be? Some of the best in the world are seniors.

There's the game's elder statesman, Doyle 'Texas Dolly' Brunson, who began by 'driving the white line' in Texas from town to town, game to game, gun in pocket to get his winnings safely from poker room to car, in the days when the problem was not winning the money but getting out of town with it. He was written off as dead with cancer, chose his pallbearers, then went into the hospital for a final operation and they found it had all gone. From then on he believed he was too lucky to do anything else but gamble. He has been world champion twice, written a famous poker book called *Super System* and is the face of an on-line poker room called 'Doyle's Room'. He's 75 now and looks like an old bulldog but still plays in the big events and holds his own. And there is the old hustler, Amarillo Slim, also from Texas, who became the most famous poker player of all time because of several wise-cracking appearances on Johnny Carson's show. He is playing in the seniors this year. He must be close to 80.

For three days we play. One by one we're knocked out. I am one of the early fallers. But regrets I have none – it's been an experience to be treasured. More than that, it's forced me to reconsider. Because it really didn't matter whether I won or lost. Or even how I played the game. What mattered was that I could play the game.

In the weird and wonderful world of poker, we oldies can still compete.

Des Wilson's history of poker, 'Ghosts at the Table', is published by Mainstream

Perfect Puglia

Patrick Reyntiens explores the hidden jewel in Italy's heel, an ancient region which combines natural abundance with breathtaking architectural achievement

It's a funny name, Puglia (don't pronounce the 'g'). I rather think it's not Italian at all, originally. I may be wrong, but it sounds to me as though the Angevin French, who were here from the 11th to the 15th centuries, spelt Apulia like that to 'Frenchify' it. We Britishers know it from our Roman history. Horace had a little house here, and I think that Cicero did too. Horace had a good time – just above Gallipoli. (No, not that one; there's another in Puglia.) Cicero was hacked to bits, so that wasn't very nice. But the Greeks came first, and Magna Graecia hangs around in lumps and clumps even today. There are funny little notices in Greek, after Italian place-names on road indicators.

The country is flat as only flat can be. It definitely isn't Holland, but there's nothing but olive trees everywhere you look. Away and away and away, 20 million olive trees clothe the horizontal landscape. They are of a graceful but slightly depressing grey-green. They are kept very well, with branches knocked off them every year or so, because olives grow on the new shoots sprouting out as a result of the pruning. They are the best in the world. Each tree is worth more than 4,000 euros and the farmers have to be very much on their toes not to let these trees be stolen and taken up surreptitiously to the north of Italy, where they command a very hefty price. There are fields and fields of vines; plenty of them. They stretch for miles. I was told that Pug produced more wine per year than the whole of Australia. I can well believe it. And there are impenetrable prickly pear hedges along the tops of the stone walls (these walls are everywhere).

Then the roads. It's all rather odd; strangely like Somerset. Little wiggly roads, for peasants and donkeys and dogs, snaking all over the country. Although they are more or less made of tar, it's difficult to drive down them because of the incessant twists, turns, upsy-daisy bridges, road halts, stops and little passing byways only some 20 yards long … you have to be very careful. But across this unending maze of roads, and connecting little Greek, Angevin or Italian villages and towns, there are 'Roman' roads of uncompromising straightness, searing through the countryside to Brindisi – and some of them do date from Roman times, as in the Appian Way.

Above: Ostuni, Puglia's 'white city'
Left: façade of the Basilica di Santa Croce, Lecce

Lecce, the capital of southern Pug, called Salento, is staggering. I've wanted to see it ever since I bought Sacheverell Sitwell's book *Southern Baroque Art* when I was 15 – and here I am, at 82, and I only just managed to see the place. I'm glad I made it, even though waiting 67 years is a bit too long: Lecce (the old town, not the modern suburbs) is beyond belief. The most extraordinary façades and interiors ever, dating from the 13th to the early 18th centuries. The monuments are amazing.

Salento stone has a curious quality. It is easy to carve when fresh out of the quarry, being so soft. But on contact with the air it hardens up and becomes very solid. So for 300 years or more, stonecarvers, from Lecce to Otranto to Bari, let themselves rip. The colossal imagination and variety of the stonecarving in Puglia, first noticed by Sitwell, makes it equal to, if not better than, any in the whole of Western civilisation. It takes your breath away.

And, talking about breath, the best book you could possibly buy to give you a taste (literally) of Puglia is *Honey from a Weed* by Patience Gray. She was the wife of a very good sculptor who fled England, America, France and elsewhere, eventually to end up in Solento, where, after a long life, he died. The book is a masterpiece of description, atmosphere – and cooking. It knocks Oliver and Ramsay into a cocked hat: sympathetic and truthful about the south of Italy in all its glory.

'All this effort just to get to Birmingham 15 hours quicker'

Taking a trip

Nina Bawden on the kindness of others

In Islington, where I live, handsome trees line the streets, but their roots lift the paving stones off the pavements, making a trip to the post box a hazardous venture. As I found to my cost in July of this year.

This is not a complaint to Islington Council about poor maintenance of its sidewalks – though that is in hand! Instead it is a hymn of praise both to the NHS and to the community spirit that we are constantly being told no longer exists in our crowded cities.

I went to the post box at the end of the street. I mailed my letters. I walked home, tripped on one of those uneven paving stones and fell flat on my face, biting through my upper lip and losing five front teeth. Not that I was aware of the extent of the damage immediately, only of pain, and blood spurting over my (new!) blue linen trousers. And of kindly neighbours and passers by surrounding me. Providing a comforting support for my back, wiping blood from my face, holding my hands, pressing ice to my nose, mouth and jaw, sheltering me from the sweltering sun with an umbrella (a pretty pink, I seem to remember), ringing for an ambulance…

The sun sweltered, but none of my comforters deserted me; holding me safe and comparatively cool, for the 40 minutes or so before the ambulance came, and I was delivered into other kindly hands, and thence to University College Hospital.

I was lucky, The maxillofacial unit were there that day. A skilled surgeon stitched me up. Merciful pain killers. I was there for 11 days, in a single room. Whenever I rang the bell smiling nurses appeared almost instantly. No private hospital I have ever been in could compare with the skilled attention and concern I was given.

And when I came home neighbours appeared with offers of help. Shopping, food, company…

This is our city, our health service. We should all be grateful.

An Orthodox Voice
The Old Etonians among us

Have you noticed how many Old Etonians there are around these days, many of them in positions of power and influence? Only a few years ago the OEs felt obliged to operate under cover. They never mentioned their old school (except guardedly among themselves under the code name Slough Grammar), gave up wearing its tie and modified their accents in the demotic direction. Mr Hurd, Mrs Thatcher's Foreign Secretary, used to apologise for being an OE, claiming that his father was a mere tenant farmer. Now they are out in the open. Through Mr Johnson they govern the capital and, if all goes as planned, they will soon rule the country. Mr Cameron's shadow cabinet is stuffed with OEs, and I hear on good authority (someone in a pub) that among Conservative MPs there are now more Old Etonians than women.

These gracious people are not just active in politics; in every other department of national life the OEs are taking over. Jonathon Porritt commands the Green battalions, Hugh Fearnley-Whittingstall tells us how and what to eat, and every move in affairs of heritage and culture is under the eye of éminence grise Christopher Gibbs (an unmistakable OE even though sacked after only one half). A protégé of Gibbs, Nicky Haslam, leads the world-famous British school of interior design. He always used to dress rough-trade style, but at a party not long ago I saw him besuited and sporting his OE tie. That is when I realised that the old Eton boys were well and truly out of the closet.

I am not sure what to think about this development. It is appropriate that government should be by those best fitted for it. But who are the fittest and how do you recognise them? That is an old problem, but certain characteristics of rightful rulers are generally accepted: that they be of good family, character and education. By those criteria Etonians more or less qualify. They are nearly all from good (meaning in this case rich) backgrounds. But at Eton they have been bullied into a sense of their own insignificance; they have had to rise early, spend hours in chapel, play rough games in the cold, study the classics, speak French and accept their place in the hierarchy. Eton has produced some outstanding cheats, cads and 'château-bottled shits', but they are balanced by the good, quiet, not ostentatiously bright boys who have gone on to manage their father's estates, sustain the beauty of old England and uphold peace and justice in their neighbourhoods. What ornaments these Etonians are. Even the vulgarians among them, sons of foreign oligarchs, sheikhs and such, are converted into liberal gentlemen and shame their parents into acceptable behaviour.

Yet I am frightened by the inevitable anti-OE reaction. Once it is commonly known that the old boys are back in power, they will be held responsible for all the disasters that threaten this realm. In the Republic it is laid down that in times of trouble, when people feel distressed and betrayed, they are whipped up by demagogues to blame their misfortunes on the richer, more educated classes, and take it out of them in Bolshevik or French revolutionary style. But that, we like to think, is not the English way. We cannot do without aristocracy, and all the pious platitudes by recent governments about our 'classless society' are a load of waffle. In the recent Olympics the bulk of our medals was won by privately educated youths in sports which receive little or no government funding. There is a lesson here for the puritanical levellers who control state education. Put the headmasters of Eton, Winchester, Westminster and our great public and grammar schools in charge, and let them produce academies throughout the kingdom where the children are proud of their education and quite capable of outwitting the Old Etonians.

JOHN MICHELL (OE)

H. CROWTHER LTD
LEAD GARDEN ORNAMENTS

www.hcrowther.co.uk
www.leadrestoration.co.uk

Phone : 020 8994 2326 - E-mail : info@hcrowther.co.uk
The Studio, 1 British Grove, Chiswick, London, W4 2NL

Three delicious blends of coffee imported from South India.

Grown below the Nilgiri mountains
Roasted beside the Thames
Delivered to your door

londongradecoffee.com

INDEPENDENT DIABETES TRUST

DIABETES HERE TO HELP

These booklets provide you with help and advice about everyday aspects of living with diabetes

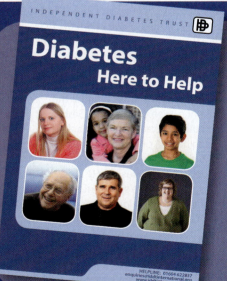

ASK FOR YOUR FREE COPIES TODAY

TELEPHONE: 01604 622837 or
EMAIL: martin@iddtinternational.org

InDependent Diabetes Trust
P O Box 294, Northampton NN1 4XS.

www.iddtinternational.org
Charity Number: 1058284   Registered Number: 3148360

words (WERDS) words. n.

An Orcadian selection, *chaft* and *rowta*

I would like to meet Gregor Lamb from Orkney, now living, I am told, in Italy. He is the author of a very important book, which he began, he says, in 1968 while in exile in England. To quote from his book's preface, he found odd words and phrases from his childhood days still being used as tools in his thought process. No longer of any value in communicating, they had been relegated to his private world, where, before long, they would atrophy and disappear. To forestall this inevitable fate, Mr Lamb began to collect his island's disappearing word hoard, and the *Orkney Wordbook* is the result. It is published by Byrgisey, in Birsay, Orkney, and I bought my copy over the internet – not the cheapest way, perhaps – for about £25.

Orcadian, the language of Gregor's island, was a Norse dialect, now almost extinct, alas. A sampler: *smoosk:* to smile in a sly manner, from Norwegian dialectal *smuska*; *skyran*: a glittering of the sky, also applied to a girl, from Old Norse *skirr*, meaning bright; *polt*, a small, chunky person, the man who was lowered over a cliff to gather seabirds' eggs (he had to be small and strong) from Norwegian *bult*, a chunk of wood; *heevie*, a woven straw basket carried on the back, from Scots *haev*, a fisherman's hand-basket, related to Old English *hyf*, a hive, and Old Norse *háfr*, a bag-net.

Had in Orcadian means both to hold and to protect. Lamb quotes a pre-Reformation 'bonie-words prayer': 'Mary Mither had thee hand / Roond aboot wir sleepan band / Had the lass and had the wife / And had the bairnies a their life.' *Boona* means a variety of things: a harness for a horse, equipment in general, and the male sex organ. It comes from Old Norse *bunaðr*, equipment – Scots has *bouney*.

As one would expect, sea terms abound here. *Andoo* is a verb meaning to row a boat against wind and tide so that it keeps in position for fishing. The verb is from Old Norse *andoefa*, to keep a boat in position by rowing.

I hope Mr Lamb is in his *ludgy pot*, in the best of health (from Old Scots legal jargon *liege poustie*, in full possession of one's faculties). He has done hero's work in collecting this splendid treasury of a beautiful Norse dialect now on its last legs. As the Irish scholar TF O'Rahilly said, not of Orcadian but of Manx, when a language surrenders itself to foreign idiom, and when all its speakers become bilingual, the penalty is death.

A letter from an old acquaintance, Jennifer Hall, who long ago transferred from Co. Kilkenny to Barnsley, contained the interesting word *chaft*, a noun often used in the plural, which means the jaw; the cheeks, chops. The word came south

> **A splendid treasury of a beautiful Norse dialect now on its last legs**

from Scotland, and it is found in most of the northern counties of England. The *English Dialect Dictionary* records 'I'll cloot his chaffs the next time I meet him,' from Fife. In Durham, in harder times than ours, pig's chaffs were a delicacy among the poor miners' wives. The old glossary, *Catholicon Anglicum*, from 1483 defines a *chaft* as *maxilla, mala*. The word is either from the Old Norse *hjaptr* or the Swedish *käft*, jaw.

I had almost given up on another word my friend sent me, one which she heard from a trawlerman from Great Yarmouth, when an inspiration hit me, a rare occurrence nowadays. Her word was *rowta*, the row bit rhyming with toe. It was a filthy day, with huge waves lashing the harbour, and the smaller boats couldn't put to sea. It was a *rowta* day, the fisherman said. Not a sign of the word in the *English Dialect Dictionary*, nor in the Yorkshire glossaries I have access to. Suddenly the Scottish Gaelic *rotach* came to mind, a wild storm with raging seas, synchronising with a flood tide. This word, Alexander Macbain's Scottish Gaelic dictionary informed me, comes from the Old Norse *róta*, storm, tempest. And Róta is the name of the Norse goddess who sent storms and foul weather, according to the Icelandic lexicographer Vigfusson.

Nice one, Jenny. I've sent your word to Oxford.

Diarmaid Ó Muirithe

'Here's your problem'

Get 10% off your order on www.shoetherapy.co.uk with code oldann

Probably the most comfortable shoes in the world!

REF: 42905 (also black)

REF: 42908 (also black grain and smooth)

SHOETHERAPY COMFORT

- Vegetable tanned soft leather uppers
- Removable leather insoles for fitting adjustment/ or orthotics
- Sheep Leather Lined
- Lightweight
- Air Circulation System for comfy healthy feet
- Leather cushioned insole
- Anti-Slip Sole
- Shock Absorbing Heel

For help and catalogue contact Distributors:
Sizeroy Ltd
info@sizeroy.co.uk
01933 665566
07774 152956

Visit us on Facebook @ShoetherapyUK
Twitter @therapy_shoe
amazon.co.uk Search SHOETHERAPY or SAPATOTERAPIA

SEE THE FULL RANGE ON OUR WEBSITE www.shoetherapy.co.uk *Estd. 1994 Sold in 70 countries*

National Churches Trust — For people who love church buildings

Some gifts are easily forgotten. Yours will last for generations.

St Peter, Winterbourne Stoke, Wiltshire

CHURCHES ARE AT THE HEART of communities throughout the UK.

The National Churches Trust is dedicated to the repair and support of the UK's churches, chapels and meeting houses.

Leaving a gift in your Will helps us to keep these precious buildings alive for future generations.

To find out how you can help keep the UK's churches alive, please call Claire Walker on **020 7222 0605**, email **legacy@nationalchurchtrust.org** visit **nationalchurchtrust.org/legacy** or send the coupon below to the National Churches Trust, 7 Tufton Street, London SW1P 3QB (please affix a stamp).

If you would like to receive information about the work we do, and how you could leave a gift in your Will please complete the form below.

Forename

Surname

Address

Postcode

If you would prefer to receive information by email, please provide your email address instead

Registered charity number 1119845

Registered with FUNDRAISING REGULATOR

Please see our privacy policy at www.nationalchurchtrust.org/privacy as to how we hold your data securely and privately. You will not be added to our mailing list and we will only use your details to send you this specific information.

★ Great Bores of Today ★

'... everybody wrote us off at the beginning of the season and I'll be honest two points from the first 15 games looked a disaster but once we got a new boss the lads started to play with confidence I mean what he said was right confidence wins games not goals dead right what are we now? 27 points behind the leaders? it's nothing it's like the boss says we've only got to win a few games and that new bloke he's bought that Brazilian what's his name? he's got to be worth ten points at the end of the season what? they've scored another goal have they? three goals down that's nothing they always come good in the second half ...'

© Fant and Dick

FEBRUARY 2009

Labour of love

You can't rush things when you're building a First World War biplane. *Ken Cooper* watches the project slowly taking shape

After 13 years of patient work, they're finally getting to the interesting part. The first five years were spent just making little bits and storing them in cardboard boxes. At last it's all coming together – an authentic Sopwith Camel fighter, built from the original 1916 plans marked 'Secret and Confidential'. In three more years, it'll take to the air, just as it did over the trenches of the Great War. The Camel is the latest product of the Northern Aeroplane Workshops, a band of enthusiasts who get together twice a week in an old mill at Batley in West Yorkshire. After 35 years of gentle part-time tinkering, this will be their third flying machine.

The body and wings look as they did in the factory more than 90 years ago – a lattice of ash and spruce, awaiting a cover of Irish linen. The pilot's wicker seat is in, and the two Vickers machine guns – original, but deactivated. And today Jim Jackson is fitting the aluminium engine housing into place. At 68, he's spent a year hammering and polishing it into shape in his garage. 'It gets quite noisy when I'm working, but nobody's complained and my wife is very supportive. I'll get my kick from seeing it flying. When I'm just a memory in a photo, this will continue long after I've gone.'

From its enthusiastic beginnings in 1973, the group is down to a hardcore of around eight men. As Jim says: 'They're a good crowd, but they do spend more time talking than working. It's a social club – a bunch of elderly gents living in the past and solving old problems, like how to drill a hole at exactly two degrees to the horizontal. But you have to admire the way they do it.'

The only nod to 21st-century working methods is the use of modern glues, for safety's sake. Otherwise, it's strictly authentic. 'When you're working from the original plans, you get a real sense of the skills those early craftsmen had,' says Trevor Foreman, a landscape architect who's currently fitting the Camel's oil tank. In a wood and fabric aeroplane, fire was a constant fear – behind the pilot's

Opposite: Bob Richardson at work on the Sopwith Camel
Right: Fellow enthusiast John Thompson
Below: A replica Sopwith F–11 Camel

back is a pressurised petrol tank. There were no parachutes, so some fliers carried a revolver to shoot themselves rather than die in flames. As Trevor says, this Camel will be a tribute to the men who fought the world's first air battles. 'I've met a few Royal Flying Corps pilots – very modest men. They were boys of 18 and 19, flying at up to 20,000 feet without oxygen, their faces smeared with whale grease against the cold, and juggling a pair of levers just to keep the engine going. Yes, and being shot at was a slight distraction as well...'

Two machines from the Northern Aeroplane Workshops already fly in displays for the Shuttleworth Collection near Biggleswade in Bedfordshire, the classic aircraft group that's commissioned and financed the Camel project. The Workshops spent 17 years building a Sopwith Triplane, and followed it with a Bristol Monoplane, which took them 12 years.

Progress is painfully slow, but the team only meet for a few hours a week, and the craftsmanship must be perfect. These are authentic flying machines; if they're not airworthy, they're grounded. The team could have built museum replicas in a fraction of the time. But they believe an old-time aeroplane, like a vintage Bentley or a classic steam engine, can only be fully appreciated in its natural environment – in the air.

As the latest project is assembled, the work is regularly checked by professional engineers from the Collection. It's one of their volunteers who'll eventually fly it. 'Our pilots may fly airliners for a living, but they start with us as tea-boys,' says Shuttleworth's Tony Podmore. 'You have to re-learn everything. It can take years to learn to fly vintage machines like ours – often they have no hydraulics or even brakes. But we're still flying while aircraft like Concorde have come and gone.'

The first Northern Aeroplane Workshops aircraft finally took off in 1992, with scenes as emotional as you could expect from a group of middle-aged Northerners. 'We shook hands when our triplane flew,' says Bob Richardson. 'This thing had grown up with us, and it was a tremendous feeling

> '**Our pilots may fly airliners for a living, but they start with us as tea-boys. You have to re-learn everything**'

after 17 years. It made all those hours of work worthwhile.' Bob is a retired police inspector. He's 64, and he's been with the Workshops from the start in the 1970s. As he admits, most of them are now past retirement age: 'They called us "The Young Ones" when we started. The youngest of us now is in his fifties.'

One of the group's founding aims was to preserve the traditional crafts of the early aviation industry – the skills of working in wood, metal and linen. 'But we're not getting any young people coming in to take over the job,' says Bob. 'It's the same in the steam engine and vintage car worlds – fewer of them are serving apprenticeships.'

Which means the next magnificent flying machine could be the last. It'll be a DH2 biplane from 1916. But at their current rate of production, Bob will be pushing 80 when it finally takes off, and he knows the group can't last for ever. That, however, is not going to put them off making a start.

Horace Darlington has just spent five years building the undercarriage for the Camel. Now, at 71, he's hoping for a job on the next project. 'It's been a labour of love,' he says, 'and it's kept me going. Without a hobby, you die, don't you?'

The last king of Laos

Jonathan Fryer danced with King Savang Vatthana in the summer of 1971

It was the summer of 1971, when I was just starting my second tour of duty as a cub reporter in the Vietnam War and its sideshows in Cambodia and Laos. I had taken a tiny motorboat over the Mekong River from northern Thailand to the Laotian capital of Vientiane – there was no bridge in those days – and then had gone to the British Embassy for a briefing. 'You should come up with us to the royal city of Luang Prabang tomorrow,' the Ambassador declared cheerfully, 'and dance with the King!'

There was going to be a celebration at the royal palace at Luang Prabang; maybe it was King Savang Vatthana's birthday, I don't recall. The entire diplomatic corps in Vientiane (which was not large) was invited to this black-tie event, which is how I ended up hitching a ride on a plane to Luang Prabang the following morning, with a British Embassy First Secretary's borrowed dinner jacket and formal trousers in my case.

We landed in torrential rain. Even for the summer monsoon season, the fury of the downpour was unusual. Gullies by the side of the road leading from the tiny airport were soon overflowing and it was a relief to arrive at the guest-house where I was to spend the night.

A young American who was also staying there ventured out into the torrential rain, determined to 'do' a temple or two before it got dark. As he recounted to me later, in the sepulchral gloom of one venerable shrine, he was approached by a little old man who started to tell him in French about the origins and significance of some of the statues. At the end of this impromptu tour, the American, wondering how much to tip this unexpected guide, asked him how he knew so much about the history of the place. 'Ah, Monsieur!' the old man replied, '*Je suis le roi!*'

> **The next thing I knew, I had received a hefty thwack from one of the Laotian courtiers as punishment for standing while the king was bowed**

I had to wait until that evening before I encountered Savang Vatthana, who was by now attired in a splendid dress uniform, with lots of gold braid. As the Ambassador had predicted, the male guests were invited in Laotian fashion to dance in a sort of slow-motion conga behind the king, waving our hands up and down gracefully, like birds. Think Graham Norton, only more limp-wristed.

Instructed to do exactly what the king did, we were meant to bob up and down as the conga wound its sedate way round the reception room. But my borrowed trousers were a size too small and, try as I might, I could not bend my knee sufficiently to lower myself more than a fraction. The next thing I knew, I had received a hefty thwack on my shoulders from one of the Laotian courtiers as punishment for standing while the king was bowed, and I fell flat on my face. I retired red-faced to a chair and calmed myself with a glass of champagne.

The following morning, Luang Prabang now cut off from the rest of Laos by the rising waters, I attended a breakfast given by the US Embassy in their local residence. A stiff invitation card was delivered to my guest-house, with the phrase 'lounge suit' crossed out and replaced with the hand-written instruction '*tenue de flood*'. The conversation over scrambled eggs and hash browns was all about how we would ever get away from the inundated city. In the end, the American air-force sent a helicopter to evacuate us, and I looked down over the roofs of temples from the chopper's open back-hatch as we climbed into the sky.

Four years later, King Savang Vatthana was deposed when the Communists took over and the civil war that had caused him so much distress came to an end. At first he was nominated as an 'advisor' to the new president. But in 1977, he and the Queen were sent to a notorious re-education camp in northern Laos, known simply as 'Camp Number One'. Reports conflict as to exactly when he died there – maybe as late as 1984, at the age of 77.

I have no grandchildren to whom I can recount this tale, but until the day I die, I will remember the night I danced with the last king of Laos.

SPORT
FRANK KEATING

My dear old thing … well, I never …Henry Blofeld, longtime buddy, 70 this summer, and *The Oldie*'s former booze-correspondent, is staging a one-man stand at the Royal Albert Hall, no less. Jonathan Agnew MCs.

Solo top-of-the-bill at the Albert Hall! Golly, Blowers, that must be worth at least a couple of peerages, five knighthoods and a whole handful of *Desert Island Discs* to swankily prove you were a national treasure who'd made the bigtime grade all right. Well done that lad…

Henry Blofeld : national treasure

We first met in the early 1960s; we were subbing on the *Guardian*, him on the sports desk, me on foreign. I'd heard Henry was a top-hole Minor Counties cricketer for Norfolk and one night in The Blue Lion, I asked how many he'd made at the crease that weekend. 'M'dear ol' thing, don't ask, it was ghastly, never managed one in the middle of the bat.' Back in the office, I looked up the scores in that morning's *Times*: H C Blofeld, 157 not out. Two or three years later I was an ITV outside broadcast producer told to find in haste someone to cover a cricket match at The Oval. It was Henry's first live commentary. A star was born.

Almost half a century later and alas for one of Henry's sometime *Test Match Special* confrères when the prog resumes this May. *TMS* can never be quite the same again… the 'Bearded Wonder' has closed his innings. Scorer Bill Frindall was also due his 70th birthday this year – born on 3rd March 1939, first day of the infamous 'Timeless Test' in Durban. Bill died suddenly in January of Legionnaires' Disease.

Coincidentally, I was also there when Bill and his coloured pencils made their debutant's curtsey in the scorers' box. It was 4th May 1966, down by the silvern Severn, first day of their tour for Garry Sobers's fabled West Indies side. It was also greenhorn Frindall's tremulous first day; alongside him in the box was John Arlott. Only the year before, at 26, Bill and his handlebar moustache had left his RAF short-service commission to train as an insurance inspector in the City. One evening, the keen young club cricketer heard on the radio that Arthur Wrigley, the BBC Test Match scorer, had died. Quite a nice job that, thought Bill. Unaware that calamity had recently struck the whole cottage industry and that the game's other two leading stats' nuts – Roy Webber and Jack Price – had also lately died, young Bill, bold as you like, bunged off an application for the job in his meticulous copperplate.

Hot favourite for the job (and Wrigley's protégé) was Arnold Whipp who, aptly somehow, doubled as ace compiler of rail and bus timetables at Manchester's transport depot. But the BBC appointments' board (head of OBs Max Muller, cricket producer Michael Hastings, and commentator Brian Johnston) swayed by young Bill's swot-appeal, gave youth its head, and told Frindall to spend the winter mugging up all (by then) 103 editions of the voluminous *Wisden*.

Bill did so with a nerdish rigour. He shaved off the flamboyant RAF 'tash, began a more scholarly beard, and having sharpened his pencils, drove down from Ashtead to Worcester at dawn on 4th May, his little Hillman Imp crammed with every reference book imaginable. Then he sat in the tiny, empty broadcasting box for hours, full of dread at being stumped at every turn by every question. Just three minutes from transmission, John Arlott ambled into the box and, in solemn ritual, unpacked his famed old leather briefcase – a large hunk of Cheddar, a packet of Ryvita, a corkscrew and two bottles of claret – then matily squeezed the nervous young scorer's shoulder in welcome: 'I hear you like driving, lad. Well, I like drinking. We're going to get on really well.'

NOT MANY DEAD
Important stories you may have missed

Police were called to a field by a worried motorist after she spotted a 'dead' horse lying on the ground, which officers found was actually asleep.
Daily Telegraph

Catherine Zeta-Jones nearly took a tumble as she negotiated a flight of stairs in a pair of impractical espadrilles… She was steadied by husband Michael Douglas, 64.
London Lite.

Dr Who star David Tennant is enjoying a break from acting and is spending it getting furniture for his new home
Mail on Sunday

Tips for meanies

Even in winter, the garden is the true land of opportunity for Meanies. When you've had your coffee, don't waste the old grinds, but tip them onto acid-loving plants like camellia, which will thrive. Ferns, on the other hand, relish old tea and tea leaves. If you've cooked pasta, allow the water to cool and donate it to your plants. There's something about the starch and vitamins they appreciate.
Jane Thynne

SEPTEMBER 2009

The world according to Enfield Snr

If it ain't broke…

The trouble with human beings is that they cannot leave things alone. By way of example, let me start with the wonderful machine that they had in our public library. When you switched it on it said 'Press any key', which is the sort of instruction I can understand. As this was followed by some equally simple instructions I was able, all by myself and with no skill other than being able to read, to order any book from the entire library stock anywhere in the country. Then, having achieved perfection, they took it away. There is now another machine which I suppose can do the same thing, and possibly some other things, but instead of pressing any key you have to fiddle about with a mouse, and I am not into mice so I have gone back to asking the ever-helpful ladies at the desk to get me the book I want, while the new machine gathers dust in the corner.

This, of course, is mere tinkering on the small scale. When done by government on the grand scale it is called Reform, which means spoiling things by way of a general upheaval. If you read, as you may well read at any moment, that the biggest reform of the Health Service for the last 20 years is about to take place, you may be sure that 20 years ago they made it worse than it was, and are now about to make it worse than it is. If anyone thinks the House of Lords is better now than it was with just hereditary peers, law lords and bishops, they must be mad.

I speak with authority because I have seen such things from the inside, as I was working in local government when Ted Heath reformed it. If you look about you for things that are all wrong, and they are not the fault of Mr Blair or Mr Brown, they are commonly the fault of the late Sir Edward Heath. Local government was all right until he started to meddle with it, since when it has become progressively less efficient, less democratic and a lot more costly.

As part of his meddling process Ted Heath commissioned a couple of reports, one from a man who I think was called Baines who drew a quite false analogy with the world of commerce and said that local authorities should become more like big business, which would, he supposed, make them more efficient. It didn't, but it gave them big ideas. Every potty little district council had to have a Chief Executive, an office which was previously unknown, such duties as there were being done in his spare time by the chief legal officer, known as the Clerk. Boundaries were changed, some people were pensioned off, more people were taken on, and lots of people, including me, carried on as before. The lawyers did not become better lawyers, the roads were not better mended, and the planners, from what I have seen, have become steadily worse, but it had all somehow got bigger so we were all paid more money.

They have developed things over the years to the point that crazy statements are made, such as that Suffolk County Council is a '£1 billion business'. It isn't. A local government bureaucracy is not a business at all, and no more like one than a primary school is like a corner shop. From time to time the newspapers get worked up at the thought of Chief Executives earning £200,000 a year or more, and retiring on vast pensions with huge lump sums, which caused the Chief Executive of the Local Government Organisation to say that they could earn 'on average more than twice as much elsewhere'. I shall believe that when I hear of one of them doubling his salary by moving elsewhere. Noël Coward described Hong Kong society as a 'lot of third-rate people living in first-rate style', and local government is now much like that, with a lot of second-rate people taking home first-rate salaries.

All of which I tell you more in sorrow than in anger, as local government used to be a humble and worthy occupation run by sufficiently capable but unassuming people. But, as it says at the front of the Book of Common Prayer, 'some be so new-fangled that they would innovate all things, and so despise the old, that nothing can like them but that it is new'. There is no stopping them and, whatever it is, they reform it.

'Guilty of something, I can tell'

SUMMER 2009

Life in the Pennines

We are a very tribal community, well aware of our individual places in the parochial firmament. We do have a social hierarchy but it does not follow normal conventions, based on power, wealth, connections on high, and accepted notions of superiority. If there is such a thing as a truly classless society in this country it is here, in what we call the Upper Dale.

Socially, we differ from communities towards the lower end, and from the dales that flank us to the north and the south, in one crucial respect: none of our land is owned by peers of the realm, and there is no such thing here as a gentleman farmer. Lacking such patronage means that none of our farmers are tenants, and the consequences of this are subtle and extensive. For a start, this means that no husbandman (the nearest arable farming is 17 miles away down the dale) owes anything to anyone but his bank manager, which has a knock-on effect throughout the community. No one feels beholden to anyone else, and no one can try to pull rank in his dealings with others, because there are no ranks to pull. We are a very independent and self-sufficient lot, and anyone who tries to challenge this is apt to get rather more than he bargained for in response. So is any incomer who decides that he (or, more frequently, she) is going to be the leader of something without being asked. We don't much care for pushers and shovers, by and large.

A small built-in hazard of this society is that, unless you are extremely certain of your ground, it is wise to be careful what you say about any individual, because the person to whom you are speaking is very likely to be his (or her) second cousin at least. For our hierarchy is based on breeding above all. And pre-eminent in the Upper Dale are half a dozen extended families who have been rooted here since the year dot.

Of these, the most numerous and probably the most self-conscious are the Metcalfes, whose collective ancestry dates back to the 12th century and who did, once upon a time, have noble lineage. This began when a Metcalfe was knighted for loyal service at Agincourt, while another led the contingent of Dalesmen at Flodden Field and became High Sheriff of Yorkshire under Henry VIII. But the family long ago came down from this high ground, its members now indistinguishable from anybody else except in small particulars. More often than not, a Metcalfe has been the official hornblower in a village just down the dale, sounding his tucket on the green at nine o'clock each evening between the end of September and Shrovetide, a custom that began in order to guide travellers home across the fells, where wolves and wild boars still lurked in the Middle Ages.

We can be very pernickety about precisely where we originate and from what stock, because this above all establishes our credentials in the natural order of things. Two of my oldest friends here had seemed on first acquaintance to be obviously local (they belonged, after all, to another of our great tribal families) and I was surprised when Joan said, 'Oh no, I'm not from here, I'm from away'. She meant that until she married Peter and came to live in our village, she had been born and had grown up on a farm just across the river, about a mile and a half from where we spoke. You can't define belonging much more sharply than that.

GEOFFREY MOORHOUSE

RANT

'O Blithe new-comer! I have heard, I hear thee and rejoice.' So Wordsworth wrote of the cuckoo. But were he with us today the poet would have nothing more to rejoice about. The cuckoo has virtually vanished from this country.

But what is this we hear instead? A strange, eerie whistling noise, a chill piercing sound that you can't quite believe is made by a bird.

KITES! Look up, and there they are slowly circling overhead like the Nazgul in *Lord of the Rings*. They call them red kites but they look black from below.

'Oh look at the lovely kites!' say the woolly-minded folk who nowadays inhabit the countryside. But the kites aren't lovely. They are black and sinister.

The late Sir Paul Getty was a saintly benefactor – he saved *The Oldie* when it was threatened with closure – but he made a terrible mistake when some years ago he introduced kites (then virtually extinct in Britain) into his Buckinghamshire estate.

It didn't take long for them to spread. And by now you can see them, often in quite large numbers, all over the home counties. Ah, say the woolly folk, the kites perform a valuable service to the environment getting rid of all the carrion on the roads. No mention of all the live things they kill – including young birds and young poultry.

What bastards! I am looking forward to my first kite cull. It can't be long in coming.

RICHARD INGRAMS

Book *your* Perfect Suffolk Escape
"Ideally located to explore Suffolk's heritage coast"

Self Catering Cottages and Studios & Caravan and Motorhome Club CL

MOLLETT'S FARM

Mollett's Farm, Main Road, Benhall,
Saxmundham, Suffolk IP17 1JY
+44 1728 604547
www.molletts.com bookings@molletts.com

Eximius
REFINED LIVE-IN SUPPORT

Eximius Live-in care – a safe alternative to a care home

Live-in care offers a safe nurturing environment for your loved ones, during this difficult time. All our carers live with their clients, supporting them with their personal, clinical and social needs. We can help with shopping, supplies, activities and social media – everything to keep them safe but still in touch and thriving.

Call us today for a chat on how we can keep your loved ones cared for and safe.

19 London End, Beaconsfield,
Buckinghamshire HP9 2HN
01494 424222   0203 794 9933
www.eximiussupport.uk
info@eximiussupport.uk

Chantry Court Retirement Village, Westbury, Wiltshire

Choice + Independence + Flexibility = A future to look forward to

- The relaxed ambience of the village, set in the heart of Westbury, provides the opportunity to retain maximum independence with the peace of mind that there is a support network.
- There is an on-site domiciliary care service, regulated by CQC, which offers one-to-one care, in your own apartment, tailored to meet your needs if and when required.
- Excellent facilities including, a restaurant, licensed bar, library, cinema room.
- Enjoy one of the few luxurious and spacious apartments, whether choosing to rent, purchase or to take advantage of our shared equity offering.
- Short-term, respite, recuperation and holiday stays are available.

Care provided in your own home by a company registered with the CQC.
In association with The Old Prebendal House www.oldprebendalhouse.com

We are delighted to offer those who book for a one week's short-term stay/respite the benefit of a second week FREE (T&Cs apply).

Call 0800 014 7552
or email sales@chantrycourt.com
www.chantrycourt.com

Chantry Court
A beautiful place to retire with care

THEATRE
BERYL BAINBRIDGE

I intended to go and see Ibsen's *Ghosts*, in production at the Duchess Theatre, off the Aldwych in Catherine Street. The traffic was so heavy and the journey so delayed by roadworks that though I set off a good hour before the curtain was due to rise I arrived very late and in something of a panic. To my relief there were still crowds of people queueing up for admittance and I was able to get a ticket and take my seat a few minutes before the show began.

Griff Rhys Jones as Fagin in *Oliver!*

There were two reasons for my wanting to review *Ghosts*: one, that I knew the director, Iain Glen, who had become a friend of my daughter when they were both students at drama school, and two, because I'd been told that the actress, Lesley Sharp, was magnificent as Mrs Alving, the tormented woman at the heart of the play. Also, I firmly believe that no work of drama or fiction comes directly from the imagination, and that its source stems from the author's own half-buried experience of life. I wanted to understand what had driven Ibsen to write it in the first place. Had his own mother been dominated by a hectoring husband?

Imagine my confusion when the lights dimmed and the stage revealed a horde of children prancing about the stage singing *Food, Glorious Food*. I was in the auditorium of the Theatre Royal watching the opening of Lionel Bart's *Oliver!*

For perhaps 30 seconds I did think of leaving, it being yet another musical, but then, even though I knew I was watching little chaps only pretending to be desperate for something to eat, I found it all rather moving – I couldn't forget that when Dickens was creating the character of Oliver Twist children really were dying of starvation, and as the music and action continued I realised I was indeed lucky to have entered the wrong theatre.

Lionel Bart wrote two other successful musicals, *Fings Ain't What They Used To Be* and *Lock Up Your Daughters*, but it was *Oliver!*, his third musical, opening in 1960, which was an instant and enormous hit. It ran for 2,618 performances in London, for more than two years in New York and eventually became a multi-Oscar winning film. He wasn't so successful with his subsequent work, drink and drugs having dulled his brilliance; he died in 1999.

This production was first staged by Cameron Mackintosh in 1977, and then again in 1994 under the helm of Sam Mendes and Matthew Bourne. The designer, Sean Kenny, was a genius whose revolutionary sets brought a new stylised realism to the stage.

This version, directed by Rupert Goold and designed by Anthony Ward, is magnificent. It's not just the list of memorable songs – *Oom-Pah-Pah*, *Consider Yourself*, *As Long As He Needs Me* – or the magic of the characters – the money-loving Fagin and the tragic Nancy in love with the brutal Bill Sikes – or even the plight of poor little Oliver that keeps one hooked, but rather the whole thing played out in the grand Victorian manner that Dickens himself so loved. Rupert Goold also directed *Enron*, the play now showing to great acclaim at the Noël Coward Theatre.

Griff Rhys Jones stars as Fagin, the miser who teaches little boys to steal. Jodie Prenger is Nancy and Julian Glover portrays Mr Brownlow, the kindly gentleman who doesn't immediately realise that he is looking after his own grandson. As for Oliver, there are four names listed in the programme, and I think I saw nine-year-old Edward Cooke in the part.

Don't waste time. Book now.

RANT

There are 350 official road signs on the road between our village and the Oxford bypass. If we lived 25 miles away that might not be excessive – but it's absurd given that the distance is only five miles. Seventy to the mile?

They range from indecipherable little discs to huge illuminated hoardings. They are repetitive, confusing and mutually conflicting (as you turn off into our village there are de-restriction signs on both sides of the road followed 20 yards later by a 30mph limit sign). Sometimes they are so close together that you can't even see the back markers. Any minute now they'll put a sign up saying 'Caution – hidden signs ahead'. The latest pair are electronic. One – solar-powered – flashes 'Slow down!' at you even if you're well inside the speed limit. The other keeps telling you to use the Park and Ride.

Heaven knows how much it all costs. And does it add to safety? Will a driver distracted by mostly irrelevant signs every 50 yards see and obey the few that actually matter? If I get done for speeding I think I'll refuse to pay the fine, plead chronic sign-fatigue and see if the magistrates have the gall to convict me.

It might be easier to live with if there were some aesthetic consistency underlying the signage. We are confronted by an incoherent clutter of colours, sizes, symbols and shapes. And it's clutter on a road that goes through pleasant countryside – you can't see the bluebells for the 'No waiting' signs.

It's hard not to suspect mis-selling. The Association of Road Sign Erectors (probably called something else for acronymic reasons) deserves a prize for persuading the authorities to commission this lucrative excess. But at least in this corruption-free nation we can be confident that there are no backhanders passing, can't we?

Mark Baker

SUMMER 2010

1963 and all that

They don't make them like that any more: *Stanley Price* recalls the golden age of sex scandals

All of us over 47 realise that Philip Larkin was using poetic licence when he wrote, 'Sexual intercourse began in 1963.' He was very specific about the timing too – 'Between the end of the *Chatterley* ban and the Beatles' first LP.'

I agree with Larkin about the year, but not the events. There were two more relevant happenings that year: the Profumo scandal and the Duchess of Argyll's divorce case. For the first time the press were totally explicit and hugely excited about the details and varieties of SI. It was written and talked about, if not actually performed, more frequently and graphically than ever before. At respectable dinner-parties words and practices were mentioned that had to be explained to the less worldly. I didn't need explanations as I'd recently returned from living in the worldliest bit

Above: Jeanne Campbell. Right: The Duchess of Argyll: a woman who had clearly outgrown normal sexual activities

of the New World – New York. I'd also had a connection with a protagonist in the Duchess of Argyll divorce scandal.

That 'connection', for want of a better word, was the Duchess's step-daughter, Lady Jeanne Campbell, daughter of the 11th Duke and, more importantly, Lord Beaverbrook's favourite granddaughter. I had met her at *Life* where we were both reporters and, as the token

> **They stole several photos of the Duchess with nothing on except a pearl necklace, performing what the judge called 'a disgusting sexual activity' on a headless man, rumoured to be Duncan Sandys or Douglas Fairbanks Jr**

English, we'd become friendly. The story about 'Jeannie', according to her American colleagues, was that she was working on the clipping-desk when Beaverbrook turned up in New York and had lunch with his fellow press tycoon, Henry Luce (*Time, Life, Sports Illustrated, Fortune*). Beaverbrook told Luce that his granddaughter was working for him. When Luce heard in what a humble capacity, he immediately called his personnel department and the next day Jeannie became a reporter.

Jeannie was fun – tall, what used to be called buxom, and not too obviously a lady. For me she was always more jolly hockey-sticks than

femme fatale, so you could have knocked me over with a feather when she confided that she had become Henry Luce's mistress. Jeannie was then 28, Luce 58.

Luce had a reputation with his staff for being aloof and puritanical – maybe something to do with being brought up in China by missionary parents. I once shared an elevator with him and he pretended I wasn't there. Anyway Jeannie had clearly broken through all that. She confided to my wife that he had told her she was the only woman who could make him giggle and make him come.

Jeannie obviously trusted my discretion because she told me about the handbag trick. She kept a spare handbag in a drawer and left it on her desk if she wanted to be away from work for a while. If anyone in her open-plan office answered her phone, they would say, 'She can't have gone far, her handbag's on the desk.' On the occasion when she confided this, she had in fact gone very far – to London for three days to help her father, to whom she was devoted.

The Duke was divorcing the Duchess, and Jeannie helped him break into her Mayfair house to get the vital evidence. She didn't tell me exactly what it was, but she was jubilant. The case took four years of legal wrangling to come to court and only then, back in London, did I read about what Jeannie and her Dad had stolen – several volumes of the Duchess's salacious diaries and the Polaroid photos of her activities, of which the best known was of her with nothing on except her trademark pearl necklace, performing what the Edinburgh judge called 'a disgusting sexual activity' on a headless man (of course he had a head, but it wasn't on the photo). The missing head was rumoured to be either Duncan Sandys's, or Douglas Fairbanks Jnr's. Many years later there was fairly conclusive proof it was the latter's.

In concluding his 40,000-word summing-up, the judge said that the Duchess had ceased to be satisfied with normal SI and had committed multiple adultery 'to gratify a debased sexual appetite'. Decree granted, the Duke lit a celebration bonfire in Argyll, and Jeannie, back in New York, her affair with Henry Luce over, married Norman Mailer. The marriage, which lasted just over a year, produced one child and much domestic violence, leading to a divorce in that magical year, 1963.

For a while I maintained a Christmas-card relationship with Jeannie and then it lapsed. Meanwhile she had returned to journalism after marrying and divorcing a rich farmer in South Carolina. Then no news till I read her obituary in September 2007 in the *Daily Telegraph*. She had died 'in her Greenwich Village apartment in her last remaining treasure – Napoleon's campaign bed'. It mentioned that she'd received a large advance for her memoirs but had blown it on a Greek villa without ever putting paper in her typewriter.

She did, however, make a stunning appearance in someone else's memoirs – James C Humes, a speechwriter for Presidents Kennedy and Johnson. He wrote that she had, in a period of 18 months starting in – yes again – 1963, slept with three presidents, Kennedy in Washington, Khruschev in Moscow and Castro in Havana. Get out the feather – knock me down.

Larkin was right about 1963. It was a vintage year.

Raymond Briggs
All tied up

The absurdity of dress codes. Where do they come from? Fashion may decree, but in the end, class dictates.

The oddest item has been the tie. Back in the Fifties, it was obligatory. Going to the doctor, dentist, bank manager – put a tie on, though the chances were, you were wearing one already. Recently, I came across a self-portrait I painted at that time, in our kitchen at home and wearing a jacket and tie. A teen-age art student!

At grammar school we were forbidden to travel home in part-uniform. So even on the hottest day we were expected to cycle several miles wearing a thick black blazer, a cap and a tie. I used to dive into an alleyway, take off all three bits and bung them into my saddlebag.

Then later, came the restaurant nonsense. Some posh places insisted that customers wore a tie. If you turned up tieless, they would lend you one. Gad! Improperly dressed, what? I only suffered that humiliation once, and of course, never went there again.

Much worse than that was the well-known story of the glamorous young woman who was asked to leave a restaurant she had just entered, because she was wearing trousers. Fortunately, she had on a trouser suit, so she marched into the Ladies, whipped off the trousers and came out with the tunic top just about long enough to pass as a mini-skirt. Apparently, that was quite acceptable. I bet it was.

But this kind of nonsense becomes ingrained. Even now, despite being an habitual sandal-wearer, I feel I cannot go to a doctor, hospital or dentist in sandals.

Consequently, I was almost shocked to see a bloke waiting in our dentist's reception wearing a stained and filthy vest. Not a T-shirt, but an underwear vest, hairy armpits and all, and apart from his skull, unshaven as well. Gad! I thought, the fellow isn't even wearing a tie.

All this piffle began for me in the early Fifties. In my transition from working class to middle class I found there was a lot to learn.

One afternoon, my girlfriend and I came back to her house and her mother asked me to stay to 'supper'. We called it 'tea' at home. Supper was something you had just before going to bed, if you were feeling peckish. Cornflakes, usually.

It was a hot summer day, so I was wearing an open-neck shirt and the usual gabardine raincoat. When I took the raincoat off, the mother's face fell.

Haven't you got a jacket?

Oh … er – no.

You must have a jacket.

Oh, no … I'm fine, thanks. Not cold at all.

Julian, darling, get him a jacket.

My girlfriend's brother led me up to his room and I put on one of his jackets and a tie. The jacket was far too big as he was a public school rugger type and I was a suburban weed. I went downstairs swamped by this green tweed jacket, with the sleeves down to my knuckles and the shoulders drooping off me.

Throughout the meal, the brother and I sat sweltering in these jackets and ties while the women wore summer blouses with low necks and bare arms. It was not a formal occasion, only the four of us.

I thought, if this is how the middle class lives, then bollocks to it.

St Dorothy of New York?

Stuart Reid reports on the uncompromising pacifist, now on the slow road to beatification, who founded the Catholic Worker Movement to provide a Christian alternative to Communism

On a bitterly cold night in January, 2004, I went down to Maryhouse in the Bowery in New York to attend a talk on Dorothy Day, the ex-communist single mother and pacifist anarchist who founded the Catholic Worker Movement and is now on the slow track to beatification.

Maryhouse is the headquarters of the Catholic Worker Movement and it was quite snug inside. I remember little of what was said, but I do remember the fellow sitting in front of me. He was reading a gay porno mag, and I watched as he tore out a page, folded it with great care, and put it in his satchel. Eventually, he fell asleep.

The movement began with a newspaper, the *Catholic Worker*, which was launched in 1933 by Dorothy Day and a French tramp and Catholic social theorist called Peter Maurin, one of 24 children of a peasant couple in the Languedoc. The aim of the paper was to 'comfort the afflicted and to afflict the comfortable' and provide working men with a Christian alternative to communism. The first issue sold for a cent – 'so cheap,' as Dorothy said, 'that anyone can afford it.' There has never been a price increase.

The launch of the paper was followed by the establishment of houses to shelter and feed the poor, first in New York, then in other major American cities, and eventually in the United Kingdom, Canada, Australia, Germany, Holland, Ireland, New Zealand and Sweden.

Dorothy lived among the poor, sharing their bed bugs, their overflowing lavatories, their second-hand clothes and their often meagre rations, and dealing on an almost daily basis with their tantrums, their dishonesties, their self-pity, their smells, their lunacy and their drunkenness. Life had been much easier for her when, as a far-left journalist in her early twenties, she was a Greenwich Village swinger.

She was married for a year. The first

Dorothy Day's last confrontation with the law, when she picketed on behalf of itinerant Mexican farm workers (San Joaquin Valley, California, 1973)

time she got pregnant she had the child aborted. In 1926 she had a daughter by a common law husband. She had the baby baptised a Catholic. A little later she became a Catholic herself, because 'I wanted to be poor, obedient and chaste.' She and her fellow split up.

Dorothy was never obedient to Caesar. For almost half a century – she died in 1980, aged 83 – she led a rebellion against what she called 'Holy Mother State' – against its wars, its lies, its cruelties and its welfarism. She was deadly serious about her pacifism, and very brave too. On 8th December, 1941, the day after the Japanese bombed Pearl Harbor, she made a speech in which she said: 'War is hunger, thirst, blindness, death. I call upon you to resist it. You young men should refuse to take up arms. Young women tear down the patriotic posters. And all of you – young and old – put away your flags.'

From time to time she was jailed for civil disobedience. She refused to take part in mandatory civil defence exercises. When the municipal sirens sounded in New York in June 1955, Dorothy was among a small group of people sitting in front of City Hall distributing leaflets proclaiming: 'In the name of Jesus, who is God, who is Love, we will not obey this order to pretend, to evacuate, to hide. We will not be drilled into fear. We do not have faith in God if we depend upon the Atom Bomb.'

Today many Christians might be able to go along with that without too much embarrassment. But in those days such an approach was seen almost as heresy, perhaps even lunacy. Her father called Dorothy 'the nut of the family'.

Dorothy was much influenced by English writers, artists and social theorists – by Hilaire Belloc, Eric Gill, G K Chesterton, John Ruskin, Fr Vincent McNabb. When Evelyn Waugh visited New York in November 1948, Dorothy was on the list prepared for him by Fr Martin D'Arcy, the society priest. Waugh was driven down to Little Italy in Henry Luce's Cadillac for an appointment with Dorothy Day and the Workers. As he wrote in a letter to his wife: 'I gave a great party of them luncheon in an Italian restaurant… & Mrs Day did not at all approve of them having cocktails or wine but they had them & we talked till four o'clock.' For some time afterwards, he sent her cheques made payable to 'Dorothy Day's Soup Kitchen'.

In the 1960s Dorothy was friendly with the anti-war crowd. She worked with the Berrigan brothers and with Daniel Ellsberg, Joan Baez, and Abbie Hoffman, king of the Yippies. But she had no time

> **Dorothy lived among the poor, dealing with their tantrums, their self-pity, their dishonesties, their smells, their lunacy and their drunkenness. Life had been much easier for her as a far-left journalist and Greenwich Village swinger**

for the counterculture. The children from affluent middle-class homes who were marching against the war in Vietnam did not always impress her. In the summer of 1967 – the 'summer of love' – she wrote in her diary: 'I felt in view of the blood and guts spilled in Vietnam the soldiers would like to come back and kill these flower-power-loving people…'

Her enemies in the Church thought she was a communist, but she was a devoutly orthodox Catholic, going to Mass daily and to confession once a week, and would have been recognised as a conservative by Samuel Johnson, though not by Margaret Thatcher. After attending a dinner in 1980 to celebrate the 25th anniversary of the right-wing *National Review*, the celebrated historian John Lukacs wrote of her 'respect for what was old and valid': her 'dedication to the plain decencies and duties of human life, rested on the traditions of two millennia of Christianity', and she 'was a radical only in the truthful sense of attempting to get to the roots of the human predicament'.

In March 2000, the Vatican opened the 'cause' for the beatification and canonisation of Dorothy Day, and she was given the title of Servant of God. No doubt Benedict XVI has other things on his mind, but I think he'd find the case for Dorothy compelling. She is the perfect saint for our time. She rejected everything that brings us misery today – wars of liberal intervention, casino capitalism, the promiscuous values of the consumer age. And her abortion? That should increase her chances of becoming St Dorothy of New York.

NOVEMBER 2010

I once met...

Ronnie Kray

A trip to Broadmoor brought *Duncan Campbell* face to face with the snappily dressed killer

A friend was popping down to see an old mate of his in Broadmoor, as one does. They had served time together in prison in the distant past and kept in touch. Did I want to come along?

And so I found myself sitting at a table in the visiting room opposite Ronnie Kray. One of the great things about Broadmoor is that, because it is a hospital rather than a prison, inmates are allowed to wear their own clothes. Ron was very snappily dressed: pastel blue suit, monogrammed silk handkerchief, silver sixpence cufflinks and military bearing. Not for nothing was he nicknamed 'the Colonel'. He could have been on his way to a night out at one of his old haunts, like the Grave Maurice or the Colony Club. This feeling was heightened by the refreshments on hand. Served by a young fellow patient, Ron drank can after can of a non-alcoholic lager called Barbican. (I think Barbican, like Ron, has now gone over to the other side. I certainly don't see it any more in pubs. It used to be advertised in commercials which showed a young man drinking it on a plane in which the pilot has just collapsed; the young man – played by a very young Sean Bean – takes control and all is well, thanks to Barbican. Somehow, I don't think they'd run it now.)

Anyway, it was the Eighties so smoking was still permitted, not to say almost compulsory, even in secure hospitals. Ron smoked non-stop: two puffs, then he stubbed the fag out in a biscuit-tin lid. I didn't smoke at the time but, even if I had, might have been reluctant to: one of the Krays' old tricks, if you had been a naughty boy, was to offer you a cigarette and, once you had got it in your mouth, whack you one in the jaw: because your mouth was half-open, your jaw was loose and thus easier to break. A useful tip.

Not that Ron was in a threatening mood at all. This was the late Eighties and he had already been inside for nearly 20 years for the murder of George Cornell in the Blind Beggar. He was aware that he would probably never be released. Where would he go, if he ever was freed, I asked him. 'Morocco... The boys and the music. I like Arabic music.' This was interesting in itself as I had read that his theme song was *Mack the Knife* and that, on one occasion, when someone had complained that there was not much atmosphere in one of the Krays' clubs, he had launched into his own manic version of *Knees Up, Mother Brown* to liven things up. Now that he was in Broadmoor, he said, he preferred more classical fare – *Madame Butterfly* was a favourite.

Out of the corner of my eye, I noticed another inmate at the next table having a visit from an elderly woman. He was in one of those dreadful wide-lapel, double-breasted velvet suits with flared trousers from the Seventies, already about 15 years out of date. As was his hairstyle and beard. He looked horribly familiar.

Oh, dear. It was Peter Sutcliffe, the Yorkshire Ripper. The visit was short, as was Ron's attention span. Time to go. Firm handshake. 'Don't print I'm mad!' were his parting words.

> **Where would he go if he was ever freed, I asked him. 'Morocco. The boys and the music. I like Arabic music'**

ADVERTISING FEATURE

HOW TREND INVESTING SAVED SALTYDOG MEMBERS FROM THE WORST STOCK MARKET CRASH IN 30 YEARS

On the 12th March 2020, 'Red Thursday', when Bloomberg terminals around the world turned crimson, Saltydog members had nothing to worry about. The Dow Jones Industrial Average suffered its worst one-day points loss ever and markets around the world were in freefall. The spread of the coronavirus and the collapse of the oil price had led to a massive sell-off, wiping trillions of dollars off the value of companies around the world.

In our demonstration portfolios we were sitting pretty as we had already reduced our exposure to the equity markets to zero.

PUTTING THINGS IN CONTEXT

Even after a buoyant 2019, and eleven consecutive years in a bull run, thing's didn't bode well as we moved into 2020. January got off to a bumpy start as tensions mounted between the Americans and the Iranians over an airstrike in Iraq. Fortunately, it didn't escalate into a full-scale military conflict.

Just when it looked like one catastrophe had been averted, another potential global crisis emerged. Health authorities in China reported the country's first death from a new type of coronavirus. By the end of January, the World Health Organization had declared it an international public health emergency. All the unrest weighed heavily on global equity markets and most stock market indices went down in January.

During February they started to recover. The Dow Jones Industrial Average had a record closing high on the 12th February, at 29,551, and the S&P 500 and the Nasdaq followed a week later.

Within a month the Dow had dropped below 20,200 and the FTSE100 had lost a third of its value – falling below 5,000 for the first time since 2011.

MARKET CYCLES

For reasons which I don't claim to understand, markets tend to move in cycles. They don't go up in a straight line, instead they have corrections along the way. It's not that unusual for prices to drop by around 10%, but they usually recover relatively quickly.

It's also easy to forget that much larger market crashes also happen with alarming frequency. There was the bursting of the dotcom bubble in 2000-03, and then in 2008/9 it was the financial crisis. Both times stock market investments could have been cut in half.

By mid-March 2020, the COVID-19 outbreak had resulted in the FTSE100 losing a third of its value in just a few weeks, and it looked like it could head lower.

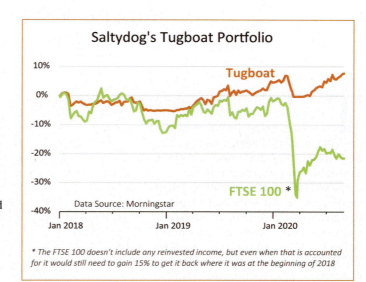

* The FTSE 100 doesn't include any reinvested income, but even when that is accounted for it would still need to gain 15% to get it back where it was at the beginning of 2018

SO HOW DID WE REACT?

At times like this it is difficult for private investors to know what to do. On the whole, the financial industry promotes a buy and hold approach. They maintain that it's too difficult to time the markets and so you shouldn't try. It's 'time in the market, not timing the market' that's important.

At Saltydog Investor we disagree.

Instead of ignoring the ups and downs of the market, we encourage our members to respond to them. As trend investors we buy into uptrends and get out of downtrends. When there are small corrections it does mean that sometimes we sell things, only to buy them back a few weeks later when the price might be higher, but it does help avoid wealth-destroying crashes.

Between the beginning of 2018 and January 2020, there were three times when we saw markets starting to fall quite significantly. On each occasion the value of our portfolios dropped and so we headed for safety. The value of our portfolios then remained relatively steady as markets continued to fall.

In each case the UK's main index recovered fairly quickly and so we stepped back into the markets.

However, at the end of February 2020 we saw one of the quickest downturns ever. Our strategy of going safe early paid off as we saw stock markets crash.

THE RECOVERY

After a few weeks, markets started to recover and we began to reinvest. As the rally strengthened, we increased our holdings and watched the portfolio rise. By the end of August it was up at a new all-time high, while the FTSE100 was still more than 20% lower than it was at the beginning of the year.

www.saltydoginvestor.com

To receive our **free guide** *An introduction to Successful Trend Investing*, or to sign up for our **two-month free trial**, please go to our website **www.saltydoginvestor.com**.

With our easy-to-use trend investing method you could protect your savings from downturns and still achieve excellent returns when conditions are favourable.

saltydog investor

Saltydog Investor Ltd is not authorised or regulated by the Financial Conduct Authority and does not provide financial advice. Any information that you use, or guidance that you follow, is entirely at your own risk. Past performance is no guarantee of future results.

So well devised

Douglas Hurd's impassioned defence of the 1662 Book of Common Prayer

The senior Church Warden noticed that their hostess had drawn the curtains of the dining room even though it was still light outside on this September evening. Obviously she was expecting a long meeting and this surprised him. There was only one item on the agenda and he did not suppose that this would take long. So far as he knew everyone present in the room was in favour of the traditional Prayer Book service although he had not bothered to check personally. He imagined that the new Rector would mumble something about keeping an open mind on liturgical change and then like his predecessor accept that no immediate change was needed.

The senior Church Warden had prepared two or three sentences in which he simply recalled that the parochial Church Council had in the past discussed changing to a more modern version but this had never found favour and the idea had quickly collapsed. He saw no reason for a change of heart now.

> 'We have erred, and strayed from thy ways like lost sheep. We have followed too much the devices and desires of our own hearts'
> **Morning Prayer**

Nevertheless he felt a certain unease as he watched the new Rector bustle into the room and take his place at the head of the table with a muttered apology for lateness caused by an earlier meeting. He carried a sheaf of notes which he arranged carefully in front of him but spoke spontaneously as if following a well-worn path. The senior Church Warden kicked himself silently for having failed to listen when an elderly colleague from another parish had warned him to

> 'Lighten our darkness, we beseech thee, O Lord; and by thy great mercy defend us from all perils and dangers of this night'
> **Evening Prayer**

expect a surprise.

He was certainly surprised by what followed. The Rector spoke with entire confidence in the rightness of his own cause. He said that increasingly the Church of England was moving to the new Prayer Book and in effect the choice before them this evening was between Rite A in modern language or Rite B which was modern in content but in wording had borrowed some of the style of the traditional Prayer Book. He spoke with some scorn about Rite B as if it was a pastiche devised simply to comfort those who were not ready to take the plunge into the modern world.

He invited the senior Church Warden as chairman of the meeting to ask for a decision between these two choices, omitting entirely the possibility that they might instead plump for the 1662 Prayer Book. There followed a short and inconsequent discussion about particular phrases which ended with the Rector taking it upon himself to sum up the discussion and declare an overwhelming majority in favour of moving at once to Rite B. The senior Church Warden had not bothered to find words for a defence of the old Prayer Book and found himself swept along.

'Since there are some of us,' he finally ventured, 'who are attached, maybe for sentimental reasons, to the old wording we could provide some way of meeting their point.'

'Yes indeed,' said the Rector. 'I thought that view might come up. I will be prepared to conduct a service according to the Prayer Book maybe at 8 am on alternate Sundays.' If this service was necessary as a concession for the time being to the opinion revealed by the

> 'A man may not marry his mother'
> **A Table of Kindred and Affinity**

senior Church Warden, he thought that 8 am would be the right hour since this would avoid any clash with the later Sunday Schools.

The senior Church Warden looked round the room to see if he could find someone to protest against this scanty concession. It would soon be dark in the early mornings and he knew he was not alone in enjoying an extra hour in bed. But no one caught his eye and he realised too late that he had been completely outmanoeuvred.

I imagine that this kind of discussion took place in many parishes during the last three or four years and that the outcome was broadly as described. My own parish of Westwell is part of a much bigger benefice and with us the outcome was different.

In Westwell church we only have the Book of Common Prayer except on those occasions when we act as host to the whole benefice, when we adopt from Common Worship the version described

> 'With this ring I thee wed, with my body I thee worship, and with all my worldly goods I thee endow'
> **Solemnisation of Matrimony**

above as Rite B. We have passed through changes of Rector in recent years and are now settled into a pattern of worship which is broadly acceptable. In Westwell and a couple of other parishes we stick to the Prayer Book; the remaining parishes adopt a modern version. There has been a revival of interest in Evening Prayer with the traditional wording. The result is that almost everyone can find a service to his or her taste within eight or nine miles of their home. The present Rector was not at first familiar with the Book of Common Prayer but he mastered it quickly and now uses it with authority and conviction.

This compromise, while it would be rejected by those who feel passionately on either side of the argument, is I think broadly acceptable and owes much to the tenaciousness of the Prayer Book Society which, better late than never, mobilised itself to defend the Prayer Book. The Society sets itself to encourage use of the

> 'We therefore commit his body to the ground; earth to earth, ashes to ashes, dust to dust; in sure and certain hope of the Resurrection to eternal life'
> **The Burial of the Dead**

familiar wording and itself organises Prayer Book services in willing parishes. The climax of the Prayer Book Society's year is the Cranmer Award. Schools compete keenly for this award which requires contestants to learn by heart a Collect or other passages from the Prayer Book and declaim the result in the Charterhouse in London or the pulpit of

> 'From fornication, and all other deadly sin; and from all the deceit of the world, the flesh, and the devil, Good Lord, deliver us'
> **The Litany**

an East London church. Contestants are divided by age into two categories which then take it in turns to declaim.

I find it deeply moving to hear young voices at work on language which has been familiar to me throughout my life. I often find listening to these voices that they refresh my understanding of familiar words, perhaps because they are uttered with that extra force which goes with youth. The Cranmer prizes are made possible by a generous bequest from Lord Charteris, lately Provost of Eton and Private Secretary to Her Majesty the Queen. He could not have found a better way of strengthening the struggle to preserve a form of worship which to many of us lies at the heart of our membership of the Church of England.

So good luck to the Prayer Book Society, and may it flourish.

● *The Prayer Book Society The Studio, Copyhold Farm, Lady Grove, Goring Heath, Reading, RG8 7RT Telephone: 0118 984 2582 Website: www.pbs.org.uk*

The sign of the cross

Jane Gardam's tale of memory and the meaning of objects

It was just before Christmas and over 20 years ago, and everyone waiting to go through Customs off a plane from Bangladesh carried armfuls of parcels. It was in the days when we were allowed plenty of hand-luggage. I remember I was struggling with a gigantic lampshade. An Irish nun came running out of the crowd towards me flapping her hands and looking rather wild. She carried nothing. 'Oh, oh,' she cried. 'Could you tell me where we pick up our serious luggage?' She was on her way home. She had not left her convent in Dacca for 20 years. I knew all this because I had sat next to her on the plane.

I showed her a notice above our heads that said 'Luggage Hall' and had a big black arrow alongside. 'Oh, how stupid I am,' she cried and looked happy. 'Now isn't there always a sign if you look for it?'

She vanished and I never saw her again.

Why do we remember some things and not others? I have quite forgotten the Christmas that followed and I have only a hazy idea of the time in Bangladesh. I remember our grand hotel and the naked children lying in the dust outside. And the rickshaw driver who gave us bananas. Not much more.

Yet I can see, like a portrait, the face of the nun. It was almost mocking. Do we really, always, find 'a sign' if we look for it?' Does hope really spring eternal in the human breast? Well not in mine.

And are we really 'never tried beyond our strength'? Of course we are. What else is mental breakdown? Was the desperate, rather over-zealous nun on the edge of mental breakdown? Had her eyes been a bit too bright? Over the years I thought about this. Why? I'll never know.

My mother, who would be well over 100 years old now, had a godfather, her elderly cousin, who would now be over 150. He had started out as a monk in the religious community on the Island of Iona. There is a photograph of him and he was the ugliest man you can imagine. He was almost as wide as he was long, he was very short, and he had the face of a frog. But above his clerical collar (he had become an Anglican priest) he had a lovely smile that seemed hooked on to either ear, and behind his glasses two loving, dazzling eyes.

He died suddenly at 41 after a lightning-storm of a life. After Iona he had been sent to a parish somewhere up near the Roman Wall where he had been a huge and charismatic success. He had married a beautiful, tall woman and they had seven children. Soon he was appointed a canon of a great cathedral and was, as Trollope would say, ' destined for great office in the Church'. He wrote a dozen (now unreadable) books of sermons.

Years after my mother died, I found among her treasures a letter from him to her at her Confirmation. It read like St Paul. She had revered her godfather, though the rest of us all thought he was a bit of a joke, and we hated the seven, saintly children and their noble mother.

He left to my mother a solid silver Iona cross which she was told had been 'blessed by the monks'. It was about 15 inches high and chased with an ancient Celtic pattern of beasts and saints and flowers and set in a lump of beautiful grey and white marble, the rock of the island itself.

My mother left the cross to my husband, and for 20 years more it stood on his dressing-room shelf alongside his toothbrush and razor, and his own 'serious luggage': the photograph of his first puppy who was as ugly as Cousin Cyril himself. Next to it was a faded photograph of his shipmates in the last war who were all drowned the week after he was transferred to another ship. And there was a photograph of me just before we got married, looking like Peter Rabbit.

My husband died in January. It had been long expected but I was not prepared. I began to behave very briskly. Dry-eyed, in a blank for many weeks and cold as ice, I lived minute by minute, neither looking for nor expecting any 'sign'. I looked only at the computer screen, and the writing-paper when I flung off slick and inadequate replies to all the kind letters.

And at last I addressed the horrible conventions of death – 'the clearing up'. The clothes went, the shoes, the lecture notes, the letters. I grew more ruthless and reached, at the very last, the dressing room. The photograph of the puppy went to our daughter and the doomed mariners to our son. Peter Rabbit finished up with Mr McGregor in the compost.

But where was the Iona Cross? It had gone too. Quite vanished. And nobody could remember having seen it for years. I certainly knew that I hadn't cleaned it for an age. We could none of us even remember what it had looked like. Somebody suggested that it had been stolen when we put the shower in. Someone else said I had imagined the story. It had never existed. Or it had simply left us. We hadn't noticed.

Then one day, six months later, sitting at my desk and staring ahead at nothing as usual, through my own 'serious luggage' on the shelf – the photograph of my old home, the three weird pebbles, the lanky wooden harlequin and the model of the Whitby schooner, I saw a hard shadow behind the schooner's spidery rigging.

Gleaming out at me, alive, with its saints and lions and the frail figure of the suffering Christ, stood the Iona Cross.

It had been there all the time.

A jewel of a show
Sara Wheeler rediscovers the magic of the circus

My slot at the Hay Literary Festival fell over a weekend this year, so I had to take the children. A Green Room heaving with artistes is not designed for under-eights. The nadir came when the smallest Wheeler spilt apple juice on Grayson Perry's shoe, a hand-made, red polka-dot number. 'Why not try the circus instead?' suggested Perry's companion, grappling with a box of Kleenex.

It turns out that the Giffords Circus tour regularly includes a stint in the castle grounds at Hay-on-Wye. Oh the glamour! This year the company presents a Forties-style musical that recaptures the magic of Continental circus in its golden age. Bare-chested Ethiopian jugglers in silk harem pants, high-heeled dancers in sparkling bustiers, highwire monocyclists and the heady whiff of sawdust and sweat. It makes Perry look like John Major in his post-circus years.

In *Yasmine – A Musical*, the troupe of acrobats, mime artists, jugglers and clowns re-enacts the life story of circus horse-trainer Yasmine Smart, granddaughter of impresario Billy. The show, conceived and produced by Nell Gifford, stars Yasmine Smart herself in the title role.

Yasmine is circus royalty. Granny Elleano Stey crossed the Thames on a high wire in 1951. Nell Gifford's script follows Yasmine from childhood in a caravan, the apple of grandpa's eye, to emergence as a big-top protégé, sessions with Parisian couturiers, and all the rest. A nice story-line follows a childhood puppet which discovers a human heart, and a lonely Yasmine who finally finds happiness through a lifelong dance with her beloved horses.

Yasmine trained seven horses for the new show, and in the second act she performs with three Arabs, great gleaming beasts snorting over wide-eyed infants in the ringside seats. Giffords is not really about animals, however – and thank God. I remember the half-starved lions and chimps from the Billy Smart's of my own youth. We used to go and see them after the performances, poking our fingers through the bars of their cages on the Bristol Downs. Instead of listless big cats, at Hay we saw a dazzling band of Giffords musicians whoop through a repertoire of Swing on instruments ranging from saxophone to banjo, double bass and saucepan.

Giffords Circus dancers

By common consent among assembled Wheelers, the best act was the hilarious German recorder wizard Gabor Vosteen. One had no idea the humble recorder could be such a star. A thin, black-clad youth with pointy shoes and a dicky bow, the captivating Vosteen played six at once (check out his demo at www.gaborvosteen.de). I also adored Olivier Taquin, a Belgian mime artist who turns into a wind-up mannequin and falls for a member of the audience.

Giffords celebrates its tenth anniversary this year. In an age of cultural sludge, it is a remarkable anomaly, a testament to the hard work, energy and vision of the entrepreneurial Nell Gifford. As a young woman, she worked for Yasmine Smart in a German circus (an experience recounted in her 1999 book *Josser: The Secret Life of Circus Girl*). 'I was carried away,' says Nell today, 'by the high art-deco style. I realised that circus could be fabulous, popular and rocking. I decided to start my own show in England, and set my heart on creating a miniature village-green circus, a jewel of a show that we could make thrilling, sexy and beautiful.'

Gifford's is a nostalgic delight. But I don't think circuses of the past were ever this good.

I once met...

Bill Cotton

Mel Hannaghan ponders an encounter with the band leader at Charlton Athletic when he was a child

I used to watch Charlton Athletic play when I was a young lad in the days when they were in the old First Division. After the final whistle I would wait for players to leave and try to obtain their autographs. One Saturday afternoon in the late 1950s I noticed a large man wearing a trilby hat which was pulled forward, and an overcoat with an upturned collar, leaving the main stand flanked by two equally large men also wearing trilby hats and overcoats. It was obvious that they were minders, which meant that the person being minded was certain to be of some importance and his signature would, therefore, be a welcome entry in my autograph book.

It was too soon after the game for footballers to be ready to leave, so other children standing near me chatted amongst themselves, not noticing the three giants scurrying along trying to look invisible. I moved away from the other children and, autograph book and pen in hand, approached the three big men. I realised that the middle one was Billy Cotton, the well-known band leader who had made so many people laugh. He peered down at me and pushed his famous head forward almost beyond the collar of his overcoat, giving me an excellent view of his chubby, bespectacled face as he shouted 'P**s awf!'

In those far off days children did as they were told most of the time. I backed off, a little shocked. One of his minders opened the door of a car parked inside the ground, not far from the main stand, and hunched over him as he climbed inside. No doubt he wanted to avoid being surrounded by a crowd of children and perhaps curious adults.

Stung by the unhappy episode, in the evening and subsequent Saturday evenings, when he shouted 'Wakey Wakey!' and his face filled the television screen at the beginning of his band show, I screwed up balls of newspaper and threw them, aiming at his wide open mouth. Our family laughed louder at that than at his antics on the show.

Genius crossword by Antico

1A is the title of a work by a person, born a hundred years ago this month, whose name is the answer to a clue without a definition part. In five clues, cryptic indications are incomplete; the parts they indicate must 1A to create the answers to be entered in the grid. Answers on page 113.

Across
1 See preamble (8,6)
8 Bit perhaps about racket supplying recipient of loan (8)
9 Poor judge led by friend (6)
10 Space station, vital, short of energy (6)
12 Minutes accepted by meeting after drama generally (8)
13 Joke capturing northern character (4)
14 Nordic folk involved in sled race (10)
17 Vessel, far adrift, breaking law at sea (5,5)
19 Money made by company at home (4)
20 Lieutenant with knight's title retreating in feeble band (8)
23 Go by stages into middle of Greece (6)
24 Film's second star (6)
25 Delay going round to catch pests, not very early (8)
27 Spiritual aim in strange test clan ran (14)

Down
1 Assorted coils kept in reserve (9)
2 Released from job stuffing cushion (7)
3 Unrefined conflict coming up (3)
4 Number suppressing rage interact in moving way (7,8)
5 Thanks for each candle (5)
6 Post learner left (7)
7 Rising knowledge about new recruit (5)
11 Cheese with force compressed (5)
15 Joint owned by crank legally (5)
16 Controls, high, set up again (9)
18 Damage after leaders of anarchic bodies decline to vote (7)
19 Odd features of iron vehicle (7)
21 Chief upset about temptation mostly (5)
22 Part of extremely rich poem (5)
26 Grass and river ahead of you (3)

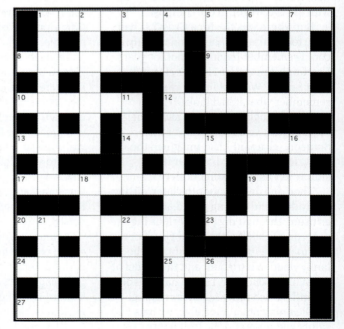

Exuberant fossils

Profitable Wonders
by *James Le Fanu*

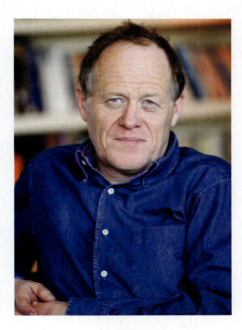

Science's ability to penetrate deep into the unimaginably distant past never ceases to amaze. It is impressive enough that we can trace our human lineage all the way back to our earliest ancestors on the plains of the African savanna three million years ago. But traversing the aeons of preceding time, palaeontologists can now provide a comprehensive account of the whole range of complex life forms that emerged during the Cambrian period 530 million years ago – so long ago that in the interim the glacial movement of the tectonic plates beneath the earth's surface has had time enough to elevate the depths of the oceans to the soaring peaks of the Rocky Mountains.

This notion of the Cambrian 'explosion' of life is scarcely novel. Victorian geologists tapping away at ancient rocks with their hammers were forcibly impressed by the dramatic transition from strata empty and devoid of life to those filled, from apparently nowhere, with the sudden influx of billions upon billions of fossilised remains.

It was not until the first decade of the 20th century that the opportunity arose to examine those fossils in the detail necessary to recognise their unique and striking characteristics. In 1909 Charles Walcott of the Smithsonian Institution in Washington was returning from an expedition in the Rocky Mountains when his (pregnant) wife's horse stumbled on a rock – prompting him to split the offending boulder with his hammer, revealing a profusion of the most perfectly preserved fossils ever encountered. Since then palaeontologists have dug out, scrutinised and categorised 70,000 specimens from the Burgess Shale, as it is known, and from more recently discovered sites in Siberia and China, the highlights of which Simon Conway Morris describes in his book *The Crucible of Creation*.

We start with the 'mud dwellers' in the ocean floor featuring the 'efficient and dangerous' worm-like predator Ottoia whose retractable proboscis sucks its prey towards its mouth, where a formidable array of sharp teeth pointing inwards and downwards extends, astonishingly, into the upper line of the digestive tract – ensuring there can be no escape. Then we encounter the remarkable variety of sponge-like 'mud-stickers' fixed to the ocean floor, such as Dinomischus, which resembles a daisy with a long stalk topped by a goblet-shaped body formed from a palisade of plates, each covered by numerous minuscule hair-like cilia that strain the sea water from food.

Next we meet the extraordinary

bestiary of 'strollers walkers and crawlers', including the famed trilobite with its armoured carapace, and Hallucigenia, so called because of its 'bizarre and dreamlike appearance', propelling itself on seven sets of stilts, echoed by seven tentacles protruding from its back. And finally there are the 'swimmers and floaters' such as the darting lancet-like Pikaia that moves by flicking its body in a series of rapid side-to-side undulations.

The exuberance of these fossils seems to contradict the common perception of the Tree of Life starting off simply enough before diversifying into ever more sophisticated and complex forms. But its true significance is even more profound.

The main virtue of the scientific method is its ability to reveal the hidden and unifying reality behind appearances – no more so perhaps than in recognising that the millions of species with which we share the planet, and the vastly greater number long since extinct, can all be categorised as belonging to just one or other of a limited number of basic 'body plans'. Thus while the diverse forms of insects (butterflies, beetles, flies, ants and so on), crustaceans (crabs, lobsters, shrimps) and arachnids (notably spiders) could scarcely be more distinct, they are all arthropods built on the same plan: segmented bodies consisting of a head, thorax and abdomen, six or more legs, and an external exoskeleton.

This is in marked contrast to, for example, the very different body plan of the legless worms, with their long cylindrical tube-like bodies, or the echinoderms such as the starfish or sea urchin, defined by the radial symmetry of their five or more similar parts. And then there are the chordates with a backbone, spinal cord and complex circulatory and nervous systems, that encompass the millions of species of fish, reptiles, birds and mammals (including ourselves).

The most astonishing of all the extraordinary observations to emerge from categorising these fossilised forms of life that arrive 'from apparently nowhere' during the Cambrian explosion, is that each of these basic 'body plans' is represented. 'Let us seek to fathom those things that are fathomable,' observed the great poet and naturalist Goethe, 'and reserve those things which are unfathomable for reverence in quietude.'

Waiting for the bird

As an aspiring writer *Ursula Holden* made ends meet by working as an agency domestic help. One night she ended up looking after her literary heroine

In the late Sixties I worked for Problem Ltd, a firm that organised the needs of London's householders. It claimed that no problem was too great or too small – it would sort it.

Armed with addresses and telephone numbers, I dealt with and cared for the needs of children of all ages. I cleaned acres of floors, washed clothes, read to the blind, cooked meals for large and small gatherings. I waited at tables, served at weddings and funeral receptions, looked after dogs and pets. My wage was one shilling and sixpence an hour paid by the householder. At the time I was trying to be a writer; flexible hours suited me.

My most rewarding job was looking after a writer whose work was causing a literary stir. I was directed to an address in Gloucester Road. The door at the top of some stone steps was opened by a Mrs

> **When I was told who was in bed I was dumbfounded – I admired her more than any other living writer**

Moerman, who explained why I was needed. Her elderly mother was upstairs. Mrs Moerman and her husband were going to the ballet that afternoon. I was to stay with her mother until after four, when someone else would take over.

As we went up she told me that Sonia Orwell, who owned the house, was in Paris. I was incredulous. I said I had read about Sonia, the wife of George Orwell, the writer who had befriended Jean Rhys.

'It is Jean Rhys who is here now. In bed.'

I was dumbfounded. I admired her more than any other living writer.

'She will be pleased you know her work.' Mrs Moerman, whose name was Maryvonne and whom I had read about,

Jean Rhys: 'literary goddess'

showed me into Jean's room at the top of the house. Her huge blue eyes under white curls looked at me from the pillows. Maryvonne introduced me but Jean just smiled vaguely and didn't speak. I think she saw me as an intruder, however well-meaning.

Maryvonne explained what I needed to do after they had left. 'Oh, and don't give her any alcohol,' she added. 'And if she should ask,' her husband spoke with a marked Dutch inflection, 'just say there isn't any.' Jean's medication precluded alcohol.

I closed the front door after them and went up. I was alone with one whom I regarded as a literary goddess. She had recently attracted notice with her novel *Wide Sargasso Sea*. Her earlier novels were being republished by André Deutsch.

I asked if I could get her anything. Tea perhaps? Or coffee? She shook her head, murmuring how nice it was here in this lovely warm place. I later learnt that she had been living in some discomfort in a remote Devon village.

Framed Picasso drawings on the walls of the stairs down to the basement looked like originals torn from his scrap book. To me, the house felt increasingly like hallowed ground.

The kitchen was bright and modern with lovely food in the fridge. I took the plate of cold sliced turkey, salad and a dainty little pudding upstairs. She looked pleased but barely ate anything.

Maryvonne had left a turkey sandwich for me. After I had tidied the kitchen, I heard pattering feet upstairs. What was Jean doing? I didn't hear the lavatory flush or taps running, but when I got back to her she was neatly in bed, asking in a pleading voice if she could have some whisky. I said I would look for some, returning to say what a pity there was none. Would she like to rest now? Or talk? I would love to hear more about her work. She was uncommunicative. She just said 'Read *Voyage in the Dark*.' When I got a copy I was entranced.

I mentioned my own ambition to write, hoping she might advise me or show interest. She only said 'Don't ever tell.'

Years later, having achieved my ambition, I understood what she meant. By discussing work in progress you risk losing an intensity of purpose. Writers are like hungry goldfish. Flattery feels like the food that keeps us going, but shouldn't be trusted.

Jean said she would like to re-read one of the Agatha Christie novels on the shelf. She never tired of Hercule Poirot which surprised me; detective novels never appealed to me.

Later, after a cup of tea, I asked if she would like her curtains drawn and the light switched on. 'No, don't. Sometimes a bird comes.' It seemed unlikely, the clouds outside were low and grey.

The doorbell rang downstairs, my time was almost up. It was Francis Wyndham, her friend and literary advisor who had done much to promote her acclaim. He ran upstairs and I heard her greeting him with animation. 'I've been thinking about what you said…'

I said goodbye and went down the stone steps to the street again. It was very cold.

I am older now than Jean was when we met, but can still hear the expectancy in her voice, telling me to leave the curtains.

'Sometimes a bird comes.'

Wilfred De'Ath
Me and my doctors

My doctor, Dr Parker, keeps me waiting, on average, 40 minutes per visit. After four such delays, sitting around in his dreary little waiting-room, I pointed out that this came to nearly three hours of my life which I can never have again. So he suggested that I take the first appointment of the day, 9am, in future; but even then he kept me waiting nearly half an hour. When I complained again, he said, 'Well, I have to look at my mail and answer my phone messages, don't I?' Yes, I guess so, but why in my time which he clearly considers is less important than his?

(After one such delay, he asked me: 'Didn't you see that I was attending a road accident just outside?' I looked through the grimy window but could see no sign of an accident – I suppose that's something they teach them to say at medical school when patients complain…)

We reached an impasse at this point, so he suggested that I go to see his assistant, Dr Krishnan: she is a much better time-keeper as well as a good doctor (I'm only suffering from a mild form of diabetes in any case). Dr K is in her early thirties but looks about 17 and cute with it (I admit fantasising about her as an Indian schoolgirl).

Things are going better now – Dr K only keeps me waiting 5 or 10 minutes tops, but I still hate their waiting-room. Why can't Dr P spend a small fraction of his (undoubtedly enormous) salary on doing it up a bit? A new carpet and some decent pictures or fresh flowers wouldn't come amiss.

Truthfully I doubt whether Dr P even knows what I look like since he spends the whole of our appointments staring into his computer screen. This is the main reason I have such contempt for the modern medical profession (Dr K, to be fair, does look me in the face now and again).

As a result of another wait for the dilatory Dr P I missed out on my next appointment which meant I lost a considerable sum of money. When I told him this he asked (in a letter) whether I wished to make an official complaint. No, I replied. I just want you to see me on time for once. 'Ah,' he said, 'you would expect me to delay the next patient if it was you who was the emergency, wouldn't you?' True, but I never seem to be the emergency. At 74, I don't feel ill inside myself; I feel about 24 and am seriously considering taking Dr K out on a date.

Meanwhile, Dr P and I are opening up the war on a fresh front – he writes to say that, in order to save his Primary Care Trust a bit of money, he wants to reduce my medication. Just wait till I see him!

Macbeth: 'They have tied me to a stake: I cannot fly'

Lady Macbeth: '…unsex me here / And fill me from the crown to the toe top-full / Of direst cruelty'

Macbeth: 'To know my deed, 'twere best not know myself'

Gore and grief in Gdansk

When the UK's smallest theatre company, Top Edge Productions, opened a prestigious international Shakespeare festival with its one-man version of *Macbeth*, adapter and director *Simon Rae* wondered how it would be received by the demanding and knowledgeable Polish audience…

I have sunk a glass of Zywiec, been to the *toaleta*, and, lurking at the stage door, thrice ignored the health warning against the dangers of *palenie* (smoking – strangely more frightening in Polish). The readiness is all.

But as the auditorium fills around me, I feel anything but ready. More importantly, I have no idea how ready David Keller is. He is the one who has to carry *Macbeth: Sliced to the Core* single-handedly through the first night of the Gdansk International Shakespeare Festival.

How did the UK's smallest theatre company get to open this hugely prestigious event? It's unnerving, especially after the rehearsal we've just had. We have a very simple set: eight chairs (forming the Scottish court when turned in, the walls of Dunsinane when turned out), two hat stands for costumes, a step-ladder and a throne.

Through nobody's fault, the step-ladder and throne provided are bigger than those we have rehearsed with. When you're trying to grab two daggers while changing costume and character having just murdered the king, a couple of extra steps can throw you. And while the throne is magnificent – a latticed golden birdcage, certainly worth wading through blood for – it blocks sight-lines and requires much last-minute rejigging.

After a fraught three hours, David is drained: not the best condition in which to undertake the toughest assignment of his acting career.

The Poles take their Shakespeare seriously. In they come, clutching their *Shakespeare Daily Bulletin*. It's going to be a full house. Is our vaulting ambition going to fall flat, our tiny company out of its depth amongst the impressive array of German, Finnish, Russian, Swedish and home-grown productions rubbing shoulders with us in the lavish programme? Are we going to succumb to the curse of the Scottish Play?

'But screw your courage to the sticking place, and we'll not fail,' I mutter, thinking of David's credentials – RADA, RSC, and many leading parts over the years, including his extraordinary performance of our other one-man Shakespeare, *Hamlet: Cut to the Bone*.

It was this, tried and tested over many

Lady Macbeth: 'We fail? / But screw your courage to the sticking-place / And we'll not fail'

Macbeth: 'Ring the alarum bell! Blow wind, come wrack, / At least we'll die with harness on our back'

years, that we had originally intended to bring to Poland, but it has an extensive, van-demanding set, and financial concerns determined a late switch to *Macbeth*, which – furniture aside – needs barely a suitcase. I hope we haven't made the wrong decision.

The houselights dim. Total darkness. A pin-drop silence, broken by diabolic playground giggling, rising to a malevolent shriek of glee, and on David skips, skittishly child-like, to scoop the voodoo doll from the throne and hail it 'Thane of Cawdor' and 'King that shall be!'

From the moment he transforms himself into Macbeth, voicing his letter about meeting 'the weird sisters' on the heath, he has them. His rich voice is the perfect vehicle for the weight and complexity of Shakespeare's language. But our production is not simply a parade of great speeches: it tells the story – albeit pared-down – of the play. This means David covering pretty much the full cast – and having to find a way of making each character distinctive. Although there are a few costume prompts – Macbeth wears a trenchcoat, Lady Macbeth is denoted by a black shawl – the challenge is to find an identifiable voice for everyone.

The different Scottish and Irish accents are probably beyond our Polish audience, but I am confident they follow the heated exchanges as Lady Macbeth tears into her husband for his vacillation over the murder of Duncan: 'When you durst do it, then you were a man'. It's a bravura performance and flings the unhappy couple down their helter-skelter descent into gore and grief.

With astonishing energy, authority and versatility, David drives through the rest, chiding the murderers for letting Fleance escape, grovelling in terror before Banquo's ghost, suffering a terrifying possession in his second encounter with the weird sisters, and fighting himself to death when Birnam Wood comes to high Dunsinane and McDuff reveals himself to have been

> Although there are a few costume prompts – Macbeth wears a trenchcoat, Lady Macbeth a black shawl – the challenge is to find an identifiable voice for everyone

'untimely ripp'd' from his mother's womb. And then, with a reprise of his first entrance, and a little-girl wave from the back of the stage, David skips off into the impenetrable darkness once more – returning to loud applause, three curtain-calls, and a bouquet of flowers.

I couldn't understand a word, but the animated conversations around me suggested we had at least engaged our audience. Irena, our wonderfully attentive minder, liked it and said David's acting was 'very Polish'. He was happy with that.

Another day, another theatre, and another step-ladder (though the same throne). We're on the main stage this time and the house seats 300. It's like doing two first nights back to back.

David pulls it off again. After a mad photo-call with 20 pony-tailed cameramen snapping away, and a lively Q&A session, we are whisked off for supper by Jerzy Limon, the festival's Founder and General Director. He enthusiastically shows us the plans for his visionary project, the new Gdansk Shakespeare Theatre, to be built close to the site of the 16th-century copy of the original London Fortune Theatre, linking back to when English actors came regularly to perform Shakespeare in Poland.

I'm proud we have played a small part in that 400-year tradition.

A Kindle convert
Superbyways: your guide to digital life, by *Webster*

Even though I love my computer, I still have heaps of proper books all over the house and am reading several at any one time. It has long been my habit to sneer at electronic books; rather I have banged on about the sanctity of the printed word, the beauty of a well-printed book, and the satisfaction of casting an eye over one's own library and finding a book worth a re-read.

So when Amazon offered to lend me their latest electronic book reader (the 'Kindle'), I accepted with a curled lip and a mocking laugh, and warned them not to expect too much by way of praise.

The chewing noise you can now hear coming from the East Anglian countryside is the sound of me eating my words. While I still stand by all my views on books, I can see that the Kindle, or one of its competitors, can be a good and useful addition to the library of anyone who enjoys reading.

If you don't know what a Kindle is, think of something about the size of a DVD case, but a bit smaller and thinner. Most of one side is screen. It uses your internet connection to download books, and can hold the texts of thousands of books in one go. It's battery-operated, of course, although one charge does seem to last for ages.

First, the good news. The big recent development is the screen; in the past, screens were lit from behind, and reading for any period tired the eyes. Nowadays, light is not involved, and the experience is as easy on the eyes as any book.

In fact, for many of us, it's better, because you can increase the type size and line spacing to suit your own eyes. This, I gather, is proving to be an astonishingly popular feature for readers of the oldie generation; many of our eyes are beginning to show their age.

There are more books available than you can count. In the case of the Kindle the simplest way to load books onto it is via the Amazon website; you simply pick the book you want, buy it, and by magic it pops up on your Kindle. What's more, if it's out of copyright, it's free; one chap I know in his late eighties has re-read all of Trollope this way, at no cost to himself, and in a much more readable typeface than that in his printed versions.

For me, however, the revelation has been subscribing to magazines. Take the *Spectator*, for example. I cancelled my subscription years ago; partly because much of the magazine irritated me, but also because I can get the bits I do want on their website. But I can't read that in bed or at breakfast. A Kindle subscription, however, is much cheaper than the printed version, and it arrives on my Kindle a day earlier than by post. For some reason the Chess and Bridge columns are left out, but otherwise it's all there, with no advertising.

It's no good for a magazine that's heavy on pictures, as the Kindle can only manage small black-and-white images, but if it's words you are after, it's the business.

Webster's webwatch

For my latest tips, and newsletter, go to www.askwebster.co.uk

www.klip.me
Klip.me is run from China and is a button to add to your browser that allows you to send anything you find on a website to your Kindle to read later. It's a bit technical to set up, but is free and works brilliantly.

https://orwelldiaries.wordpress.com
Orwell's domestic and political diary entries, republished each day, 70 years to the day after they were written. Made to look like a daily Blog, a style which makes them feel vital; worth dipping into regularly.

What's more, subscribing to foreign magazines means no higher overseas rates, and no waiting for the post.

There is some bad news. I don't like the on-screen keyboard; it's not a touch screen, so it is slow and laborious to use, but one seldom needs to use it in any event.

Also, you can't lend your books or magazines to anyone else (they are tied to your Kindle) but you can have more than one Kindle using the same Amazon account, so everyone in the house can have the same stuff on theirs, and the words need only be paid for once.

All in all, I'm sold. There may be better machines than the Kindle, but I am now a convert to the principle of reading books, and especially magazines, on one. What's more, I might well give up buying printed magazines altogether, or at least those that offer an electronic edition.

'No, you listen to me – like everyone else on this bus'

WORLD'S WORST DUMPS

MARCH 2012

MediaCityUK

Fine if you are partial to Soviet-style ambience and zero nightlife – but don't get stuck in the lift with a dalek, warns *Norman Deplume*

Surely nothing could be cooler than saying you work at MediaCityUK. It sounds so groovy and sexy that you don't know whether to go there or ask it out on a date. Three hip and happening words all blancmanged into one delicious-sounding place. Impressionable people will be so jealous when you say you work there – right up until the moment they hop off the tram at Salford Quays to see this supposed media utopia for themselves. And then, oh dear!

Salford Quays has succumbed to a bad attack of 'regeneration'. Diagnosed by the local council, there have been large doses of ugly modern office blocks, concrete wastes 'landscaped' with tubs of low-maintenance shrubs, and cant about regenerating redundant old dockyards. During the day, the place is a gloomy dystopia; after dark, you'll find more nightlife down at the local cemetery (the exception is the bar at the Holiday Inn where you can watch desperate travelling salesmen hit on sneering eastern European barmaids, if you have nothing better to do – which you won't).

It's now three months since the BBC moved decisively into MediaCityUK. In the last year, thousands of BBC staff have been torn from their hearths in west London and deported en masse to what has become known throughout the organisation as 'Outer Salberia'.

The sense of exile hits you full force as you trudge across the wind-blasted plazas and into the pitiless sleet coming off the Manchester Ship Canal. After that, you head past slab-faced security personnel and into the revolving doors of one of the grey Lubyanka-like buildings that make up MediaCityUK. Welcome to Auntie's very own gulag.

Among the many irritating features in the Lubyanka are the lifts. You can spend all day going up and down to floors you don't want until you realise that the damn things are only operated by pushing the buttons outside the lift. The lifts themselves have no buttons at all, not even for emergencies.

The BBC has attempted to stamp its own identity on the place by placing daleks in areas where the public may see them. (The Corporation does the same to daleks at its current HQ, that other notorious dump, Television Centre in Wood Lane.) But by far the most sinister aliens are the security guards who zoom around the place on their daft two wheeled 'Segway' machines like demented Terylene-clad wizards in some sort of creepy Harry Potter-meets-Securicor world.

Some shiny-faced BBC staff will tell you how much they love MediaCityUK, but there is something sinister about them and you suspect they would be just as happy in North Korea beating their breasts and crying their eyes out over Kim Jong-il.

Soon Granada TV will join the BBC here. Work has already started on the new *Coronation Street* set which rises remorselessly from a muddy patch opposite 'Quay House', the BBC's grim new HQ. Rumour has it that the Queen will officially open MediaCityUK, but only on condition that she can pop back a week later and declare it officially closed.

As for the daleks, BBC managers beware: it's a fact little appreciated that by nature daleks are gentle timid creatures who love nothing more than crocheting baby booties for their tiny grand-daleks and listening to *Desert Island Discs*. But if they are used in dumps as product placement, or poked at endlessly by small boys or tour parties of Scandinavian youths, they can be driven to paroxysms of hate. Yes, stairs are a problem but they have figured out the lifts and know where you lurk. Exterminate!

Harry Potter meets Securicor: a MediaCity security guard whizzes by

Stats and statins
Dr Stuttaford's Surgery

The limits of formulae

A 60-year-old London artist has read recent reports of the advantages of taking a daily dose of statins. Excited by the prospect of limiting the influence of a worrying family history of cardiovascular disease and diabetes, she approached her doctor. He was less enthusiastic. After reading her blood test results he told her that she only had an 8 per cent chance of a heart attack or stroke in the next 10 years. What should she do?

General practice is as much an art as a science. The art is in balancing a single patient's needs against the dictates of statistical formulae which only determine a standard treatment for an average citizen. Currently NHS treatment is balanced so that maximum benefit is achieved for as many people as possible for the minimum cost. This is usually good quality off-the-shelf practice, but inevitably one size doesn't fit all.

The reader tells me her doctor is kindly and approachable – but NHS appointments are so short it could be she hasn't fully disclosed all the relevant facts. The doctor may not know about the family's history of cardiovascular disease (both parents) and diabetes (two first-degree and a host of second-degree relatives), or the patient's history of pulmonary embolism and Reynaud's disease. Is he aware that she used to smoke, drinks more alcohol than is recommended and takes little exercise? He knows that her total cholesterol and her LDL, the pernicious low density lipoprotein, are raised. I suspect that his opinion is influenced by her higher than average HDL, the 'good' cholesterol.

The reader's doctor has fed her data into the computer which has assured him that she has 'only' an 8 per cent risk of cardiovascular disaster within 10 years. Currently the NHS advises prescribing statins when someone's risk exceeds 20 per cent. It is easily overlooked that NICE guidelines state: 'Healthcare professionals should always be aware that all CVD (cardiovascular disease) risk estimation tools can provide only an approximation of CVD risk.' It adds 'Interpretation of CVD risk scores should always reflect informed clinical judgement.' In other words, a patient's treatment should not be based solely on the results of statistical formulae but should take into account clinical findings and lifestyle following discussion between the GP and patient.

Like all drugs, statins can have side effects. The common side effects – mild insomnia, a slight increase in tiredness, aches and pains in the muscles – do not interfere with everyday life. Rhabdomyolysis, a serious muscular condition, is rare, as is significant liver or renal disease.

My practice was to order kidney and liver function blood tests before prescribing statins. My patients were initially given a low dose, but after six weeks, if tests were satisfactory, the dose was progressively increased until cholesterol control was achieved. These blood tests were repeated after three months, six months and then annually. If a patient developed severe muscle pain specific blood tests could exclude rhabdomyolysis. Unfortunately the cost-conscious NHS does not recommend periodic testing, either to judge the benefit or the undesirable side effects of statins.

The *Lancet* has published an analysis of 27 research projects involving 175,000 people taking statins. Whatever their initial risk of CVD, the incidence of heart attack and strokes was reduced by 21 per cent in those on statins. This has prompted NICE to consider reviewing their recommendations on statins.

If the reader was about to get on the bus to carry her through life, would she travel on one where the management accepts a life-threatening risk to one in every five of the passengers? Wouldn't she prefer to travel on the bus that offered her the promise of reducing her chances of a possibly fatal incident by 21 per cent? Statins are her ticket for the safer and longer journey. The reader's GP has treated her according to the book. He should reassess her case, making certain that he is up to date with her complete history.

Hairy nostrils

A reader is troubled by the long hairs that flourish in his nostrils and ears. However often he plucks them out they are soon replaced by a host of longer, stronger, thicker and darker reinforcements.

This is usually a male problem. It is also a familial characteristic – if our reader looks around the family table next Christmas it is likely that there will be others with hairy nostrils. Hirsutism is excessive hair growth in unwanted places. Nearly all older men have some degree of it. Unfortunately for the reader, recent research, possibly of questionable soundness, showed that women found that an older man's bushy eyebrows were attractive whereas a man's hairy nose or ears were not. Plucking and cutting doesn't encourage the next crop of hairs – research shows that whether cut, plucked or ignored, the hairs become progressively thicker as well as stronger and more stubborn with age. I wouldn't recommend agonising electrolysis or expensive laser therapy. There is nothing for it other than a simple, battery operated nose trimmer.

'First Little Bo Peep loses her sheep. Then all of a sudden, Mary has a little lamb. I say we bring her in for questioning'

COOKERY
ELISABETH LUARD

Soggy summers have their compensations. A fabulous crop of fungi is anticipated for our woodlands and pastures this year, though you'll have to get there ahead of the slugs.

Traditions in mushroom-gathering are regional. In Italy, it's the porcini – the spongy-gilled, brown-capped *Boletus edulis* – which is prized above all others. In France, they pay good prices for the chanterelle, the pretty golden trumpet with fluted underparts sometimes known as the girolle, a name also applied to its close relative, the black-capped yellow-leg. In Catalonia, gatherers go for the saffron milk-cap, *Lactarius deliciosus*, a bright orange mushroom that bruises blue and exudes a milky juice. In Poland and Russia anything goes, while in Switzerland there are more cases of mushroom poisoning than anywhere else on the planet.

Britain favours the field mushroom, *Agaricus campestris*, ancestor of our white-capped, pink-gilled cultivated mushrooms, which may come as a surprise to our Continental neighbours, who treat the family with well-founded suspicion since they can be mistaken for a couple of deadly members of the *Amanita* gang, the death cap and the destroying angel. Go with what you know.

Field mushrooms bordelaise
Cook English mushrooms as they like them in France. If you prefer, you can cook the mushrooms whole and use the breadcrumbs as a topping. Life's never too short to stuff a mushroom. Serves 4 as a starter.
- 1 lb open-cap mushrooms (wild or cultivated)
- 4–5 tablespoons olive oil
- 4 tablespoons chopped parsley
- 2 garlic cloves, finely chopped
- 4 tablespoons fresh breadcrumbs

Wipe over the mushrooms and trim the stalks. Slice thickly.

Heat the oil in a roomy frying pan. Add the mushrooms when it's hot enough to fry but not yet smoking. Salt lightly and cook the mushrooms gently till they yield up their water and begin to brown. Add the garlic and parsley and plenty of pepper, and allow everything to cook together gently for another few minutes. Stir in enough breadcrumbs to absorb all the juices. Turn the heat up for a moment so the crumbs brown a little. That's all. Serve with a crisp salad.

Alison Uttley's mushrooms in cream
The creator of the *Little Grey Rabbit* stories, no doubt encouraged by her publishers to dip into a popular adult market, published *Recipes from an Old Farmhouse* in 1966, an account of an idyllic Derbyshire childhood:

'Mushrooms, magical fruits of the pastures [were] gathered by the servant-boy when he went to the fields to call up the cows. When the mushrooms were brought into the kitchen they were peeled at once and the tips cut from their stalks, and then they were put convex-side down into a saucer or two of cream. Salt and pepper were sprinkled over them and the saucers were placed at once in the hot oven. They were cooked and ready for the early breakfast. They were poured over hot buttered toast and they made a "dish fit for a king".'

Summer pudding
Just in case you've forgotten what summer looks like, help yourself to sunshine on a plate from *Messy Cook*, Michael Raffael's assembled wisdom on kitchen behaviour. Make two with the last of the summer berries and freeze one for later. Serves 4.
- 4 oz blackcurrants
- 6 oz redcurrants
- 8 oz sugar
- 1½ lbs raspberries and strawberries
- 7 slices diet white bread, crusts removed

Simmer blackcurrants with a cup of water for 5 minutes. Add redcurrants and sugar. Stir to dissolve. Bring to the boil, take off the heat, empty into a sieve set over a bowl. Slightly crush remaining fruit with a fork and add to the sieve. Leave until juices stop dripping. Cut up the bread to line a two-pint pudding basin. Taste and adjust the sweetness of the juice. Line the basin with clingfilm. Dip pieces of bread in juice and line the basin's bottom and sides. Fill with the mixed fruit. Cover with the last of the bread. Weight the pudding and leave to stand for at least 24 hours. Turn it out. Boil any leftover juice to a glaze and brush over the pudding.

PEDANTS' REVOLT
This month's irritants

Faint praise
Bradley Wiggins's achievement in the Tour de France is 'impossible to under-estimate', says the *Daily Telegraph*'s leader-writer on 23rd July, so doing precisely that.
ALAN BROAD

An object lesson…
According to an email recently received from Amazon, 'Your Amazon.co.uk order has dispatched.' Dispatched what?
PHILIP BONE

Having a tautological turn?
Heard recently on both BBC and ITN: references to a '180 degree U-turn'. What other sort can there be?
RODNEY BENNETT

Past imperfect
What has happened to the immediate past tense as in 'sunk a 10ft putt' or 'he drunk a cold beer'. Where did sank and drank go?
DONALD MCPHAIL

Misleading…
Misplaced – useful word for politicians who dump constituents' letters in wastebaskets
Mis-selling – useful word for bankers who commit fraud
Misspoke – useful word for Hillary Clinton to use after lying about coming under sniper fire in Bosnia
Miscount – useful word for election cheats
Miscreant – useful word to describe slippery public figures who use the 'mis' prefix

House Husbandry
with *Giles Wood*

In which Mr Wood is no longer a man who went to mow

'A man is known by the company he keeps' runs the proverb, but my late mother-in-law, an Ulsterwoman, had another method of detecting desirability – or its opposite – in a human:

'A man is known by his garden,' she decreed as she stood in mine on one of her rare visits to the mainland 22 years ago.

There was no use trying to explain my gardening philosophy to her, nor even of attempting to endorse it by citing Lord Tennyson, who also revelled in a 'careless-ordered garden, close to the ridge of a noble down', on the Isle of Wight. In her opinion the careless-ordered garden was symptomatic of a careless-ordered mind.

The attraction to mown lawns may be hardwired into the pleasure receptors of our brains. From the Neolithic period onwards, cropped grasses denoted wealth, as they signalled ownership of grazing animals such as sheep or cattle. There may even be Compulsive Mowing Disorder caused by the need to keep busy so as to avoid confronting painful emotional issues.

Too bad my mother-in-law is no longer around to witness my latest experiment, for a great peace has descended upon my acre since I started to obey the injunctions in *The Natural Garden Book*, written by Peter Harper of the Centre for Alternative Technology. In a classic case of Jungian synchronicity, I found my lawnmower had seized up and was no longer functioning on the same morning that I happened upon the section of the book where Harper urges 'Relinquish control' and 'Don't keep mowing the grass'. I stopped mowing and the sky did not fall in.

The silence from our own acre only served to magnify the machine noise coming from the gardens of other villagers. Fortunately, this only takes place outside office hours because the unemployed villagers – who could mow or strim at any time – always prefer to do it when their employed neighbours can hear the racket. My wife, who is an expert on the subject, has characterised this as an instance of 'display working' – jobs only enjoyably performed when there is an audience to witness them being done.

Many people go to great lengths to suppress wild flowers on their billiard-table lawns, lavishing petrol and pesticides on stretches of grass which serve no useful purpose except, perhaps, for those who think along the lines of my mother-in-law, that they suggest the owner has a 'well-ordered mind'.

These 'squaddie haircut' lawns are hopeless for biodiversity and offer no cover to fledgling birds. The irony is that the shorter the grass is cut, the less it grows – but the more moss and weeds come in. The longer you leave it, the more dew the lawn collects, and the stronger and deeper the roots grow. Making peace with the long grass, as I have done, therefore makes a lot of sense and, as we saw at the Olympics, the wildflower meadow is right back in fashion.

I have found that the time freed up from the tyranny of mowing can be used to identify different native grass species.

'Look, Mary,' I said. 'This Yorkshire Fog grass waving in the evening sun with insects hovering like dust motes...'

'Why do you want to attract more insects?' groaned Mary.

According to new research from the University of Western Australia, maize plants may be communicating with each other by making clicking noises with their roots, an idea that John Wyndham had in his masterpiece *The Day of the Triffids*.

I am not suggesting that lawn plants yet have the intelligence to gang up and take revenge on those of us who mow them, but the implications of plants as sentient beings presents a legal minefield. Earth jurisprudence lawyers may soon be wrestling with the concept of whether lawns have the right to express themselves fully by flowering and seeding, and how often. This calls into question the future of the centre court at Wimbledon.

Ahead of the game as usual, I have been pioneering equal rights for lawns in what might be described as a grass roots movement – one that my family would like to kick into the long grass.

GRANNY ANNEXE

Playtime

By *Virginia Ironside*

It was a call from my cousin, Nell, which set me off. She rang to say she'd found my old doll's house in her attic – she'd inherited it when I'd grown out of it. Not only had she found the doll's house, but also a box full of furniture and little people. And yes, the bendy 'father' of the house was there, with wool bound round his wiry limbs, and the dressing-table with the tiny round bit of glass stuck on.

'Next time you come to stay we'll play with it together!' she said, jokingly.

But she'd hit on one of the major problems about being an adult. You can't play with them. I suppose you could, self-consciously, in an earnest therapy group. But every time your teddy hit another person's stuffed dog, a ponderous counsellor would be on hand to tell you that it signified the rage you felt for your father. Not a hell of a lot of fun.

But is there ever quite so much fun to be had as playing with children?

A lot of my granny friends clearly do not go in for playing. They love their grandchildren, but beyond a bit of colouring or making biscuits together, they can't join in the fun. They are quite prepared to go to the park to feed the ducks, and read endless books to them. They will help them collect dried leaves and stick them into a chart and buy them toys galore. But they won't actually play, say, goodies and baddies or hide and seek with them.

I'm afraid to say I enjoy it. And I say 'afraid' because I'm worried I'm a bit weird.

There was nothing I liked more, when my grandchildren were smaller, than pretending the sofa was a boat, and the cushions we'd thrown on the floor were fish. We used a string bag to catch them with and every so often my grandson would dive off onto the carpet to kill a shark, which I would then cook and we'd eat – unless, of course, the shark escaped from the oven, as he so often did, and we had to start all over again.

Once, we built an entire city out of cardboard boxes on the lawn. There was a prison (his) and an art gallery (mine) and a hospital and a post office, and luckily I took a photograph before a huge monster came down from the sky and destroyed it by jumping up and down on it until it was flattened.

When my son was tiny we used to play dinosaurs in the bath. I'd make my hands into a couple of these creatures, my fingers as legs and my middle finger as their waving heads. This pair would walk along the edge of the bath making rude remarks, occasionally pushing each other in to the water and constantly demanding hats and coats from my son, who would obligingly cover them in bubbles. My son talked to them as if they were real, in a completely different voice to the one he used to me.

Until they are about six, children regard their grandparents as huge playmates. And is there anything nicer than hearing: 'You be the bad bear, granny, and I'll be the good bear'? Or 'Watch out, granny! He's coming to eat you up! I'll save you!'?

I once taught in a pre-nursery school and I'll never forget one little boy painting an elaborate picture of a house. Together we built up a picture of its inhabitants and added a car, a kennel, a dog, until a rich story emerged. Every event was painted to cover the last, but you could still see the faint outlines of the old story underneath. At the very end, he got out some black paint and proceeded to cover the entire picture.

'Why are you doing that?' I said. I'd been looking forward to showing off his imaginativeness to his mother when she picked him up.

'It's night-time,' he explained, perfectly rationally, 'And they've all gone to bed.'

Playing is like that. Nothing to show for it except a whole treasure trove of memories and laughter.

Oh dear. Sentimental old me. Can't wait to see the doll's house again, though.

Finding your final resting place

It began with simple walks with the dog; then *Peter Stanford* found himself visiting the graveyards of Europe on a journey in the company of death

My grandmother had very precise ideas about where and how she wanted to be buried, right down to the hymns and the seating plan in the church. She had even saved up – with the Co-op – to pay for it. In her latter years, it became one of her favourite topics of conversation. Perhaps the memory of her banging on about 'my goodbye' was why my parents resisted making any plans at all for their own final resting places, save for when my father, towards the end, wistfully wondered if anyone would turn up at his funeral. They did.

In the storm of grief surrounding the loss of a parent, always so much worse than you've imagined even when you've had months to prepare your defences, there is that frantic rush to make funeral 'arrangements', a grabbing at any solution proffered by men in black, and the painful business of reaching a consensus with siblings without mum or dad to keep us in check. And so my parents have both ended up in a ghastly municipal plot next to a dual carriageway on the way into Liverpool.

Much of our lives is shaped by

reacting against what our own parents did, or had done to them, and so (hopefully well in advance, but you never know) I have already chosen my final resting place. It wasn't really what I'd intended, but with hindsight was the inevitable outcome of spending far too much time of late in graveyards.

It started with my children insisting on a dog. They made all the usual promises about the care they would lavish on it and, even though I knew their pledges were about as reliable as a party political manifesto, I was worn down into submission. And so began my daily ritual of walking the poor neglected creature around our local cemetery. Thankfully she is black, so fits in seamlessly if there is a funeral in progress.

It should be my cue to look death in the eye – a habit most of us have lost in this secular, scientific and sceptical age where we willingly lap up those who sell

Opposite: view towards the sea from Saint Margaret's churchyard, Burnham Norton, Norfolk. Grave details from the same cemetery. Bottom: Peter Stanford. This page: Keats's grave in Rome

us the myth that we are immortal. And I do try to ponder mortality as I pick my way between the gravestones, black bag at the ready for when the dog chooses her spot. But I've long subscribed to the theological school that says that heaven, if it is to be worth anything, has to be ineffable, beyond our imaginations. Mark Twain dismissed pictures of angels on clouds playing harps and happy scenes of eternal family reunion as 'a mean little ten-cent heaven', and that barb echoes in my head.

So I end up reading the inscriptions and cataloguing the architectural A–Z of the memorials – our local burial ground belonging to the wave of grand Victorian cemeteries that are littered with broken columns, mausoleums, obelisks and outsized angels. And from there it is a short step – over fallen masonry – to wonder when and how we ended up treating dead bodies in this extraordinary way.

To find the answer, I have spent 18 months, sometimes in the company of the dog, who appears never to let such surroundings get her down, wandering round cemeteries in Britain and on the Continent which plot the history of burial, and cast light too on how we have regarded death itself down the ages.

From the pagan mausoleum or 'Scavi' that is locked away in the cellars of St Peter's in Rome (they built the original basilica on top of it), via catacombs, medieval ossuaries, Père Lachaise (where burials were taken out of the control of the church and entrusted to municipal authorities) and the war graves of northern France, to contemporary eco-burial grounds, I've journeyed in the company of the dead in all of them.

Undoubtedly the most beguiling was the Non-Catholic Cemetery in Rome, beside the 1,800-year-old Aurelian Walls, part meadow, part formal graveyard under a canopy of trees, all in the shadow of a giant pyramid, and the place where Keats lies beneath a stone that shows a

> **I have spent 18 months, sometimes in the company of the dog, wandering round cemeteries in Britain and on the Continent which plot the history of burial, and cast light too on how we have regarded death itself**

lyre with a broken string but not the identity of its occupant. 'Here lies One Whose Name was writ in Water,' it begins, following the last instructions of a poet 'half in love with easeful Death', who believed himself a failure to be quickly forgotten.

Shelley is here too, and a big part of the pull of the Non-Catholic Cemetery (so-called because in the early 19th century, when Rome was under papal rule, a cardinal finally conceded that a discrete plot was needed for heretics) is that shrine-like aura that surrounds poets' graves, over and above those of other artists.

Robert Graves – whose surname should allow him to expound with authority on the subject – once offered the following explanation: 'An aroma of holiness still clings to the title "poet" as it does to the titles "saint" and "hero", both of which are properly reserved for the dead. It is only when death releases the true poet from the embarrassing condition of being at once immortal and alive in the flesh that people are prepared to honour him; and his spirit as it passes is saluted by a spontaneous display of public emotion.'

But Rome is too far afield, and so I have ended up opting as a final resting place for a graveyard overlooking the sea on the north Norfolk coast. Why? I'm tempted to say because I like the view from Saint Margaret's churchyard at Burnham Norton. I do, of course, but when I'm six feet under and past caring…

Surely, though, our own burial is one of that dwindling number of subjects over which we can be utterly illogical? Research suggests that the average length of time that relatives visit a grave after a death is just 15 years. That feels too short, and so I am hoping that my children might be tempted to come for longer to this place, nestling on a ridge around a 1,000-year-old church, within sight of the beaches where we have spent so many happy family holidays. Graves, in that and so many other senses, are properly about the living.

MUSIC
RICHARD OSBORNE

The relationship between music and the mind has been discussed by writers and thinkers back to the time of Plato. You won't find much about the subject in specialist music literature but occasionally a book comes along that's laden with unexpected insights. *Guardian* editor Alan Rusbridger's *Play It Again: An Amateur Against the Impossible* is just such a book. Ostensibly it's the diary of a 57-year-old amateur pianist's attempt to master Chopin's G minor *Ballade* whilst attempting to edit a newspaper that finds itself cosying up to maverick WikiLeaks mastermind Julian Assange even as it pursues the News International phone hackers. It's all riveting stuff. But as Richard Ingrams pointed out in his review in the April *Oldie*, this is not where the real general interest lies. He cited the book's exploration of the nature of memory (Rusbridger being a self-confessed amnesiac). But that's only one of several music-and-mind strands that crop up during the course of the author's encounters with all manner of interesting folk from neuroscientists to celebrated pianists.

The conversations about memory are fascinating, not least about different kinds of memory, of which 'procedural' memory – memories which cannot immediately be called to consciousness but which are there embedded deep in the mind ready to be summoned in a given context – is the most important to a performing musician.

These days our knowledge of brain function isn't just speculative. A brain scan can reveal to the naked eye how a violinist will have developed an unusually large area of somatosensory material in the right lobe (receptor of the left-hand's complex fingering) whereas a pianist, whose prestidigitation occupies both hands, shows no comparable enlargement.

Music is unique among the arts in the complexity of the challenges it presents to both the performer and the listener.

> Music is unique among the arts in the complexity of the challenges it presents

It's also unique in the variety and power of its inputs into the human brain. Anyone who has read Oliver Sacks's collection of case histories, *The Man Who Mistook his Wife for a Hat,* will recall the brain-damaged musician who'd lost touch with reality but who could still bathe, dress himself and eat provided he did so whilst singing.

I came across a lot of this kind of thing when I was writing my biography of the conductor Karajan, where questions of mind and music cropped up repeatedly.

One of the most quoted passages relates to his shock at listening to tapes of the nine Beethoven symphonies he had recently recorded in Berlin. The tempi seemed unduly slow, until he realised that he was listening in St Moritz, a mountain location where his heartbeat was faster. (I often think that anoraks who pontificate about one conductor's superiority over another take too little heed of their own biorhythms.)

Another involved the English mezzo Josephine Veasey. She had been rehearsing *Das Rheingold* with Karajan in New York when he announced that he was off to LaGuardia airport for a flying lesson. He already had a pilot's licence but he was retraining to fly jets. Jo wondered why. 'Because I don't want to end up like my father,' was his cryptic reply. What Jo didn't know, until I told her 25 years later, was that Karajan's father, a distinguished surgeon, had suffered from Alzheimer's in his final years. Karajan had long been convinced that exposure to activities involving complicated structures – music-making, flying jet aircraft, speaking several languages – helped create and maintain those neural networks on which cerebral function depends.

Karajan was also fascinated by memory – how, for example, pianist Walter Gieseking could learn a piece simply by studying it during a train journey. In Rusbridger's book neuro-psychiatrist Ray Dolan explains that this is an unusual gift but not uncommon, one that involves imagining the physical act whilst studying: a process that helps lodge the material in the procedural memory. Unbeknown to himself, Karajan, an experienced Alpine skier, had used this process to learn to water-ski. After silently studying skiers on Lake Lucerne for a couple of hours, he strapped on the skis and to the amazement of onlookers performed more or less perfectly from the word go.

A new film documentary *Karajan: The Second Life* has just appeared on DVD (Deutsche Grammophon 073 4983). Directed by Eric Schulz, maker of the superb Carlos Kleiber documentary *Traces to Nowhere*, it draws on hours of previously unseen footage of Karajan working in rehearsal and in the recording studio. I've never seen a better documentary about a conductor. I guess even a non-music-lover would find it fascinating.

'Look -a wild bore'

Whiteboard jungle

'Plastification' has marginalised inspiration. We need to reverse that trend, says *Kate Sawyer*

A young lady I know wants to be a teacher – not a career I would necessarily urge anyone to enter right now, but that's another matter. She is currently working as a teacher's assistant while studying for a degree in 'Teaching and Learning', one of those flash in the pan degrees that the government dreams up and then decides isn't really worth much and stops, leaving people stuck halfway through.

Realising that this degree was perhaps not such a good idea as she had first been persuaded, she tried to transfer to a degree in that wonderful old-fashioned subject, English, and was accepted at a reputable university to do so. Lovely – except that Student Finance would not pay for the extra year this would involve and asked her to stump up thousands of pounds. She is from a very humble background; her father ran away when she was six weeks old, her mother is a supermarket assistant, her partner is a trainee builder, her wage as a teacher's assistant is laughable. So there is not a chance in hell she can do that.

Being a determined young woman, she went to the head of English at her school and asked for help. (The head of English is not even an English specialist – make of that what you will.) She wanted to be seconded to the English department, and to know what she could do to give herself a better chance of a job as a teacher when she finishes her degree. 'Go away and come back in September with some plans of what you can do for us' was his only response.

What he did not ask her was: why do you want to teach? What have you seen in this school that interests/ enlightens/ disturbs you? Why English? What do you read? Do you write?

Why not? Because none of that matters any more. The Teaching and Learning degree was set up to make better teachers, but the fact that it is not subject-related says it all. A graduate of this degree will know how to use an interactive whiteboard; how to group children; how to use a whoosh ball (a ball of brightly coloured rubber bands you throw around the room); how to manage a variety of activities such as 'marketplacing' and 'table-topping'. They will learn to have washing lines strung across their classrooms on which to peg symbols of learning, how to use Plasticine models to put across concepts. They will be much better than I am at display boards.

When my children were young my father used to say, 'I love having the children around but I do hate the plastification of the house when they're here.' The plastification of education is a million times worse.

It is absolutely right that teaching should be improved. It is absolutely true that an entirely teacher-led class will turn off a lot of children. Of course children learn more by doing than by watching. But does everything have to be done as a game? We are forgetting the most important element of teaching; whether your subject is English or Physics or even PE, you want your pupils to love it and to learn not just the subject itself, but to learn from the subject.

I am entirely in favour of ensuring that children learn to write grammatically (although I'm more relaxed about spelling), but much more than that I want my pupils to leave me having talked about reading, having enjoyed writing, having come across new ideas and knowledge and delight in words and energy from English, and from my classes.

I have known the young lady in question since she was 14. She used to come to me to borrow books and talk about them, show me her work and ask for help. She has patience, intelligence and a love for her subject and, realising that she is at a disadvantage because of the route she mistakenly took, she is doing everything she can to overcome this.

Can we not, occasionally, halt the plastification of teaching and look, not at the medium of teaching, but at the people we need to be teachers? Can we not remember that it is they who in the end have more influence over the children than the latest educational craze?

We have all heard famous writers or scientists saying, with a wistful look in their eyes, 'It all began with Miss…' Have we ever heard one say 'It all began with pinning a drawing of Macbeth to a washing line just behind the witches?' I don't think so.

Unwrecked England
Luxulyan Valley Viaduct, Cornwall
Candida Lycett Green

From the heights of Helman Tor with its strange granite monoliths you can see the Luxulyan Valley deepening to the south, half hidden in meandering miles of luxuriant woodland. The lane, high-banked with bracken, bramble and patches of bedstraw, leads to Luxulyan village past scrappy farms and an abandoned quarry, hidden now by scrubland and flooded with the deepest, iciest, ink-blue lake I ever saw.

The workmanlike village, edged with new, slate-roofed housing, sits above the valley, its church constructed of massive glistening blocks, its tiny station platform just long enough to accommodate a single-carriage train. Nearby is the Kings Arms railway pub, built in the 1870s for passengers travelling on the 22-mile line from Newquay, through St Columb Road, Roche, Bugle and along the Luxulyan Valley to Par.

We took the lane out of the village towards St Blazey, from where you could see the soft undulations of the windblown woods on the skyline ahead. At the bottom of the valley, granite gateposts gave onto steep little fields and the woods, in the full leaf of high summer, began to feel tropical and jungle-like. The shallow River Par ran beside us, sometimes rushing over boulders, sometimes sliding slowly through golden pools. Beside the river were enormous oaks and beeches, their branches smothered in bright green moss and a proliferation of delicate ferns. Coppiced two or three hundred years before, with their roots so well watered, they had grown out of all proportion. The trees in themselves were enough to amaze us, but then suddenly we saw it – the mighty Treffry Viaduct towering up into the small patch of sky above. We hadn't been expecting it and the shock was tremendous.

In the early 19th century Joseph Austen inherited through his Treffry mother a vast Cornish estate, including Place House, an ancient turreted pile in the middle of Fowey. He took his mother's name and began to develop his considerable mineral assets as well as acquiring other people's. He saw that the Luxulyan Valley was a convenient route between the coast and the high ground where many of the mines lay. After building a new artificial harbour at Par, a canal up the valley to Ponts Mill and two cable railways to his mines, he then bought the dilapidated harbour at Newquay.

Treffry employed the engineer James Meadows Rendel to design a railway linking the two ports so that minerals and granite could be transported easily. In the late 1830s the building of the viaduct began, using some of the immense granite boulders scattered among the trees on the valley floor. Great square blocks were cut and the structure rose above the treetops to nearly a hundred feet, spanning the 670-foot-wide valley. Beneath its railway track, the viaduct carried a channel to bring water to one of Treffry's mines and to power the mammoth waterwheel at the Carmears Incline. It was a wildly ambitious project for the time and it wasn't surprising that the great Cornish entrepreneur had his coat of arms carved on the viaduct's face.

Today, rising among crags, outcrops of ivy-covered boulders and paths zigzagging up steep banks of hart's-tongue ferns, the viaduct, now in the care of the Cornwall Heritage Trust, remains awe-inspiring – even though it has long been redundant (the present railway uses a lower route to cross the valley). Directly beneath the arches our voices echoed eerily, and during the hour we lingered there we saw no one else. Just up the road the Eden Project has a million visitors a year. Give me the peace and wonder of the Luxulyan Valley.

NOVEMBER 2013

MIND THE AGE GAP

Lizzie Enfield

I bump into someone in the street who I last met years ago. 'I think it was 25 years ago, actually,' he says. 'I can look it up in one of my old diaries.'

'You are just like my mother,' I reply.

My mother has drawers full of diaries, dating back years. These are not Samuel Pepys-style, elaborately written tomes which a social historian might one day unearth and use to throw light on daily life in the 20th century. They are just notebooks in which my mother has written who was going to the dentist or coming for lunch.

She often refers to them to try to settle the dates of things no one can quite remember – things that arise around the dinner table, and things that are largely unimportant.

'You remember that time we went to Cornwall and Joe came with us?' someone might say.

'Oh yes, that was 1976. I remember because it was very hot,' another will comment.

But we are a fairly argumentative family and if we spot a flaw in someone's anecdote we tend to point it out.

'No, it wasn't '76. I remember going to Cornwall that year and we met the Hubbles and Joe definitely was not with us then.'

This is all wholly irrelevant to the point of the story. The point of the story may be that the dog fell off a cliff and had to be rescued, or we saw dolphins in the Camel estuary. 'Years ago' would suffice for most people. But not for us. The exact date needs to be fixed in our heads before whoever it is can carry on with the story.

My husband deplores this trait in me.

'When I was in New York,' he may say, about to tell an assembled gathering about something which happened to him in New York.

'Which time?' I will interrupt, stopping him in his tracks. 'The time you went at Easter or the time you were there in October?'

'I don't remember,' he says, anxious to get on with the story.

'Was it after they introduced the smoking ban?' I will ask, trying to help him pinpoint a date he does not find it necessary to pinpoint.

If I was my mother I could refer to a diary.

'It was in 1977,' Mum will say, after rooting through the drawers and discovering that she has written 'to Cornwall with Joe' in an entry in August 1977.

I asked her, the last time I visited, if I could have a look at one of these diaries, just to see what, if anything, it revealed.

I chose 1982, the year I was the age my daughter is now. I thought we might be able to make some sort of comparative study of life then and now. It has not changed a great deal. We went to the dentist, we still do. People came to lunch, they still do. It rained. Say no more. The next-door neighbour was burgled. That happened to us, too.

In the midst of all the regular stuff there are a few entries that can't be explained. A visit to Mr Ede, a name no one can recall, a trip to a place which means nothing to anyone and a rather strange 'Jesus Christ via satellite' on a Wednesday.

I ask what this means and my mother say she has no idea. I wonder if this is code. My mother used to work in Intelligence and 'I have no idea' is code for 'I signed the Official Secrets Act and am not going to tell you.' I wonder who the mysterious Mr Ede really is and who was really on the other end of the satellite link. I know my mother is a good practising Catholic but I don't think even she has a direct hotline.

A few days after meeting the person I had not seen for 25 years, I get an email from him. He'd been through the drawers of his desk and had dug out the diaries. 'The trouble with keeping those diaries,' he says, 'is I thought they would remind me of things, but instead they just remind me that my memory is failing.

'I do remember meeting you but can't find a note of it anywhere and yet we appeared to meet up with the Maxwells on a very regular basis and I have absolutely no idea who they were!'

RANT

The AA wrote to me at the beginning of June and informed me: 'Dear Mr Heath, There's never been a better time to renew your AA Membership – with a special 25 per cent discount.'

You can imagine the adrenalin that pumped through my veins, synaptic transmissions sparking off one another, as I contemplated the joyous news that rather than paying £46.80, I would receive a 25 per cent discount, which would mean that for my 19th year of membership I would be charged just £35.10p.

Having read the renewal letter, which had been sent to me by none other than Andrew Strong, the Chief Executive of the AA's insurance division, I turned it over to confirm how much I would pay. Rather than confirming that I would have to cough up £35.10, it read as follows: 'Total Renewal Cost including 25 per cent discount is £110.29.'

So even after taking into account the 25 per cent discount, the AA intended to increase the cost of my annual membership by 135.66 per cent. Although this is not as bad as payday loan sharks, is this the behaviour that one would expect of an organisation that likes to refer to itself as the '4th Emergency Service'?

A telephone call ensued. I was calm, cool, collected and had my facts to hand. After pressing a few buttons, followed by a ten-minute wait, I got through to a human being.

He mentioned something about inflation. (This was a bit silly given that inflation is around 3 per cent, not 135.66 per cent.) I was then told that he could do something to bring the price down. First it dropped to £65. Then I was told I could have my 'Home Start' removed and this would reduce the cost of my membership to £35.10, leaving me with roadside cover only. In fact for the last nine years I have been paying for Home Start without knowing it, having been led to believe that it was complimentary and had been granted due to my 'loyalty'. All of which is not that far removed from such matters as the PPI scandal…

Stephen Heath

Happy Birthday, Briggsy

Author, illustrator and *Oldie* columnist Raymond Briggs turned 80 in January. *Russell Davies* marks the occasion by looking at his unique contribution to children's literature and the graphic novel

This page: Raymond Briggs, Hyde Park 2008, and below, extract from *Ethel & Ernest: A True Story*. Facing page, clockwise from top: pages from *Fungus the Bogeyman Plop up Book*; illustration from 'Notes from the Sofa', Briggs's *Oldie* column; illustration from *Father Christmas*; and 'The Biggest Hip Bone Ever' from The Roald Dahl Treasury

Raymond 'I'm not a fan of Christmas' Briggs has of course become the national standard-bearer for the festive season. The last *Radio Times* Christmas cover is credited (in minute print) to the Assistant Director of the animation feature *The Snowman and the Snowdog*, but it's Briggs's Father Christmas just the same. *Radio Times* might have thought to remind readers that Mr Briggs would be celebrating his 80th birthday on the 18th of January.

It's unlikely that his Sussex village was disturbed by any noisy celebrations – the Briggs guise as a miserable git was adopted long ago, and officially moving onward into the category of miserable vintage git won't make a lot of difference. His wardrobe, as before, will come largely from the charity shop, where his avowed attendance has been checked by journalists suspecting a Scrooge-like pose adopted for myth-making purposes. But no: Mr Briggs really is a habitué of the shirt and jacket racks.

If his general aim is to present himself as sparse, ungenerous and even emotionally starved, there is a large part of his life which denies it, namely his style of drawing. He belongs to a generation otherwise dominated by spiky, nibby draughtsmanship, the legacy of the great Ronald Searle erupting into the the barbed-wire entanglements of Scarfe and Steadman. But Raymond Briggs's impulse is all towards roundedness: chunky bodies and spherical heads. It's a taste that emerges in semi-academic drawings as well as comic art. The Roald Dahl Treasury, for example, groups Dahl's writings into sections, each one introduced by a 'straight' drawing from Briggs, who trained at the Slade. The most striking of them, attached to a piece called 'The Biggest Hip Bone Ever', lavishes on the exhibit in question a Henry Moore-like devotion to its monumental bulbous smoothness. Briggs, incidentally, once went to one of

Dahl's birthday parties, and found the writer 'fairly curmudgeonly'.

Briggs's own most successful curmudgeon, 40 years ago now, was his Father Christmas, a grumbling anti-stereotype regarded with horror by many parents, especially when the saintly grouch was revealed on the lavatory. But Santa's resemblance to their own wheezing, fallible grandpas was precisely what children loved. Emboldened by the success of this brassed-off benefactor, Briggs progressed to *Fungus the Bogeyman,* an inexhaustible wallower in beastly secretions. This time the principle of roundedness extended even to the depiction of a plump bicycle – a prophetic design, this, since many bikes today are indeed constructed from oddly fattened pipework.

One of Briggs's early aims had been to raise the prevailing standard of writing in children's books, and *Fungus* is a remarkably wordy production, often more caption than drawing. So when *The Snowman* arrived, it offered two reversals of policy: innocent cleanliness in place of the fungoid world, but also wordlessness instead of prolixity. As everyone knows, it's literally an uplifting piece, and yet a great sadness lurks – less to do with the necessary 'mortality' of the Snowman than with the smallness of the suburban world to which the dream must return.

And here, below all the rounded surfaces, is Raymond Briggs's real subject: the little family into which he was born, the son of a milkman and a domestic servant. Its undisguised emergence came in 1999, with *Ethel & Ernest: A True Story,* his parents' own progress shown in pained detail. He draws them standing stolidly side by side, doorstep-snapshot style, and we see how optimistic and stoical they are, but also how hapless, and bound for defeat.

We have met parts of them already, in Jim and Hilda Bloggs, from *Gentleman Jim* and the post-Bomb *When The Wind Blows* (a 'nuclear family' if ever there was one). All they really wanted was each other, and a bit of cosiness, and I suspect the same applies to Mr Briggs. When Puffin Books requested his favourite memory, he described coming home from the Army: 'The warmth and comfort of our little kitchen… Carpets on the floor! Curtains! The women in pretty clothes. A cloth on the table. China cups and saucers. A comfortable bed. Food you could eat and no one shouting at me.' Not too much to expect for your birthday.

Adlestrop: himself at last

P J Kavanagh celebrates Edward Thomas's famous poem *Adlestrop*, inspired by his Midsummer's Day train journey 100 years ago

Edward Thomas: sometimes wrote for 16 hours at a stretch

Adlestrop, written when Edward Thomas suddenly turned to verse at the end of his short life, puzzled his friends. Its language is so spare, stripped down: only one line, 'No whit less still and lonely fair', is in the 'poetic' style of its time. He had certainly 'wrung all the necks of my rhetoric', as he wrote to Robert Frost in 1914.

He was on his way to stay with Frost, the American poet, when his train stopped 'unwontedly', on Midsummer's Day of the same year, under the shadow of approaching war, and he wrote the poem six months later, after the Great War had begun. He was wondering, in his usual indecisive fashion, whether to enlist. Now *Adlestrop*, so peace-filled, has become an anthology favourite: there is even a book of articles called *Adlestrop Revisited*, in which contemporary railway timetables are consulted, questions asked: why did the 'express' train stop? (No answer found.)

He was born in 1878, published his first book of essays while still an undergraduate, married in 1899, his wife pregnant, and to keep himself and his family fed, for the next 15 years found himself in a whirlpool of deadlines, underpaid commissions for 'country' books – he called it 'the Norfolk Jacket school of writing' – and biographies. Sometimes he wrote for 16 hours at a stretch. Friends such as W H Hudson and Walter de la Mare feared for his sanity and he feared for it himself. There were breakdowns, brief flights from his family (three children), as much for his family's sake as for his own. He felt, increasingly, that much of what he wrote (not all) was somehow false, was not the real him; but then, what was that? Because of the poetry that was in his prose he was often asked why he didn't write poems: 'Me? I couldn't write a poem to save my life.' Then, late 1913, in London, he met Robert Frost.

They were of remarkably similar temperament, melancholic, mood-swingers; more or less coevals. It was Thomas's reviews of Frost's poems that established Frost's reputation in England, which helped him to success in America. It was Frost ('Edward Thomas was the only brother I ever had') who did not ask Thomas why he did not write poems, who told him that parts of his prose were poems.

It unblocked the dam. 'I might as well write poetry,' Thomas wrote to Eleanor Farjeon in 1914. 'Has anyone ever begun at 36 in the shade?' Over the next two years he wrote poems, often daily – 140-odd – while groaning over a commissioned biography of the Duke of Marlborough.

Between 7th and 9th January 1915, he wrote four poems, one of them *Adlestrop*. He found the name in the previous year's June notebook, one word ('only the name'). Publishers turned his poems down, and the diffident Thomas was quite undeterred: 'Sorry about the rejection because I feel utterly sure they are me.' At last.

He joined the Royal Artillery; asked why, when that was so dangerous, he answered, 'Because it would give a better pension to my wife.' At Arras in 1917, shortly before he was killed by the close passing of a shell that did not explode but left him dead, the last entry in his notebook, found 'curiously crumpled' in his pocket: 'I never quite understood what was meant by God.' You cannot be more honest, or more your Self, than that.

Adlestrop

Yes. I remember Adlestrop –
The name, because one afternoon
Of heat the express-train drew up there
Unwontedly. It was late June.

The steam hissed. Someone cleared his throat.
No one left and no one came
On the bare platform. What I saw
Was Adlestrop – only the name

And willows, willow-herb, and grass,
And meadowsweet, and haycocks dry,
No whit less still and lonely fair
Than the high cloudlets in the sky.

And for that minute a blackbird sang
Close by, and round him, mistier,
Farther and farther, all the birds
Of Oxfordshire and Gloucestershire.

Jeremy Lewis
LIVING HELL

Gripes and grumbles from *The Oldie*'s resident sage

One of the generational gaps between those of us who grew up in the post-war years and younger folk has to do with central heating and the wearing of woollies. I'm devoted to our daughters, but when they come to see us in the winter months they make a 'Brrrrr' sound, flap their arms around their bodies, ask us how we can bear to live in such a cold house, and – without a by-your-leave – flick up the central heating. It never occurs to them to wear a jersey indoors, let alone to emulate my wife, who often wears mittens while watching telly when it's cold outside. I'm always amazed to see young men striding about frozen streets in lightweight suits and open-necked cotton shirts: my wife thinks that because they spend their days in over-heated houses and over-heated offices, they accumulate a residue of warmth, rather like a camel's hump, which enables them to survive the cold as they hurry from one inferno to another. Heaven forbid that we should go back to the austerities of the early Fifties – I remember only too well the agony of chilblains after playing football at my prep school, and making matters worse by warming my purple hands on the radiator – but with energy supplies about to dwindle or be cut off altogether, jerseys, scarves and mittens might not come amiss.

Nearly 50 years ago I made my first and only foray into practical politics. It lasted a matter of days, and I realised almost at once that this was a world to which I was hopelessly unsuited. I was living in Victoria at the time, and, in a rare flush of idealism, I decided to join the Labour Party. I was given some pamphlets to read, and was told to drum up support for the party in the Churchill estate, a series of concrete blocks running along the river in Pimlico, distributing the pamphlets as I went. I banged on my first door, and was immediately in trouble. An angry-looking man appeared, disputing everything I said and demanding to know the Party line on matters far beyond my understanding. 'Oh dear, I'd never thought of that' and 'I'm so sorry – I haven't a clue' became my stock responses as I moved from door to door, outwitted at every turn.

Cyril Connolly once said that he believed 'in God the Either, God the Or and God the Holy Both' and I know exactly how he felt. I have firm views on books and music and clothes and which wallpaper to choose, but when it comes to politics I dither as much as ever. I am left-wing, I suppose, in that I instinctively side with the workers, but I am right-wing in my dislike of change and a soft spot for ceremony, tradition, obsolete uniforms and judges in wigs. I am right-wing on some matters, Left on others, but much depends on the company I'm keeping. If surrounded by *Guardian*-reading north London folk, I whizz sharply to the Right; confronted by ladies in the Home Counties, I unroll the Red Flag. It's all very confusing.

Tattoos are taking over the world, and very hideous most of them are. The other day on the Tube I found myself standing behind a girl with a very low-cut dress, and what read like the first chapter of a romantic novel tattooed on her back. My reading was interrupted by her bra strap, but as far as I could see the story continued into her nether regions. We all know about the problems faced by demented tattoo-lovers who want to replace 'Fred' with 'Tom' or 'Mary' with 'Jane', but will this poor girl – who may well live to be a hundred if current trends persist – spend the rest of her life with a bad novel printed on her back?

GARDENING
DAVID WHEELER

As a child in the 1950s I looked forward to those Saturday mornings when I had saved enough pocket money for a new toy. A shallow, rectangular Elastoplast tin held eight half-crowns in two layers (I was given one half-crown per week) and when it was near full, the window-shopping would begin. In those largely pre-plastic days my prize was a metal helicopter measuring some 14 inches from nose to tail, and the whirring noise of its friction 'motor' (which also turned the blades) convinced me of a future RAF career.

As it turned out, a misspent youth led me into newspapers, with longish spells on one of the country's most respected if not bestselling Sunday titles and a political weekly.

I still give myself pocket money (if there's anything left over from the state pension – I receive no other) but instead of toys it's plants. Nor do I have to wait for Saturdays, although, with a past spent largely in a nine-to-five regime, I still regard Saturdays as holy play-days. And nothing quickens my pace more assuredly than a proposed trip to a nursery in search of a few desirables from my garden Wants List. Of course, the one pound equivalent of eight half-crowns (however it might translate in present-day dosh) doesn't go far in the garden centre these days. I recently came across some admittedly rare hydrangeas (a new passion) priced between £60 and £80 … each. Needless to say, they'll remain on the Wants List until, and if, some kind benefactor passes this way.

I'm not shy about asking for cuttings, but draw the line (usually) at stealing them or begging them from a nurseryman whose livelihood relies on sales. Instead, I have a more or less binding rule that I only buy hydrangeas from which at least three cuttings can be taken immediately. When rooted, two are sited near the original plant to make a pleasing group of three and one is to sell when the garden is open, thus repaying my initial investment. Fortuitously, hydrangeas are fast growers in this garden and it's not long before I can raise more than the Golden Three, giving me – perhaps – the start of a slush fund that might, just might, go towards one or two of those costly rarities.

Living on England's border with Wales often involves a considerable drive to a renowned nursery, although the botanically fabulously rich Hergest Croft, at Kington, is just six miles away … and sells plants. If, however, my desirables lurk in far-flung places (Loder in West Sussex, for example, Crûg Farm in north Wales, or Sally Gregson's Mill Cottage in Somerset), I try to tie in a visit with something else, another nursery or an overnighter with pals en route or close by.

The choice of vehicle is important when plant-shopping. I have one-and-a-half cars: my own ancient, tidy and nippy but far too small sporty number, and a half-share in a four-wheel-drive workhorse whose interior is beginning to look and smell like a compost heap. The latter is slow but will, if packed sensibly, take 30 or 40 shrubs or small trees. Said sporty has no room for such beasts, but will safely transport numerous smaller treasures such as auriculas, hellebores, ferns and pelargoniums in shoeboxes neatly stowed in the boot.

From foreign nurseries, when travelling by plane, it has to be cuttings or seeds, although I do have ways to ensure a plant's suitcase survival. Sadly, it's too late to embark upon that fabled helicopter career – leaving me to ponder what those pilots do actually ferry around in their smart leather bags.

Lacecap hydrangea in the author's garden

The 104-year-old woman who broke up my marriage
BLOG LIZ HODGKINSON, 2020

When Dadi Janki entered my life in 1980 I had no idea of the upheaval she would cause to my home, my marriage and my entire outlook on life. My husband and I were living a comfortable, middle-class life in Richmond, Surrey, with our two young sons Tom and Will, and then, wham!, a tiny, elderly Indian lady managed to overturn everything we had previously held dear.

Dadi Janki – the term means 'elder sister' – has just died, aged 104. She was the head of the Brahma Kumaris, a worldwide spiritual movement led by women. The organisation now has thriving centres in most countries in the world, and in India runs many hospitals, schools and charitable programmes. Yet when Dadi arrived in London in 1974, the BKs had no presence in the West: she had nowhere to live, no money, spoke no English, was in poor health and had no followers at all.

But by the time she died, she had acquired an English stately home, many imposing residential retreats, thousands of followers and, crucially, had claimed my former husband for herself.

How did she do it? Dadi had a seemingly simple message: to impart the true word of God – she had a total, utter conviction that God was guiding her in everything she did.

Once Neville had met Dadi and fallen under her spell, he began to invite her followers and students to our house to hear a talk and practise meditation; thanks to these weekly classes, everything began to change. Neville gave up his previous life and went to live in a BK retreat centre.

Our marriage, of course, could not survive and in 1988 we went our separate ways; but we have remained friends, thanks to Dadi.

I'm with the uke band

Up and down the country people in droves are taking up the ukulele. *Trevor Grove* is one of those enchanted with four strings

Last summer I bought a ukulele. I didn't know I was part of a musical revolution, but apparently so. All over the world people are overcoming any sense of ridicule that attaches to the tiny instrument and strumming away. Celebrities such as Johnny Depp, Gary Oldman and Pierce Brosnan have come out. Ukulele bands, clubs and societies are popping up all over the place, from Manchester to Munich. In Tokyo there's an outfit called Ukulele Afternoon. They meet in Yoyogi Park, wearing eccentric clothing, to play un-ukulele-ish numbers like 'Twist and Shout'.

I've learned all this from Get Plucky With the Ukulele by Will Grove-White. It is not just a jollier than usual teach-yourself manual, which was what first drew me to it, but also an encycolpaedia-cum-history of 'all things uke', as the subtitle says. For example, did you know that the immediate ancestor of the ukulele was invented in Madeira and was a called a machete (pronounced not as in the jungle-clearing implement but 'ma-shet')? In 1858 Lewis Carroll took a photograph of Alice (in Wonderland) Liddell holding a machete which her father had brought back from a Madeiran holiday. When Portuguese emigrants sailed to Hawaii in the late 19th century, they took their machetes along. The locals went wild for the new music. They re-christened the instrument ukulele, which means jumping flea.

Will Grove-White was uke-struck at a tender age, when his mother took the lad along to the Empress of Russia pub in Islington in 1987. There, in an upstairs room, they heard a perfomance by the recently founded Ukulele Orchestra of Great Britain. This magnificent ensemble of eight singer-strummer-pluckers has since become a national musical treasure, playing gigs in China and the Arctic Circle, Carnegie Hall and the Sydney Opera House, while building up a doting audience at home. The adult Will is one of its star performers.

The UOGB is the main reason for the worldwide ukulele explosion. Lots of Oldie readers will have been to their concerts. They are funny and funky as well as musically ambitious. The repertoire ranges from George Formby (pictured) and Tiny Tim to Tchaikovsky and Isaac Hayes. Copycat ukulele orchestras are springing up daily.

In primary schools, the uke is replacing the descant recorder as the instrument of choice in music classes. Hooray. I first learned to strum a ukulele back in the 1950s when I was six years old. I had to sing a song called 'Rose, Rose I Love You' at a Christmas concert. I was taught to tune the four strings – G, C, E and A – to a mnemonic: 'My Dog Likes Fleas'. This stuck in my head long after I had given up the recorder and sticks there still, despite the ukuleleless decades that have intervened.

The great thing about the ukulele, besides being cheap, cheerful and ultra-portable, is that since you strum not blow, you can sing along. This helps disguise any lack of skill in the fingers and frets department. Barely had I glanced at this book than I had mastered not just 'Row, Row, Row Your Boat' but even quite a difficult blues number, 'Baby Please Don't Go', using just one chord and just one finger. On what other instrument could a novice proceed so far so fast?

Yet from such low beginnings great heights have been reached. Tessie O'Shea with her banjolele (the banjoid version, as favoured by Geo Formby) was a huge hit in her day. Israel Kamakawiwo'ole was even huger in ours. The fifty-stone Hawaiian enchanted millions of YouTube devotees with his sweet-voiced rendering of 'Somewhere Over the Rainbow', though it wasn't easy to spot his minuscule uke among the folds of flesh. George Harrison was a ukulele man. Joni Mitchell, Brian May and even Jimi Hendrix struck their first chords on four strings instead of six. Neil Armstrong played his ukulele as soon as he got back from the moon. Billionaire Warren Buffett played his on state TV in China.

> **Barely had I glanced at this book than I had mastered not just 'Row, Row, Row Your Boat' but even quite a difficult blues number, 'Baby Please Don't Go', using just one chord and just one finge**

What an endearing little instrument it is: capable of wonders in the hands of virtuosi, but never concealing its comical qualities – a kind of crafty double entendre. Remember Marilyn Monroe in Some Like It Hot, one minute belting out 'Runnin' Wild' with her white ukulele in her hand, then telling Jack Lemmon (as Daphne): 'If it wasn't for you they'd have kicked me off the train. I'd be out in the middle of nowhere, sitting on my ukulele.'

Thanks for reminding me of that, Will. Now I must get back to learning the G7 chord and 'Oh My Darling, Clementine'. With the door shut, though. I recall that Jeeves memorably gave in his notice when Bertie wouldn't stop practising 'I Want An Automobile With A Horn That Goes Toot-Toot' on his banjolele.

BIRD OF THE MONTH

The lapwing

BY JOHN McEWEN * ILLUSTRATED BY CARRY AKROYD

No bird captures the zest of spring so flamboyantly as the lapwing (Vanellus – little fan – vanellus), when the males sculpt the air on humming wings with an ecstatic, tumbling display over the nesting grounds, whether new-sown fields or upland pasture and moorland, uttering that thin, wheezy call by day and night, perhaps best mimicked by its east Scottish name, 'peasiwheep'. 'Lapwing' describes its normal flight, as it flops along on those fan-shaped wings, their black and white contrasts lending a flicker to a travelling flock. Yet one derivation is from an Anglo-Saxon word that does not describe the flight, but rather the long, black, curving crest, the bird's most singular feature. In flight, lapwings look black and white, but close up the secondary name of green plover does scant justice to the olive mantle and wing coverts, shot through with emerald, iridescent bronze, purple and pink, and apricot tail coverts.

The collective noun for lapwings is a 'deceit'. The 'false lapwynge, ful of treachery' wrote Chaucer in 'The Parlement of Foules'. And Shakespeare's womanising Lucio boasts in Measure for Measure:

> ...'tis my familiar sin
> With maids to seem the Lapwing,
> and to jest,
> Tongue far from heart...

The reputation unfairly comes from the bird's defence of its young, when it lures away a predator by hirpling off, dragging a wing to appear wounded and therefore easy prey. The chicks precociously run at birth and Ben Jonson (The Staple of News) described rash people as 'lapwings with a shell upon their heads'.

Lapwings were prized for their meat and eggs. Hunting for the eggs was customary until forty years ago; the clutch was left if it pointed inwards, meaning incubation. More refined in every sense than black-headed gulls' eggs and similarly camouflaged to resemble stones, they can still be collected on licence until 15th April – but not for sale. As for the meat, it is a protected bird. This reflects a grave fall in numbers – a two-thirds decline since 1970. Lapwings remain our most familiar and widespread breeding wader but have ceased to nest in most of south-west England, west Wales and the west of mainland Scotland, while in Ireland the number has halved. Nesting pairs remain most numerous in north-west England, the Outer Hebrides, Orkney and Shetland. Modern farming, notably autumn sowing, appears the principal cause of this headlong decline.

Winter sees lapwings congregate in flocks, the numbers bolstered, subject to the weather, by influxes from the Continent. Sometimes winter flocks are peppered with golden plover, which, grounded, look contrastingly brown and thrush-like. In recent years lapwings have shown a preference for wintering on or near Britain's eastern estuaries, and rooftop flocks can now be seen in towns.

Lapwings are haunting. From faraway Samoa R L Stevenson remembered them, in his poem 'To S R Crockett':

> Be it granted me to behold you again
>   in dying,
> Hills of home! And to hear again the call;
> Hear about the graves of the martyrs
>   the peewees crying,
> And hear no more at all.

Queen of the flies

Fishing is the perfect antidote to stress, says Jean Williams, consummate fly-maker and angler's best friend. By *Patrick Bishop*

An old-fashioned bell tinkles as you push open the door of Sweet's tackle shop. Once you cross the threshold, the modern world vanishes. Inside the dim interior it is forever 1978. Odd bits of fishing equipment and faded photographs line the walls haphazardly. A monster 35½lb salmon looks down from a dusty glass case. And there behind the counter is the smiling face of Jean Williams who has presided over the place for nearly 40 years.

'Fishermen hate change,' she says. 'They love coming back and finding everything exactly as they remembered it – not all white and clinical.' Amid the clutter on the counter is an envelope addressed in an elaborate copperplate hand to 'the amazing Jean of Sweet's – the one and only fount of fishing knowledge'.

It's a bit of an exaggeration perhaps, but indicative of the devotion that she inspires. The phone rings frequently as anglers call from far and wide, inquiring about river conditions and what the fish are up to. There is a constant stream of visitors, from elderly male dog walkers dropping in for a chat to young lads reporting their successes.

Sweet's is in the little Monmouthshire town of Usk where Jean has happily spent all her life. As a teenager she wanted to be 'a hairdresser or a telephonist'. Instead, a chance encounter between her aunt and Mrs Sweet in a tobacconist's led to a job as an assistant in the shop.

The owner, Lionel Sweet, was a famous fisherman who was able to cast five rods at once – two in each hand and one strapped to his foot. She learned how to tie flies and then Mr Sweet took her fishing. She caught first time – a trout on a Claret and Mallard. When Mr Sweet died in 1978 she and her husband, Mike, bought the business. Mike is a golfer and rugby man, and the shop is very much her domain. In the years of her reign it has become a mecca for anglers coming to fish the Usk river; they go there to buy her beautiful flies and listen to her talking wisely in her soft Marches accent, about trout, salmon and life in general.

> **Lionel Sweet was a famous fisherman who was able to cast five rods at once – two in each hand and one strapped to his foot**

'Fishing is a wonderful leveller,' she says. 'You meet people from all walks of life and all temperaments.' Her customers have included rugby star Sir Gareth Edwards, comedian Billy Connolly, actor Timothy Dalton and, rather surprisingly, the American crooner Gene Pitney, who was playing a local country club. She also believes it is much better for you than pills or psychotherapy. 'People get so tensed up these days,' she says. 'They might be very important or do very stressful jobs, but when they get on the river they forget all about time. Nothing else matters except the water and the fish, and all your cares and worries drop away. When they get home, they are a better person. Some wives would do well to realise that…'

Fishing is still a predominantly male activity, and often an obsessive one. Women tend to react to their menfolk's enthusiasm for it in two sharply different ways. Category A resents their frequent and often open-ended absences. Category B shares the view expressed in a poster displayed in the shop: 'Give a man a fish and he will eat for a day. Teach a man to fish and you will get rid of him for the whole weekend.'

For Jean, it is a sublime activity. Most

A place of peace and reflection: fly-fishing on the River Usk in the Brecon Beacons

of her fishing has been done on the Usk, a broad and powerful river for much of its length that is well populated with feisty wild brown trout, though salmon numbers are much reduced. 'The river is a magical place,' she says. 'There is nothing to match it for beauty early in the morning when the sun is coming up and there is a wreath of mist still lying on the water, or at sunset when there is a hatch on and the fish are rising.'

To catch them, of course, you need flies. Jean's are exquisite creations, conjured out of feathers, fur and fluff. In her time she has invented a few patterns of her own. The Rupert Bear is a lemon and red confection (inspired by the little chap's jersey and trousers remembered from Christmas annuals long ago) which mimics a yellow mayfly, and the dark-hued Desperate Dan is a salmon fly for the Usk.

There are thousands and thousands of fly patterns. Jean believes that most of them are redundant. Fishermen are as gullible as golfers when it comes to kit. They convince themselves that lack of success can be explained by the fact that they have not got the latest miracle rod, reel, line or fly, a delusion that keeps the tackle industry alive. My fly boxes contain hundreds of patterns which have never caught a fish, and I find myself using the same half a dozen old faithfuls all the time.

In Jean's opinion, you need only five to cover almost all eventualities: 'You can get by with a Greenwell's Glory, a Pheasant Tail, a Hare's Ear, an Olive and maybe a Sedge.' I bought a selection of her creations before setting out to fish the evening rise on the Usk town water just up the road from the shop. A cloud of sedges flickered over a promising-looking glide but were ignored by the trout which stayed down. I tied on a pheasant tail nymph and eventually hooked a reasonable sized brownie, but after a few seconds it had twisted free.

The following day was spent on the Wye after salmon. I had a brief, ecstatic moment when a six- or seven-pounder that had been thrashing about at the tail of a pool tugged at one of Jean's Desperate Dans. But that was that. I couldn't go home without catching, and in the early evening was back on the Usk. I had to return to London that night (my wife is Category A) and by seven was getting desperate. Some fish started to rise and I reached for a Williams-tied sedge. I landed it delicately a foot above a sturdy-looking brownie who surged forward and took it. I felt the electric jolt as man and fish connect, the thrill that never fades. It was no more than half a pound but a beautiful creature. I returned it gently to the river and headed for home, thanking God and Jean Williams.

Jean Williams in Sweet's tackle shop

Tintin as saviour

Hergé's hero, being celebrated at an exhibition in London, was a refuge and salvation for *Craig Brown*'s generation of schoolboys

We were about a fortnight into our second term at prep school when a new boy with the unusual name of Carmichael Theobald arrived in our dormitory. I forget now why he was allowed to arrive so late. It must have been a severe illness or some sort of family bereavement: no other excuses would have been accepted.

All of us in that dormitory would remember the arrival of Theobald because every night he would have the same nightmare and wake us all up with the same anguished scream: 'TINTIN! HELP ME! TINTIN! TINTIN! SAVE ME!'

Heaven knows who or what had been threatening him, but, quite clearly, his plea never fell on deaf ears: within a couple of minutes, Tintin would have come to his rescue, and Carmichael Theobald would be fast sleep, leaving the rest of us wide awake, speech bubbles with '!!!' and '???' tethered to our eight-year-old heads.

Eight-year-olds are no strangers to the joy of teasing. But none of us teased Theobald about his midnight screams, presumably because we recognised the sense in his choice of Tintin as his saviour. Though ours was a Catholic prep school, few of us would have wanted to ask Jesus to save us from, say, falling off a rope into a waterfall while being chased by baddies. He would have made too much of a song-and-dance about it, and would have ended up by delivering a knowing little homily. He might even have embarrassed us by inviting his disciples along to watch. But, more than anyone else in the world, you could always rely on Tintin to get you out of a scrape with the minimum of fuss. Tintin was amiable, intrepid, good-humoured, quick-thinking and, perhaps above all, straightforward.

The Crab with the Golden Claws, Red Rackham's Treasure, Prisoners of the Moon, The Seven Crystal Balls: all of us had read, and re-read, and re-re-read all the Tintin books. Our real-life parents might drop us off at school at the beginning of each term and not see us again until half-term, but Tintin and Captain Haddock would be there for us every day, our refuge and salvation from irate Latin masters and freezing football pitches and muscle-bound matrons. Without getting too Freudian about it, I suppose that Tintin was our mother, loving and clean-shaven, while Captain Haddock was our father, crankier, more crotchety ('Billions of Blue Blistering Barnacles!') and a great deal more hirsute.

Tintin's creator, Hergé, came to feel that his need to escape the drab straitjacket of Catholic Belgium was what had originally driven him to create the world of Tintin. Half-man, half-boy, a reporter untroubled by the burden of reporting, Tintin travels the world – Peru, the Congo, Scotland, America, even the Moon – and is always guaranteed the most exciting and colourful of adventures.

And what colours! They dance off the page: the bright blue of Tintin's jersey, the contrasting greens of the jungle, the rich yellows and reds of the native robes. Of course, as children, we read Tintin for the adventures, desperate to find out what happens next, but the richness of the colours and the beautiful clarity of the drawings must have contributed to their subliminal appeal.

Hergé was painstaking in his art, but, like all the best artists, took every effort to make it seem effortless. By the time he came to create his 18th Tintin adventure, *The Calculus Affair*, in 1954, he was insistent that every object and setting be drawn from life. This meant that he went with his camera and sketchbook to Switzerland to record Cointrin Airport, Cornavin Hotel, Cornavin Station, and to Nyon for Professor Topolino's house. For one page, in which the baddies force Tintin's taxi into Lake Geneva, Hergé scoured the lakeside road just to find the one corner at Trevon where the incident could occur.

Over the years, Hergé became, to some extent, a victim of his own obsession. After hundreds of letters from Tintin fans were posted to Professor Calculus in Room 122 on the fourth floor of the Cornavin Hotel, the management sent Hergé a huffy letter pointing out that such a room number did not exist. But in the end, art triumphed over reality, and, when the letters kept coming, the management were obliged to introduce a Room 122 where none had been before.

Needless to say, there are adults for whom the adventure and delight of the Tintin books are never quite enough: behind every waterfall and in every crevasse, they search for a symbol of something deeper. One French intellectual, Jean-Marie Apostolidès, has written a number of books – *L'Archipel Tintin, Tintin et le Mythe du Surenfant, Dans la Peau de Tintin* – in which he attempts to psychoanalyse the key characters. For him, *The Calculus Affair* represents both Calculus' 'triumph and his defeat', and the scene at the end in which the Professor burns his plans for an ultrasonic weapon represents 'a symbolic castration'. Another French intellectual, Pierre-Yves Bourdil, published an essay called 'Tintin: A Myth in This Century', in which he said of the Tintin oeuvre that 'We use it, in a sense, like the Bible' because it 'reveals to us the essential'. Tintin himself is, he says, 'a hero to whom the gods have given a destiny' and Hergé, 'through the delicious music of his work, makes us participate in our century'. And so on and so forth: like a latter-day Thompson and Thomson, Apostolidès and Bourdil arrive on the scene as smart, self-important authority figures but, more often than not, end up flat on their faces, their bowler hats hopelessly askew.

On the other hand, there is something deep-seated, even primal, about our need for Tintin. Hergé was at least partly aware of this. For a year in the late 1950s, in the process of leaving his wife for his girlfriend, he himself experienced recurrent nightmares of a world covered in snow. In the most frightening of these dreams, he found himself in a white tower, his surroundings covered in dead leaves. 'At a particular moment, in an immaculately white alcove, a white

skeleton appeared that tried to catch me. And then instantly everything around me became white.'

Hergé travelled to Zurich to visit a psychoanalyst, Franz Riklin, a pupil of Jung, who concluded that the white symbolised his obsessive quest for purity, and advised him that if he didn't abandon his obsessive work on Tintin it would eventually destroy him. Hergé accepted the analysis, but refused to accept the solution, believing, like his plucky hero, that problems are best confronted head-on. 'What would Tintin do?' remains a pretty good question to ask oneself, particularly now that so many former childhood heroes – Rolf Harris, Jimmy Savile, JFK, etc – have taken such a tumble.

So instead of retreating into retirement, in 1959 Hergé embarked on what he came to regard as his greatest work, *Tintin in Tibet*, the pages of which are filled with snow. It is, says Hergé's sharpest biographer, Harry Thompson, 'a book of overwhelming whiteness and purity'. Once Hergé had completed his masterpiece, he divorced his wife and married his lover, never again to be visited by one of his snow-white nightmares. Tintin had saved his creator, just as he was to save young Carmichael Theobald, night after night.

God

SISTER TERESA

Recently a facilitator paid a visit to the community, with a view to helping us talk to one another properly, something which is known nowadays as communication skills. In practice, for most of us and, I would suspect for the majority of people outside the cloister also, this means listening as opposed to speaking – we can all be too eloquent by half, especially when annoyed.

Initially I was surprised that the facilitator took mercy as her theme but as she went on to explain that communicating requires compassion at all times, her choice made sense. We all know that we should be charitable in speech but we find endless snags in putting this into practice. St Paul waxes eloquent on the subject in his letter to the Ephesians 4:29–30 'Let no evil talk come out of your mouths, but only such as is good for edifying, as fits the occasion.' Then comes a surprise: 'Do not grieve the Holy Spirit of God.' There has been endless theological debate as to whether or not God can experience pain, but St Paul has no such qualms and states categorically that it is possible for us to make God sad.

We did a number of group exercises, the most interesting of which consisted of a list of 16 quotations from writers as diverse as St Luke, St Catherine of Siena, St Thomas Aquinas, T S Eliot and Carl Jung. With the exception of St Luke and Eliot they were all authors of whom I knew very little, and to whom I have never been drawn. We were asked to choose one quotation and to give, in a sentence of less than 30 words, the reasons for our choice.

The excerpt from the *Benedictus* leaped from the page: 'Through the tender mercy of our God whereby the dayspring from on high hath visited us, to give light to them that sit in darkness and in the shadow of death, to guide our feet into the way of peace' (Luke 1: 78–9).

When compared and contrasted with Jung's 'The greatest and most important problems in life are fundamentally unsolvable. They can never be solved but only outgrown', or 'What is a normal goal for a young person, becomes a neurotic hindrance in old age', it seemed to me that there was no contest. Luke is poetic, full of hope, points to something far beyond ourselves to which we are fully entitled and shouts out for all to hear 'He won': a far cry from Jung's accurate yet, dare one say it, pedestrian musings.

No one could possibly want to go back to the bad old days of religious triumphalism with its exclusive assertions and its aggression, but there is no harm in winning and in being thrilled to do so. I was born after the Second World War but am always left with a lump in my throat watching films of London on VE Day. The same lump is clearly to be found in ardent supporters of football teams, those allegedly safe substitutes for actual war, with the excitement left in and the slaughter (one hopes) left out, though sitting in a magistrates' court in the Home Counties after the home team has lost leaves one with the impression of the aftermath of a very bloody battle.

The victory of which Luke writes is the Resurrection, the ultimate success story and the most difficult to explain. Sunrises are pointers, and the dawn in the *Benedictus* prophesies the daybreak of Easter Sunday some three decades later.

LEARN LATIN
Lesson for today

We are still living on Roman time. The origins of the names of our months go back, according to legend, to a calendar set up by Romulus, the mythical founder of Rome, in the 8th century BC.

Romulus' calendar had ten months: Martius, Aprilis, Maius, Iunius, Quintilis, Sextilis, September, October, November and December.

You'll see that those last six months literally mean 'the fifth', 'the sixth' etc. And that we still use September, October, November and December, even though they are no longer the seventh, eighth, ninth and tenth month of the year.

We owe the 12 months of the year – again according to legend – to Numa Pompilius, the second king of Rome after Romulus. He added in Ianuarius and Februarius, our January and February. They were originally added to the end of the year, so September, October, November and December still rang true as the seventh, eighth, ninth and tenth months.

It was Julius Caesar who messed it all up, by making January the start of the year – as it is now. And so, suddenly, December – once the tenth month – became the twelfth month. In 44 BC, Mark Antony declared that Caesar should bequeath his name to Quintilis, which had been the fifth month, but was now the seventh month, Iulius, or July. And in 8 BC, it was ruled that what had been the sixth month, Sextilis, and was now the eighth month, should be named after Julius Caesar's successor, Augustus. August was born.

Julius Caesar was also responsible for the most famous date in Roman history, the Ides of March – March 15th – in 44 BC, the day he was assassinated. All Roman months had three principal days, around which the calendar revolved: the Kalends, or the first day of the month; the Ides, the 13th day of the month, except in March, May, July and October, when it was the 15th day; and the Nones, which was eight days before the Ides.

Any day immediately before the Kalends, Nones or Ides was called 'Pridie'. So Prid Non Mart – as it was abbreviated – is 6th March.

All other days were worked out by counting back from one of those three principal days. Bear in mind that the principal day itself is counted in counting backwards. So, III Id Mart is the third day back from the Ides of March, i.e. 13th March, counting 15th March as the first day.

HARRY MOUNT

RESTAURANTS
JAMES PEMBROKE

SAINSBURY'S CAFÉ, PASSIM
WILTONS, JERMYN STREET,
LONDON SW1

'People typically spend 25 minutes here,' so says Google of Sainsbury's Café. I very much doubt Alexander Chancellor ever spent less than an hour and 25 minutes on lunch. It was not only his favourite pastime but his preferred way of editing a magazine. When interrogated by Algy Cluff about his daily disappearance from the *Spectator*'s offices between 11.30am and 3.30pm, he replied, 'How else can one fill the day?'

During his glorious reign at *The Oldie*, he looked quite distraught when at noon he found his diary was empty, and was always relieved to be invited out. He preferred snug Italian restaurants like Da Paolo, in Charlotte Place. It was at the table that his famous chortle was most in evidence. He wasn't a raconteur armed with rehearsed set pieces; rather, he enjoyed his own and others' hypocrisy. His real gift was his openness: his willingness to share his personal highs and lows, and to empathise with his fellow diner's. He was my greatest ever lunch companion.

He used to frequent the Waitrose café in Towcester. I wish he had been with me at Sainsbury's café in Chichester. He would have laughed at the menu's addition of the calorific value of each dish. I opted for baked potato with tuna and sweetcorn (439 calories) but my wife overindulged in a lentil dahl soup (536 calories). Both were surprisingly good and were very courteously brought to our table by a lady who offered me the holy of holies: salad cream. She then brought us a pot of Earl Grey tea for just £1.20 each.

When Alexander became editor, I stupidly took him to Otto's to share an entire pressed duck. He barely ate a slice of the enormous bird whose grandfather must have been an emu. After his friend Harry Mount accepted the job, I thought a fellow cyclist would have a hearty appetite so I took Harry to Wiltons. This really wasn't Alexander's type of place: it was too clubby and formal for him. He would have been worried about bumping into bellowing patricians.

> He barely ate a slice of the enormous bird whose grandfather must have been an emu

Wiltons, undoubtedly the best purveyor of English grub in Britain, is a treat, and one needs to order carefully if straying from the £30 set menu. But who goes to Wiltons to be stingy? The oysters are irresistible. I had the juiciest lamb's kidneys and bacon for £18; Harry went for the brill at £23.50.

The wine list is where some equity release will come in handy. At £46, the Ronan by Clinet was the cheapest bottle of claret. I hadn't realised that Harry only drinks white wine, so I was forced to complete the entire bottle.

Like Alexander, I hate waste.

Da Paolo, 3 Charlotte Place, London, W1T 1SD; www.dapaolo.co.uk; 020 7580 0021. Generous two-course lunch for £19.95.

Wiltons, 55 Jermyn Street, St James's, London SW1Y 6LX; www.wiltons.co.uk; 020 7629 9955. £30 for two courses (including the carvery trolley at lunch).

Genius crossword solution
(from page 82)

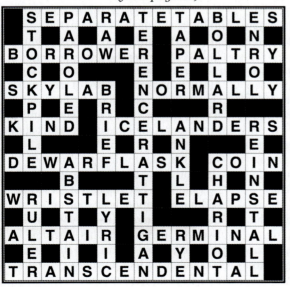

Classic read

MATTHEW PARRIS encourages us to reread George Eliot's *Romola*

Many books disappoint on rereading. Some prove just as good and some even better. But there are a few that are such heavy-going the first time round that they should *only* be reread.

Unfortunately this presents a logical difficulty. So I'm afraid you must battle grimly through a first reading of George Eliot's *Romola* purely as homework for the second reading – and leave a good pause between, so that Eliot's profound and sometimes overwrought attempt to enter the mind of 15th-century Florence can sink in, and all its strange, sideways reflections on people and politics in our own age filter through.

Eliot's most popular and accessible novels – *Middlemarch*, *The Mill On The Floss* and the rest – were written about the England she knew so well. *Romola*, however, places human types who are familiar and eternal in a time and place that may seem strange. She labours mightily, and with wonderful flashes of success, to make us feel at home among the scheming, gossiping Renaissance Florentines, and worked tremendously hard to achieve this, travelling, researching and straining every imaginative sinew to show us that the past is not another country.

She found the effort exhausting, she says. Anthony Trollope warned her not to 'fire too high above the heads of her readers' (not a fault Trollope can ever be accused of) and maybe she had. Yet once you know the plot, once you've remembered who everyone is and absorbed the atmosphere, chaos and intrigue of a vibrant, intelligent city-state at a time of fear and uncertainty, Eliot's favourite people spring so powerfully to life.

Her trademark false hero – handsome, beguiling and selfish with a yellow streak running right through him (Tito here) – and her trademark heroine – devoted, passionate and tender (Romola here) – are joined by the cruelly wronged old Baldassare: an iron will punching through a faltering memory.

Perhaps I'm getting more like Baldassare – who knows – but I shall be rereading *Romola* well into old age.

DECEMBER 2017

'Just a Minute' is celebrating its 50th birthday. In all that time, the panel game has been presided over by only one man: 94-year-old Nicholas Parsons. *Valerie Grove* salutes the show and meets its vintage ringmaster

Sixty seconds that hooked the nation

Radio 4 is festooned with candles and balloons this year. So many favourite programmes are celebrating birthdays.

I'm Sorry I Haven't a Clue, the funniest and most surreal panel-game, is 45. The *Today* programme is 60, as it reminds us daily, and so is *Test Match Special*. The venerated *Desert Island Discs*, an ideal formula that pleases both castaway and audience, is 75. As for the *Shipping Forecast* – our 'nightly litany of the sea', as its presenter Zeb Soanes calls it – at 150, it predates even the earliest crystal sets.

And then there is the panel-game *Just a Minute* or, as it is fondly known to participants, *JAM*.

JAM celebrates 50 years on air on 22nd December, when Nicholas Parsons, 94, can flourish his unique trump card: he has been in the chair for the entire half-century. He even chaired the pilot.

It was not an instant success, as Parsons likes to relate: 'My manner can best be described as laborious, rather pompous.'

Audience Research found the show 'dangerously thin'. The male panellists (Derek Nimmo and Clement Freud) overshadowed the women.

There were annoying hesitation challenges, irritating bursts of applause, and silly extra restrictions like not using the word 'the'. But hey, as Parsons now reminds us in every episode, over the decades *JAM* has become utterly brilliant, vibrant with talent, a favourite 'all over the world!'

And, while there may be those who look on *JAM* as Marmite, the panellists absolutely love participating.

Stephen Fry says, 'It's like being asked to join the MCC or the Athenaeum.' Sue Perkins calls it 'my favourite gig of all time'.

Why else would Fry, Paul Merton, Ross Noble, Julian Clary and Graham Norton bother? They don't need the money, but they love Radio 4. They enjoy the unrehearsed spontaneity of *JAM*, where you turn up half an hour before and record two shows before supper.

If their jokes are its appeal, Nicholas Parsons is the keystone. I met Parsons – at 94, impossibly dapper and spry – at the Park Theatre, where he and his wife came to see Gyles Brandreth's family production of *Hamlet*.

This reminded me that, on *JAM*, Brandreth spoke of having once played Hamlet: 'I was so poor, the audience threw eggs at me,' he said. 'I went on as Hamlet and came off as omelette!'

What is the key to *JAM*'s success?

'Fun,' says Parsons. 'Intellectuals come on to show how good they are at the game, but that's not the point. The point is to increase the fun.'

The doyenne of radio critics, Gillian Reynolds, is certain that the entire show depends on Nicholas Parsons's professionalism and comic timing.

Parsons was a doctor's son, raised in London; he read engineering at Glasgow, acted in rep, and became straight man to the comedian Arthur Haynes.

Sioned Wiliam, Radio 4's comedy commissioning editor, sings his praises: 'He's amazingly alert, very astute, does two shows a night, is hugely loved, and never undercuts the panellists.'

Certainly not: he enjoys being the foil to them all. Gyles Brandreth gets away with saying outrageous remarks about him. 'He even claimed once to be my love-child!' says Parsons.

Another time, given the subject 'The chairman's darkest secret', Brandreth began, 'Nicholas or, as close friends know him, "Susan", is the first transsexual to host a panel show in this country.'

But it is the chairman's great age which is most guyed. Sheila Hancock coined the term 'Nick-baiting'. When Parsons recalled playing at the Globe Theatre, Paul Merton interrupted, 'Shakespeare gave you the job, didn't he?'

Here are Paul Merton and Graham Norton bantering about Oliver Cromwell:

Parsons: 'Well, it was 1653, not 1563…'
Norton: 'Nicholas remembers.'
Merton: 'To be fair, he was doing the warm-up act for Charles I's execution.'
Norton: 'He's still got the bladder on the stick!'
Merton: 'Unfortunately, for different reasons these days!'

Or there was the time Merton said, '*Just a Minute* has been recorded in French, Belgian, Flemish, Walloon, Greek, Latin.' (BUZZ)

Norton: 'It has not been done in Latin.'
Merton: 'Well, when Nicholas first did it, it was.'

When the BBC threatened to take *JAM* off the World Service, there was such an outcry across the globe that they relented. After all, in India they even have *JAM* clubs. So Parsons and the *JAM* team flew to India, and did a show from the Mumbai Comedy Store with garrulous Indian counterparts.

The programme was devised by Ian Messiter, master inventor of radio panel shows. In his schooldays at Sherborne, a history master caught him daydreaming in class, and challenged him to talk about Henry VIII's wives for two minutes without hesitation or repetition; the alternative was a caning. He was caned.

Talking on one subject for 60 seconds, without repetition, hesitation or deviation, is harder than anyone thinks. Even Stephen Fry, with his 'fearsome intellect', found it hard, and started using cod archaisms like 'howmever'. (At the end of the programme, an announcer

Time lord: at his Buckinghamshire home, with one of his antique clocks

reassured listeners that 'There is no such word as howmever.')

Messiter's programme was originally called *Off the Cuff*. Then *One Minute, Please*. In 1967 came the new name, and new mainstay: chairman Parsons.

Parsons had been at school (St Paul's) with Clement Freud in the 1930s. He had also worked in rep with Kenneth Williams in the 1940s.

'Re-stoking Kenneth's ego' became his role. Williams, when introduced, 'would stick out his little bottom and strut across the stage'. KW's catchphrase was 'I'm a cult figure! I'm a cult!'

'Kenneth Williams was good at the game,' says Parsons, 'but what he was brilliant at was funny improvisation.'

Gyles Brandreth first met Parsons at Fanny Cradock's Christmas party in 1969.

'A minute's speech is no problem for Gyles,' as Parsons reminded me. 'In 1982, he established the world record for talking non-stop, twelve-and-a-half hours.'

What gives long-running programmes their staying power?

'Familiarity, in a word,' says Joby Waldman of the independent production company Reduced Radio. 'And that can't be achieved overnight.'

He used to produce *Gardeners' Question Time* – 70 this year; so he should know.

Even the most familiar show has to be 'replenished' – a favourite Radio 4 word – to appeal to the 35-40 generation, who may regard ancient panel games as stale buns. *My Word* and *My Music* faded out. But '*Clue*' and *JAM* – prompted initially by the Grim Reaper's carrying off Freud, Nimmo, Williams, Peter Jones and Humphrey Lyttelton – have been refreshed by younger, funnier blood. On '*Clue*', Jack Dee has been a brilliant replacement for Humph. Paul Merton – who originally proposed his services to *JAM* – became its star.

At a book launch for Miles Jupp (another *JAM* recruit), I asked Merton if he could imagine the BBC ever replacing Parsons with someone younger.

'Well, they could hardly replace him with someone older,' he zipped back.

For 50 years, the laughs have become as much part of our comfort zone as slippers by the winter fireside.

So how about any of us pitching a new game show that might flourish for five decades? Highly unlikely, everyone in the business agrees. But Sioned Wiliam assures me that Radio 4 is open to ideas. Must have potential for wit and sharpness, cleverness and silliness.

Recent arrivals in the repertoire include *Would I Lie To You?*; *Heresy*; *It's Not What You Know* and *The Unbelievable Truth*. These have staying power. The time to pitch your panel game idea – look on the Radio 4 website under 'commissioning' – is next spring.

The deadline for quiz show ideas has gone, but I told Sioned Wiliam my proposal anyway: a quiz, *I Remember It Well*, for the pre-Google generation who think their memory is wonderful but get things wrong all the time.

Who can tell what will work? Parsons says *JAM*'s formula makes it 'forever refreshed and unpredictable'.

'I've tweaked the game to introduce more fun, adding bonus points for laughs,' he says, 'The family of the show's inventor are happy for me to tweak.'

Parsons admits that *JAM*'s success is inexplicable: 'The essence of comedy is that you pause for effect, you repeat for emphasis, and you deviate for surprise. Yet these three things are exactly what you can't do in *Just A Minute*. And it's a comedy show, played for laughs!'

Long may Master Parsons continue to produce laughs, at the helm of *JAM*, with his Tiggerish enthusiasm and ebullience. Perhaps there should be a new *JAM* subject – the secret of eternal youth.

Nicholas Parsons died in 2020, aged 96

Getting Dressed

Perfectly prudent

As a food tycoon and *Bake Off* star, Prue Leith smartened up her act

BRIGID KEENAN

Oh dear! No sooner had I finished writing about Jossy Dimbleby for last month's *Oldie* than I realised that *The Great British Bake Off* was ending and I had to interview Prue Leith.

'Too many cooks' you might say, but I don't think so. The only thing these two share, aside from their culinary skills, is a penchant for bright colours.

Leith was born in South Africa in 1940. She was sent to Paris, where she did a university course and earned money as an au pair; and where she first became interested in food – and clothes.

As a teenager, Leith had worn 'what my mother called "bottom-of-the-pond" colours, dark and dingy. She had a pink ballgown made for my first school dance and I threw a sickie rather than wear it.'

In 1969, Leith moved to London and, with a Cordon Bleu cookery course behind her, Leith started making business lunches in her bedsit in Barons Court – luckily, her landlady had no sense of smell, she says. A decade later, she launched Leith's Good Food and her own restaurant, Leith's.

Her boyfriend, later her husband, Rayne Kruger – their union lasted more than 40 years – was her guiding spirit and chairman. She had one posh frock which she wore for the restaurant opening but all her other clothes were either from M&S or home-made.

She remembers a sheath dress done in shiny black lining material, another cut out of curtain fabric. But, from then on, she says she was mostly to be found in 'chefs' kit'.

Twenty-six years later, having written newspaper cookery columns and 12 cook books as well as running her food empire, she decided to slow down and write novels and she sold her businesses – by then turning over a huge £15 million a year. (She used some of her profits to open a catering college in her native South Africa).

But hers has been no languid retirement. Over the years since, Leith has been appointed to more boards than you could shake a furled umbrella at – from British Rail to the Halifax – and she has been awarded the OBE and the CBE, partly for work on school food.

Becoming a tycoon required a more serious way of dressing, but Leith never fell back on the office palette of black or grey. She loved bright colours ('I don't have any recipe called after me, but there is a daffodil with my name') and well-tailored, simple, but comfortable clothes – the arrival of the trouser suit had been a boon to business women, she says. For years, her favourite garments were two plain jackets that she wore so often that they frayed at the cuffs. But when, a year ago, she married John Playfair, an ex-fashion designer, he found her a tailor (www.orhanlondontailoring.com) who copied them for her. (She wears one of them in our picture, with an Orhan shirt, Long Tall Sally trousers, and earrings she made herself.)

Her new husband is a near neighbour in the Cotswolds but they decided to keep their separate houses. 'I couldn't live with all his junk – thousands of books piled up on the floor, chests of fabrics, his hat collection... I keep my own house quite tidy.'

Leith follows a disciplined schedule – she is finishing her eighth novel – and, though she likes to go to bed at about ten, she will stay up to 4am, if on deadline. *The Great British Bake Off* persuaded her to put on her apron again. A new cookbook is in the pipeline.

Leith has her own stylist, Jane Galpin, who did her outfits for *My Kitchen Rules*,

At the opening of Leith's, her restaurant on Kensington Park Road, London, 1969

the TV series she left to move to *Bake Off*. 'In the past, I've had stylists who were too young and chose baby-doll dresses for me, but Jane understands. She gets that I have to be comfortable, in flat shoes – and that the combination of my middle-class, bossy voice, determined personality, glasses, and height (five foot eight) can seem formidable but can be tempered by wacky jewellery and bright colours.'

Leith has recently hired a personal trainer to help her lose weight – 'I go to her studio to puff and pant.'

Forty years ago, she had the bags under her eyes 'done'. 'Now I could do with a neck lift, face lift, arm lift, leg lift – the lot. But what's the point? It is not going to make me young and beautiful and I would rather be me than risk looking like an alien.' She has her hair cut locally, and coloured 'in an obvious mix of fake colours' by Ritchie at Billi Currie (www.billicurrie.com).

In the past, she has had her teeth whitened 'expensively' at the dentist, but now uses whitening toothpaste. 'No idea if it works.' Her beauty products are 'Anything to hand – Boots mostly; just soap and moisturiser.' Her reading glasses are hand-painted by Ronit Fürst.

Leith has succeeded in so many fields; I wondered which one she is most proud of? Surprisingly, it has nothing to with any of them. It is that she created, and led, the campaign to put sculpture on the fourth plinth in Trafalgar Square.

Anne Robinson – Short Cuts

Help! I haven't been groped
But some well-known men have certainly tried it on

I have become a grave disappointment to the editor of this magazine. Despite a lifetime careering around newspaper offices, Westminster, television studios, several visits to 10 Downing Street and even – oh, the shame – a meeting with Harvey Weinstein, who wanted to get his hands on *The Weakest Link*, my incidents of Groper-gate are practically zero.

Worse still, younger members of the sisterhood have now pretty well disowned me.

This is since I sat in a BBC radio car in my drive in Gloucestershire, being interviewed for the *Today* programme. Unfortunately, I sighed and giggled when one of the two female guests in the studio was explaining how inappropriate it was for a male barrister to have described her as stunning.

I didn't actually say so but, if the truth were told, I have been known to perk up considerably when described thus.

More seriously, I believe that my generation paved the way and lifted the barriers for younger generations of women. Yet, puzzlingly, we failed to pass on our fighting spirit and natural sense of the absurd.

To save face, I do have a handful of examples of indecent proposals.

At a Labour Party conference in Brighton, I walked into breakfast and was hailed by a man who had been chief policy advisor to two prime ministers.

I joined him and we chatted agreeably like seasoned conference attenders while making our way through a full English.

Then, as I gathered my belongings and made to leave, he leaned over and whispered, 'Shall we go up to my bedroom and read the *Guardian* together?'

I would like to say I responded with a withering putdown. But I was too busy looking at him with a mixture of pity and contempt. Never mind, it illustrates, although it is hardly necessary, that you can become a member of the House of Lords, while simultaneously being a complete tosser.

My second, I have always marked up as 'highly commended'.

At the end of an official prime ministerial tour of Japan, China and India with Margaret Thatcher, we had one last stopover in Hong Kong. And an evening ahead at the governor's mansion.

In the afternoon, the phone rang in my bedroom at the Hong Kong Hilton. It was my favourite travelling companion. He was at the time the *Observer*'s most gifted writer.

'Anne,' he said, 'May I ask you a question?'

'Of course,' I replied.

'Is there,' he continued, 'any chance that, between now and Heathrow, we might go to bed together?'

'No,' I said. 'But, Clive, now we've cleared that up, why not join me in my room for tea?'

The third, I can only describe as stylishly artful.

The late Alan Clark invited me to lunch at the Savoy Grill.

'He'll just want to get into your knickers,' said my then husband. I disagreed.

However, as the waiter cleared away our Dover soles, Alan put his head to one side and said slowly, 'Annie, why don't we fast-track you into a safe Tory seat and then we can make you arts minister?'

I mean, what girl doesn't like to be thought of as clever?

I've always considered there not to be much difference between a night in the London Clinic and a first-class BA flight to Los Angeles.

Both operate a policy of what Shirley MacLaine once described to me, in relation to being on a movie set, as 'hurry to wait'.

You hang around for hours while nothing happens.

Lying in a bed in Devonshire Place recently, before being taken down to theatre for a tiny procedure, a flurry of nurses saw to my every need.

The tranquillity was only briefly broken by the arrival of a tall, slightly greying man in a black raincoat, carrying a rather chic, black briefcase.

'You,' I said, 'must be the incredibly handsome anaesthetist.' And he was.

Only later did it occur to me that, in the current climate, I might well have been out on my ear in my nightie and needing to grab a cab home.

Five of us had a lovely time at the Literary Leicester festival, as the panel invited to chat about our friendship with the late editor of *The Oldie*, Alexander Chancellor.

I had forgotten to mention in my last column that, along with Craig Brown, Alexander Waugh and Ferdy Mount, the author Geoffrey Wheatcroft joined us.

I am so glad he did.

It is more than 30 years ago but, as I gazed at him in his Garrick Club bow tie, it came to me that Wheatcroft is my one example of a man making an unexpected and clumsy lunge.

It was a sudden full-on grab and kiss on the lips by someone I hardly knew. Phew, I trust the editor will now be less dissatisfied.

The ruthless guide to parties

'Tis the season for enforced jollity, but don't let it get you down. Serial partygoer *Rachel Johnson* gives her tips on how to make the best of it

Take from my three score years and ten a half century and – as A E Housman might have put it – that only leaves 20 Christmases more.

I do not want to fritter my last remaining evenings in December in the nether regions of West End 'eateries', fending off bores with champagne breath, spraying me with flecks of fishy canapé, while asking me what I think about 'Pestminster'.

There's something borderline fascist about the festive season: the invitations for Advent that arrive in August, jingle tills in September, Winter Wonderland in Hyde Park halfway through November…

It all puts me in a bad mood, as the secret to most enjoyment is spontaneity. Carol services and nativity plays are a lovely, enduring tradition but Christmas parties are the essence of a regulation revel that comes earlier every year. All the forced jollity from Christmas fascists – you know, the sort who make you wear paper hats and dangle mistletoe – are the enemies of fun.

Nicky Haslam is the grandest guide to the day itself. Here are my Pippa-style anti-tips on how to survive the Christmas party season:

Arrivals Unlike book launches, Christmas parties don't have a sweet spot to hit which is just before (or just after, depending on the author) speeches. Peak time is between 7.15pm and 8pm for an early-evening drinkies. If you're the life-and-soul type, you will want to know that C Northcote Parkinson (as in Parkinson's law) has identified the throbbing epicentre of a gathering will always be slightly to the right of the centre of the room, so head there.
Bores If you see one bearing down, hide your drink, so you greet them empty-handed. Maintain eye contact, and then gasp, 'Gosh, I must get a drink! Can I get you one?' and fade away. Giles Wood, of this parish, always makes a beeline for bores as he is too lazy to make sparkling conversation with noted wits. 'I'm very lazy and uncompetitive,' he admits, 'and I enjoy rehashing clichés with legendary dullards, pretending I'm in a Mike Leigh play.'
Circulating A good trick is to stand right by the entrance. Guests will be so anxious to penetrate the throng themselves that you can process them efficiently in transit. *Gogglebox*'s Mary Killen (the *Spectator*'s agony aunt) has a tip for 'working off' auld acquaintances: stand on the pavement outside – which is what she did for many years for the annual *Spectator* summer party (maybe not so amenable in December.)
Dress I disdain the custom that women have to suddenly abandon their funereal black onesies (my favourite outfit) or LBDs for sweeping velvet dresses in jewel tones, sequins, and sparkly tops. I refuse. I don't have a 'Christmas Party Dress'. I will never have one, and nor should you.
Drinks I am a terrible champagne snob. I mind terribly if champagne is anything but ice-cold. Cava or prosecco don't even count as 'bubbly'. Mulled wine is the devil's work. Eggnog is obviously out of the question in England. I boringly stick to white or red wine if I'm pacing myself, to no ill effects.
Exit The problem with Christmas parties is not just the getting ready, the getting there, then having to be in a hot, loud, crowded room, with people asking you what you're doing for Christmas; it's getting the hell out again. I never check in my coat and bag, and sometimes don't even remove my outer garments, so I am already poised for flight.
Festive fayre You can't go wrong with honey-and-mustard, baked chipolatas.
Gossip Parties are essentially a Gossip Exchange, where information is traded. But never ask outright, 'What's the gossip?' or say to a journalist, 'Now you won't put this in a newspaper, will you?' It's a cast-iron rule that only ocean-going crashers, who have never uttered anything interesting in their lives, say this. Start with 'Have you heard…' and drop a delectable titbit. There is nothing people love more than gossip and no greater pleasure than feeling in the know. Wait for return confidences to flow.
Invitations I try to go to parties I've accepted – or at least do a 'drive by'. But at Christmas, as in July, there can be several gold-platers on the same night. Just as I would encourage chaps to try to be 'one-woman men', I advise social butterflies to be 'one-party women'. Commit, people!
Merrie music One society hostess has carol singers at her annual bash at a storied London establishment but music should be discouraged. People go to talk, not to listen to music or dance, and most men bitterly resent being forced to do either.
Tinsel and other seasonal decorations. If you must, but baubles in reds and golds and glass, please.
Yule Logs Just no.

I hope no hostesses will read this and think me an ungrateful guest. The truth is, as anyone who knows me will confirm, I can't resist a party – however grim – and am always thrilled to be asked.

And I almost always turn up – so let that be a warning to you all.

Rachel Johnson is author of 'Notting Hell' and 'Shire Hell' (Penguin)

'Party like it's 99!'

Italy

Content on Como

Henrietta Bredin was in need of R&R. She found it on a lake

At the dusty end of August my friend Patrick and I supped a little wearily together and agreed that what we were both pining for was a thoroughly old-fashioned sort of a holiday, in a small and charming hotel, maybe on a Swiss lake, accompanied by a large pile of novels (no e-readers for us, thank you very much). The following day he was buying stamps in his local post office and fell into conversation with a woman who was bemoaning the Swiss franc exchange rate and the expense of holidaying there. Dismissing Switzerland on the spot he wondered rhetorically whether an Italian lake might be an appealing option. His new acquaintance promptly endorsed this idea with enthusiasm and commendably specific detail, saying that the place to go was Lenno, on Lake Como, and that we should stay at the Hotel San Giorgio.

So we did. We booked rooms in the first week of October, by which point we were dustier and wearier, the holiday had shrunk into a long weekend and we were quite incapable of contemplating more than one novel apiece, and a light one at that. I was travelling from London and Patrick was coming from Budapest, so I got an early flight, he took the night train from Vienna and we met, in honey sunshine and in time for late-morning coffee, in front of the stridently shouting flagrantly fascist eagle-embellished monument that is Milan Central Station. The coffee was excellent and the trains – they would hardly dare do otherwise from this Mussolini-inspired building – ran on time.

After an easy hour, rattling past market gardens and sparkly stretches of lake, we were in Varenna, where we paused for a leisurely outdoor lunch, feeling immensely smug at having stolen back some late-summer warmth, before catching a boat to Lenno. The journey, chugging gently via Bellagio, Villa Carlotta and Tremezzo, was improbably pretty, we were the only passengers to disembark and there, immediately to our right, was an arching sign over an open gateway, leading through a garden that sloped down to the water's edge to a green-shuttered, wide-terraced, sleepy-looking hotel. After a very brief interlude to deposit bags in rooms and admire views, we were on the terrace, watching the sun go down and raising a Negroni apiece in a grateful toast to the woman in the post office.

There are some fascinating places to visit around Como but there is nothing so punitively great that it would be shaming to return home without having been to have a look. Within easy walking distance of Lenno is the Villa Balbaniello, which has extremely eccentric opening hours but, once you've worked those out, can be reached by a track winding through mushroomy woodland with a thick carpet of fallen chestnuts underfoot. The villa belongs now to the Italian equivalent of the National Trust and was owned before that by Count Guido Monzino, who bought it in 1974 and filled it with his own joyously eclectic collections of Tang horses, Beauvais tapestries, Inuit carvings, paintings on glass and an entire roomful of mementoes from his various expeditions, that included a 1971 sled journey from Cape Columbia to the North Pole and the first Italian ascent of Everest in 1973. We also enjoyed the bedroom that he'd fitted up for his mother, with silver faux-bamboo headboards and dressing-table, and the library in which all the books are devoted to mountaineering, each one bound in faded tobacco-brown leather so that a first edition of Guido Rey's *The Matterhorn*, with hand-coloured plates and pen-and-ink drawings, is hard to tell apart from Chris Bonington's *Boundless Horizons* published in 2000. In the 1970s and in the wake of the kidnapping and murder of Aldo Moro, Monzino was afraid of similar threats and constructed a series of hidden passageways down to a landing stage on the lake in case of the need to make a hurried exit.

We loved the motorboats (and one vintage steamboat) that stitched their way about the lake but were covetous of the Balbaniello launch, with its gleaming polished wood and neatly coiled white ropes, and wouldn't have said no to a hop in the seaplane that we saw every now and again, skimming insouciantly across the water trailing a crisp white wake.

Chestnuts featured on every menu in this gluttish autumn month and made delectable rib-sticking gnocchi, slick with the local olive oil. And when we had to leave, with considerable reluctance, we discovered that the station bar at Varenna, keenly attuned to the train timetable, can soften the blow of departure by providing a midday Campari and soda at a platform-adjacent outdoor table, accompanied by tiny warm anchovy pastries.

On the eve of a retrospective exhibition at the British Museum, *John Julius Norwich* recalls the remarkable life and tremendous spirit of his friend Patrick Leigh Fermor

Paddy the Great, king of Greece

A new show at the British Museum – about three great lovers of Greece – takes me right back to the 1950s. The English painter Johnny Craxton (1922-2009) was a joy – the only dinner guest we ever had who came on his motorbike and left his leathers in the hall. He always came on his own; we were all intrigued by the idea of his long-term boyfriend, whom we never met. I think Johnny saw Greece as a larger Crete – just as Neville Chamberlain was always said to see Europe as a larger Birmingham. Johnny loved Crete with passion.

The Athenian painter Nikos Ghika (1906-1994) provided me with my first breath of Greece in the summer of 1954, when we went to stay with him in his lovely old house on the island of Hydra.

Also staying there were Paddy and Joan Leigh Fermor. Ghika later designed the serpentine pebble mosaic floors at Kardamyli – the Leigh Fermors' enchanting house in the Mani. It was Paddy that I knew best of the three. Our friendship lasted from the 1950s until his death in 2011 at the age of 96.

In the spring of 1955, when we were living in Yugoslavia – I was working at the British Embassy – a letter arrived from my mother. She had been offered a caique for a fortnight's sail among the isles of Greece. Paddy and Joan Leigh Fermor were coming; could we come, too? At the end of August, we drove down from Belgrade to Athens, and boarded the *Eros* at Piraeus.

It was my first time in the Aegean, and my best. Paddy lived and breathed his beloved Greece – fluent in its language, encyclopaedic in his knowledge of its history, people and literature. And nobody has ever carried his learning more lightly.

As we sailed from island to island – and, in those days, there were almost no tourists, and I can't describe what a difference that made – he talked about Greece, Greek beliefs and traditions, about Byron and the Greek War of Independence, about those monstrously magnificent Greek heroes – men such as Mavromichalis and Kolokotronis, whose names roll so satisfactorily across the tongue – and about the Greek Orthodox Church and its quarrels with the West over words such as 'filioque' and 'homoousion', his talk taking in all the mystery and magic of the Byzantine world. Twenty years later, I was to write a history of Byzantium myself; but I doubt whether, had it not been for that fortnight on the *Eros*, I should ever have done so.

One day we were in a taverna on Santorini. Britain and Greece were then at the height of the Cyprus dispute and Paddy was, of course, firmly on the Greek side. Suddenly a member of the party at the next table, hearing us speaking English and being slightly drunk, launched into a stream of anti-British invective. We pretended not to notice. Then, suddenly, he and his companions burst into song.

'Quick,' whispered Paddy. 'National anthem – everybody up.'

We leapt to our feet while he, naturally knowing all the words, sang them at the top of his voice. The mood of the other table changed immediately; and they were still more impressed when he continued with all the following verses – solo by now, since no one else knew them. Abject apologies followed: the ouzo went round once more, and we all departed friends.

It was characteristic of Paddy that, when he and Joan decided to build themselves a house in Greece, they chose the remotest corner: Kardamyli, at the far end of the Mani, the second of the three peninsulas that form the southern coast of the Peloponnese. And oh, how they loved it.

Paddy basically designed it himself. I remember him saying, while the building was in progress, 'I want it to be part of outdoors, so that, if a chicken were found wandering through the library, no one would be a bit surprised.'

By November 1969, with its vast supply of bookcases, a huge desk and plenty of room to pace over a stone floor, the 'powerhouse for prose', as Paddy liked to call it, was ready at last. The two books describing his teenage walk across Europe, *A Time of Gifts* and *Between the Woods and the Water*, were both written there, together with hundreds of letters, articles and the jeux d'esprit which he so loved, and of which he was such a master. But those dread enemies procrastination and distraction were always hovering behind him, tempting him away. And as we shall see, they were to get him in the end.

Kardamyli was a huge success. It became the epicentre of Paddy's world. For the first time, at 54, he had a home of his own. He continued to travel around Europe to see his innumerable friends, but it was here, I feel quite sure, that he

In a Grecian paradise: from left, Nikos and Barbara Ghika, John Craxton and Paddy and Joan Leigh Fermor together at the Ghikas' home on Hydra in 1958

was happiest. Outside Europe he was seldom tempted to roam. Except, surprisingly, for the Caribbean. A year or two after the war, he and Joan were persuaded by their old friend (and mine) Costa Achillopoulos to accompany him on a longish tour of the islands.

The result was Paddy's first book, *The Traveller's Tree*, which was published in 1950, and also his second, *The Violins of Saint-Jacques*, an exquisite little novella which was his only venture into fiction.

The islands fascinated him. His chapter on voodoo is a masterpiece. And then, when he got to Barbados, what did he find? A tablet in the churchyard of St John's, carved with Doric columns and the cross of Constantine, reading: 'Here lyeth ye body of Ferdinando Palaeologus, descended from ye Imperial lyne of ye last Christian Emperor of Greece. Churchwarden of this parish 1655-1656. Vestryman twentye years. Died Oct 3. 1679.'

Later, Paddy discovered that Ferdinando's son Theodore had returned to England and had settled in Stepney, where he left a posthumous daughter baptised with the typically 17th-century name of Godscall Palaeologus.

She may have married, and had countless children; but, for the time being, this little girl in Stepney remains the last authentic descendant of the Palaeologi, the last imperial family of Byzantium.

Of course Paddy was a superb linguist; but I have never known anyone who enjoyed his languages so intensely. He loved on-the-spot translations: 'To be or not to be' in German, for example – occasionally recited backwards – or *D'Ye Ken John Peel* in Italian, which my daughter Artemis (his biographer) and I sang at his memorial service:

Conosce Gian Peel, con sua giacca tanta grigia?
Conosce Gian Peel, prima cosa la mattina,
Conosce Gian Peel, quand' è lontano, è lontano,
Con suoi cani e suo corno la mattina.

And then there were the letters – letters that could have been written by no one else. Reading them, written at such terrific speed that sometimes they grow faint because the fountain pen can't deliver the ink fast enough, one marvels at Paddy's facility and fluency. And yet, when he was writing a book for publication, every sentence was a battleground. When, in July 1988, Sotheby's sold the autograph manuscript of *A Time of Gifts*, it was described in the catalogue as follows:

'c.450 pages, the majority written on rectos only, some on both sides, the first chapter on lined foolscap sheets, some cartridge paper, others lined, heavily revised and corrected, revised passages frequently written on separate sheets and pasted or clipped over the original, corrections or elucidations often in red ink, foreign or difficult words printed in the margin, many sheets with encouraging notes to the typist, often stapled or stitched with coloured thread into gatherings, generally of ten pages.'

I have an idea – I hate to have to say it and desperately hope I'm wrong – that Paddy's last years were not as happy as the rest of his life had been. He missed Joan desperately after she died in 2003, he was getting old and he gradually had to face up to the fact that he would never complete the third volume of the story of that glorious European journey in his early youth. He produced bits and pieces for it by the dozen, but something always prevented him from organising them, connecting them and making them into a single coherent document. It was, I suppose, a kind of writer's block.

He would seize on anything – letters, articles, translations, those ingenious word games he so loved – rather than face one of two facts: the first, that he must finish the job; the second – far worse – that he couldn't. Eventually he knew that the second was the truth. When he came to London, people would say breezily, 'How's Volume III coming on?', little realising that they were driving a dagger through his heart.

Volume III is not entirely lost. *The Broken Road*, compiled by Colin Thubron and Artemis, breathes Paddy through and through. And anyway, he has left us so much more to revel in.

As a travel writer, he was surely in a class by himself. But he was much more than a travel writer; he was the most extraordinary literary – and social – phenomenon I have ever known, and I am proud to have been his friend.

The Ghika, Craxton, Leigh Fermor exhibition at the British Museum ran from March to July 2018

On the 50th anniversary of the classic TV sitcom, *Ian Lavender* recalls only great actors and great friends

A Dad's Army feud? Who do you think you are kidding?

If I had the proverbial pound for every time I were asked the question... It would have to be two questions, really, at 50p a time. The first question is: 'Can you say your line for us?' Well, strictly speaking, it was Arthur Lowe who said, 'Don't tell him, Pike!' And the one that so many people get round to, eventually, is: 'Go on, tell us, what were they really like, Mainwaring and Wilson?' And it saddens me.

It saddens me that the majority of enquirers are either incredulous or disappointed to hear, from me at least, that John le Mes and Arthur Lowe were not permanently at daggers drawn; and never needed to be persuaded to be available at the same time next year for the next series.

Over ten years, we made 80 TV episodes, 67 radio recordings, played the stage show in the West End for a year and worked together in various other TV, plays, radios, and pantomimes, in various combinations. We played together – and I use the term 'played' advisedly – for about 20 per cent of those ten-plus years; and I never heard the word feud used until a few years ago.

When, three years ago, the research began for the mildly amusing and mildly truthful docudrama of how *Dad's Army* got to your screens, I asked the researchers why they wanted to speak to me. The show was already in production when I auditioned for Pike and I knew nothing about how it got to our screens. 'Ah yes,' the reply came, 'but we think it will be far more interesting when we get to later on and find out the truth about the feuds between the cast.' Well, I'm sorry, but there are no 50th birthday revelations of that awful truth about *DA* – from this direction, at least.

We spent an awful lot of time working together – and playing – but we none of us lived in each other's pockets. Some saw more of each other than the rest, but isn't that true in any group who work together? I saw quite a lot of Clive Dunn and Arthur Lowe, but it doesn't follow that Jimmy Beck and I couldn't stand working with each other. What did follow for me was that each year brought the joy of another couple of months to learn from John Laurie and Arnold Ridley about their very different wars and lives. There was more time to learn about jazz and movies from John le Mes at Ronnie Scott's; more to learn about variety theatre from Clive and Bill Pertwee; more to learn about doing my job.

My theatrical education as a kid in post-war Birmingham had been essentially variety at the Hippodrome, pantomime, all those radio comedies and plays, and Saturday morning cinema at the Danilo cinema in the shadow of the Austin motor factory. A few years later, in 1968, there I was, this sprog of sprogs, in a hotel lounge on location in Thetford, literally sitting at the feet of this crowd of childhood heroes, listening to the story of their lives. It took no time at all to realise that here was a group of disparate people and players from all parts of the business who, like any gathering new cast, had got to find a way of working together.

David Croft told me a few years later that he had said to Jimmy Perry after the first recording, 'If this lot can get on, we could have a hit here.'

On the middle weekend of the location filming of each new series, David Croft and his wife, Ann, would host a dinner party for us. On one of the later occasions, dear John Laurie had the floor and began to speak along these lines. (Imagine, if you will, his beautiful Dumfries accent.)

'David, Ann, once again we have to thank you for a splendid evening and once again, let's not forget, for continuing to employ this strange mixture of strolling players. And we are strange – make no mistake. Let's just look at ourselves. There's young Lavender here, green, wet behind the ears, peely-wally but enthusiastic. I've taught him everything he knows, but not everything I know, and he's kind enough to give me a lift now and then.

'Billy Pertwee, who keeps us entertained with his jokes from the end of the pier and folderols. Yes, Billy, you keep proving to us with those jokes that the old ones are indeed the old ones.

'Clive, who started playing his 70-year-old man when he was 17 in a prisoner-of-war camp and still plays the same character to this day.

APRIL 2018

Don't panic! From left: Jones (Clive Dunn), Walker (James Beck), Wilson (John Le Mesurier), Mainwaring (Arthur Lowe), Frazer (John Laurie), Pike (Ian Lavender) and Godfrey (Arthur Ridley)

'My dear friend Arnold, who has tried everything but not quite succeeded: playwright, producer, film-maker, and actor, of course, recently to be heard in *The Archers*.

'John le Mesurier, occasional stage work, much television and every other British film made since the war but, if truth be told, a dilettante.

'Arthur, our dear leading man, who started in weekly rep after the war, progressed to singing second tenor in Harry H Hanson's number-two tours of indifferent musicals, on into TV soap and then situation comedy.

'And that leaves me… me, with an extensive stage career… who has appeared in quite as many films as John, some of them quite good to me, too, who has played every one of Shakespeare's leading men except for Henry VIII because I was too thin. Me, who was considered by many the finest Hamlet of the Twenties, now settled into a bucolic semi-retirement and now, now, I have become famous for doing this crap!'

We all laughed a bit, only a bit, because we were now almost laughed out into silence. He had summed all of us up in a couple of sentences each, and we all knew each other pretty well; so we could and did laugh at ourselves and each other mightily. I like to think that we knew each other so well on and off stage that we knew our bad bits as well as our good, but I was unaware that any of us had to get over a feud in order to do more television shows. On the other hand, none of us was required to be bosom buddies when we finished work.

John and Arthur may not have spent a lot of time together socially – how many double acts do? But you don't produce some of the most delicate touching scenes and then pure physical farce, like John and Arthur, did with a feud going on around you. There was not a lot of feuding around when Arnold and John Laurie would be found talking, talking late into the night about their awful common bond, the First World War.

We are all of us using part of ourselves in our characters; so, yes, Arthur was at times pompous – which is what people want to know – but before that he was something of a shy man, a very private man. He chose, like anyone else, to decide who was and was not allowed into his bubble.

Until then, he took the social risk of using the pomposity to keep people at their distance. In *Dad's Army*, there were at least another seven people ready to burst Mainwaring's bubble. In real life, it was Arthur who did the bursting.

Little did I know, on that first day we all met to go off on location filming, that he was going to become not only one of the seven new people to work with; but one of my seven new teachers each summer, and eventually seven new friends. The down side of having these seven new older friends was that I was going to lose them early in my life. I was not long out of teens and they were my dream oldies.

The Oldie Annual 2021 **123**

Grumpy Oldie Man

Why can't waiters speak properly?
I'm the most irritable person on earth, particularly in restaurants
MATTHEW NORMAN

At the door of an Edinburgh restaurant, my son stayed me with an arm and gave the pep talk. 'I know you're the most irascible person on earth,' it began, 'and never more so than in restaurants.'

That may be true. For the 20 years during which I reviewed them, professional etiquette mandated an appreciative grin whenever a waiter offered to 'explain the menu', or delivered a keynote address about the beach from which chef foraged the pebbles moonlighting as butter dishes. A return to civilian ranks has slightly loosened the shackles.

'And I also know you're tired after a very long drive,' he went on. 'But I like this place, and want to come back, so do you think we could get through dinner without an incident?'

It had been a long drive from London to collect him and his gear from his vacated student flat. But despite the sequence of losing battles with ostentatiously unmanned M6 roadworks, I assured him the mood was good.

He nodded sardonically at that, asking if he should activate the iPhone stopwatch to time the first eruption. The average, he claims, is four minutes and 27 seconds.

'Not necessary,' I said. 'I'm, like, totally chilled.' He shot me a piercing glance, but eschewed the stopwatch.

In the event, this was a mistake. It might have recorded a new personal best, or worst, though without official timing that cannot be ratified.

What broke me wasn't the young waiter's 'Can I bring you some menus for yourselves this evening?' The years of reviewing inured me to reflexive pronouns. As for that equally superfluous 'this evening', although it struck me as clear entrapment – a temptation to reply, 'I'm tired after a long drive – so I'm going to sleep now. If you could bring us the menus for ourselves tomorrow morning...' – I resisted and said that menus would be a delight. The reprieve proved short-lived. 'No bother,' said the waiter.

'I'm trying,' I hissed across the table, 'I really am, but what is it with "no bother"? It's always that, or no problem, or no worries. Why do they say it?'

Shushing me with practised ease, he promised to explain later.

We ordered from the vaguely pan-Indo-Chinese menu. In every regard but one, my papaya salad (crisp, shredded vegetables, good glass noodles and fresh herbs in a good sesame oil dressing) was a triumph.

The solitary flaw, being pernickety, was the lack of papaya. We rooted around the bowl with chopsticks, after the style of Basil Fawlty searching the trifle for hidden duck. Not a molecule.

I received grudging permission to alert the waiter. 'Forgive me if this seems pedantic,' I told him, 'but there is literally no papaya in this papaya salad.'

'Ah,' he said, plainly unbothered. 'Would you like more papaya?'

'You're very kind, but I wouldn't like more papaya. What I would like is papaya.' 'No bother,' he said, 'I'll talk to the chef.'

After reviewing close to a thousand of them, I assumed I'd encountered every imaginable restaurant eccentricity. In a way, the novelty of a dish bereft of its solitary advertised ingredient was refreshing. We discussed the matter, my son and I, over hot water boldly masquerading as tea. 'It's an intriguing ontological question,' said this philosophy undergrad. 'Can a papaya salad truly be said to be a papaya salad if it contains no papaya?' I thought the answer fairly simple. But, as ever when I try to engage him in philosophical debate, it was incalculably more complex than I could appreciate or begin to understand.

'Chef says he's had to be a bit sparing with the papaya,' reported the waiter on his return, 'because those people waiting for a takeaway ordered the salad as well.'

The ontological symposium having developed not necessarily to my advantage, it was a relief to move on to the semantical. 'It's not so much that he's been a bit sparing,' I posited, 'and more that he hasn't spared any.'

'Well, he's sorry for being a bit sparing with the papaya. Can I bring some beef for yourself for the salad instead?' I said that he could. 'No bother.'

We finished and paid up. When I thanked the waiter for knocking the £8.50 off the bill, he revealed that this, for him, had been no bother.

'Jesus wept, why do you millennials use the phrase like broken parrots?' I spluttered on the walk to my son's flat. 'Isn't being bothered an integral part of the job? Of any job?'

The point, he explained, is that young people in service industries want to put us at our ease. The one thing that bothers them is the customer being made to feel awkward by the power imbalance implicit in the relationship. 'No bother' consoles us that they aren't feeling dangerously oppressed.

I flashed back something witty. 'Cobblers', if I recall correctly.

'Everything annoys you, old man, doesn't it? Every tiny, trivial, minuscule thing,' he observed. 'You're a snowflake.' I thought he had a point. 'Now is there any chance that we can finish packing up the flat without any outbursts about the filth or the flimsiness of the bin bags?' The power balance implicit in this relationship had been duly reasserted.

'No bother,' I said. No bother at all.

Theodore Dalrymple: The Doctor's Surgery

Raise a glass to tee-totalitarianism

My definition of a moderate drinker is someone who drinks as much as I do; a heavy drinker drinks more than I do; and a miserable killjoy drinks less.

In other words, I consume exactly the right amount of alcohol, that happy mean between drunkenness and sobriety. Personally, I have not found teetotallers to be much fun, though no doubt there are exceptions.

A recent paper in the *Lancet*, however, wants to make teetotallers of us all. After immense statistical labours, which not one in a thousand doctors would be able to understand, the authors came to the conclusion that the only safe level of consumption is none. Their prose, the work of many hands, is not exactly a pleasure to read:

'The present study aims to build upon pre-existing work and to address several limitations found in earlier research. First, the available studies have assessed the risk of alcohol use by relying on external meta-analyses, which do not control for confounding in the selection of the reference category within constituent studies. This approach is problematic because of the so-called sick quitter hypothesis, which emphasises the importance of reference category selection in correctly assessing risk among drinkers, along with other confounding study characteristics such as survival bias.'

In essence, the authors compared the consumption of alcohol per capita in a very large number of countries and correlated it with death rates from diseases known to be associated with or caused by alcohol. They found that there was no level of drinking that did not increase the chances of dying earlier than might otherwise have been expected.

I was reminded of a speed awareness course I attended after I had been caught speeding in Swindon. It was very good and I have been more careful to observe speed limits ever since; it provided clear evidence that the faster you drove, the more likely you were to kill or be killed. In fact, there was no completely safe speed at which to drive.

It follows from this that, if you want to avoid death by road accident, the only safe thing to do is never to leave your house. Only the other day, for instance, my wife was knocked over by our mechanical wheelbarrow when she accidentally put it into reverse; luckily, I was on hand to change gear and the sole

> To avoid death by road accident, the only safe thing to do is never leave home

damage was to some hollyhocks on to which the wheelbarrow had pushed her.

It is, I suppose, only natural that a medical journal should concern itself with health to the exclusion of all other considerations. As everything is a nail to a hammer, so every pleasure is a potential cause of illness to a medical journal. Even those things that are temporarily found to be health-giving, such as moderate drinking, are sooner or later found to be a serious threat to health. As Richard III said to his brother, 'We are not safe, Clarence, we are not safe.'

What to me was astonishing in the paper in the *Lancet* was the willingness of the authors to prescribe policy to the entire world on the basis of very complex calculations that must by their very nature be uncertain, and will almost certainly be shown to be full of mistaken assumptions. Moreover, they commit what ought to be a criminal offence in medical authors, namely that of expressing risks only relatively and not absolutely. Even if it were true that moderate drinking raised the death rates from certain diseases by 50 per cent among 30-year-olds, this would be trivial because the death rates were so low in the first place.

We live in an age of advancing health totalitarianism.

KITCHEN GARDEN
SIMON COURTAULD
APRICOTS

In the 18th century, the naturalist Gilbert White opined that apricots could only be grown to perfection in England; and a hundred years later it was fashionable for landowners to grow apricots on the walls of their tenants' cottages. The huge number cropped every year at Aynho, in Northamptonshire, gave it the name of Apricot Village, but the 'dangling apricocks' mentioned by Shakespeare are not much seen growing in this country today.

A resident of Aynho told me the other day that, despite the hot summer, he had no more than three or four apricots on his one tree this year. Due to the cold spring, there were not enough bees to pollinate the flowers. Last year, however, following a cold winter, an early spring and a warm summer, his tree had produced 104 fruit. The change of climate which we keep hearing about may well provide better apricot-growing conditions in future.

Most importantly, an apricot tree grown outside should be against a south-facing wall, in well-drained soil rich in lime. It should be planted in autumn and ideally trained in the shape of a fan. If few insects are around in spring – apricot is usually the first fruit tree to flower – the blossom should be pollinated by hand with a small paintbrush.

Of the varieties recommended, Sibleys can be grown in a large pot near the house, and Tomcot has large fruit with deep orange flesh. Moorpark, which is said to have a rich, juicy taste, must have improved since Jane Austen's day when, in *Mansfield Park*, a dinner-party guest stated that this same variety had no more flavour than a potato.

Most of the apricots which we may buy in a supermarket at this time of year, from elsewhere in Europe, tend to be dry and woolly, and can only be enjoyed if stewed first. I have eaten deliciously fresh apricots in France, but I think the French keep the best for themselves. However, by growing them in the garden at home, one may come close to agreeing that Gilbert White was right.

The Oldie Emporium

UK Travel

....book a holiday with us today
info@andersenboats.com / (+44)(0)1606 833668
www.andersenboats.com

Pattard Cottages

Located N Devon Coast in ANOB. Well equipped holiday cottages sleeping 2-8. Pets welcome. Now with fine dining on site.
01237441311
www.pattard.com
on site restaurant
www.pattardrestaurant.co.uk
01237 441444 for table reservation

The Penn Club

The Penn Club is a Members Club with a strong Quaker ethos, open to non-members for B&B. We are located just off Russell Square, close to the British Museum, the British Library, several buildings of the University of London and other attractions and places of interest.

"Home from Home"
PENNCLUB.CO.UK
020 7636 4718
office@pennclub.co.uk

Overseas Travel

Found under the apple tree by the sheep

Once upon a time, before swimming pools, there was a Dordogne of rare butterflies, even rarer wild orchids, strange edible fungi, midnight moths and fossils unearthed by farm animals, you could hear the midwife toad….That Dordogne still exists. Come to La Chaise, off-season, find your own fossils, fungi – make your own foie gras...

La Chaise, 24350 fr.
doinap917@gmail.com

Self Catering Holiday Cottages in Sandwich, Kent

Cottages 2 & 6 are available for holiday let. Ideal for 2. Town centre but in peaceful private garden (parking) WiFi.
2 nights £180, No6 £450 pw, No2 £520 pw
01304 613270 • www.sandwichcottages.co.uk

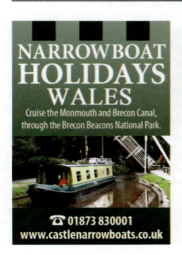

NARROWBOAT HOLIDAYS WALES
Cruise the Monmouth and Brecon Canal, through the Brecon Beacons National Park.
☎ 01873 830001
www.castlenarrowboats.co.uk

Self-catering for two
in the Shropshire Hills AONB:
Quiet countryside near Wenlock Edge;
starry skies; walks from the door;
open all year; 4* comfort

www.ferndaleflat.co.uk
email: mike@brogden.info
phone: 01584 841649

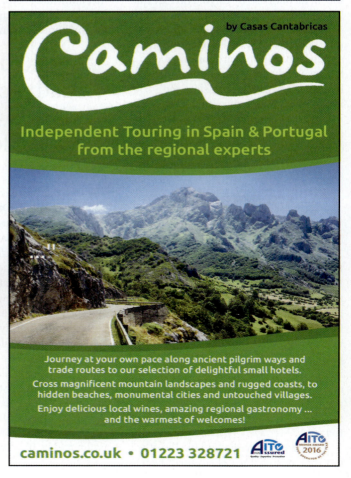

Caminos by Casas Cantabricas

Independent Touring in Spain & Portugal from the regional experts

Journey at your own pace along ancient pilgrim ways and trade routes to our selection of delightful small hotels. Cross magnificent mountain landscapes and rugged coasts, to hidden beaches, monumental cities and untouched villages. Enjoy delicious local wines, amazing regional gastronomy ... and the warmest of welcomes!

caminos.co.uk • 01223 328721

To advertise, contact Kami Jogee on 0203 859 7093 or via email kamijogee@theoldie.co.uk. scc rate £45+vat.

Books & Publishing

Confused about self-publishing?

YPS are the one-stop-shop for self-publishers

- Copy-editing & proofreading
- Full book design service
- Printing & binding
- Promotion & marketing
- Book distribution
- Commission-free online bookshop
- eBook production & distribution
- Free & friendly advice
- Cup of tea and a chat!

As featured in the Writers' & Artists' Yearbook

York Publishing Services Ltd
tel. 01904 431213
enquiries@yps-publishing.co.uk

www.yps-publishing.co.uk

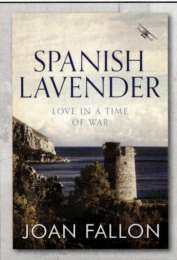

SPANISH LAVENDER
LOVE IN A TIME OF WAR
JOAN FALLON

"A riveting read that spans three generations."
(HISTORICAL NOVEL SOCIETY REVIEW)

Elizabeth is visiting her parents in the south of Spain when the Spanish Civil War breaks out. She refuses to evacuate with them and remains alone, in the devastated city of Málaga, where she makes friends with two young men, Juan, an idealistic Spaniard, and Alex, a pragmatic Englishman. As the Nationalist troops grow ever closer they decide to flee along the coast to Álmeria.

During the Spanish Civil War Elizabeth fell in love. 70 years later her granddaughter wants to know more.

www.joanfallon.co.uk
AMAZON LINK: http://amzn.eu/ia20aPJ

Gifts

Fire-Drake Jewellery
A small business in rural Herefordshire, creating jewellery in precious metals.

firedrakeuk.com 07944 669446 facebook.com/FireDrakeJewellery

Amazing New Technology Lamps take the strain out of reading. Back by popular demand. The Reader ultra high definition reading lamp.

The Craftlight Company — better by design.

Ultra High Definition lighting making a difference

1.5 mtr high

SAVE OVER £26

Virtually no heat and consumes just 6watts

Add a second lamp for £59.95

Elegant all metal antique brass finish.

converts to table or desk lamp

Very low heat

British Design

Unlike a traditional filament bulb, our lamps produce a brighter more concentrated light which will transform your reading experience. Small and large print will appear crisp and clear with more vibrant colour. This light makes black blacker and white whiter for better contrast. The focussed beam of light is similar to direct sunlight and is ideal for reading books, magazines, newspapers, along with hobbies including painting, jigsaws, sewing, geneolgy, and much more.
Each energy efficient lamp can convert to half height to be used as a desk or table lamp.
Making it the essential lamp for your home, office, or workroom.

TO ORDER or for more information.
visit www.craftlights.co.uk
look under newspaper and magazine offers for special offers.
or call 01502 587598
for help or advice.

The Reader 1.5 mtr was £96.00 Now only £69.95 inc p+p

The Oldie Annual 2021 127

The Oldie Emporium

Books & Publishing

BARBARA J HOLTEN
Editing & Proof-Reading Services

Here to help your writing shine at its best

Contact Barbara at
info@barbarajholten.com
Quality service at reasonable rates

www.barbarajholten.com

From manuscript *to* beautiful books *by Carnegie*

We produce every kind of book for every kind of author

Over 36 years' experience, friendly, tailored approach, free estimates & honest advice

Carnegie Scotforth Books
www.scotforthbooks.com
anna@carnegiepublishing.com 01524 840111

Your Book Is Written To Be Read
Books published - novels to academic
History, Biography, Autobiography
Submission to:
Janus Publishing Company Limited
The Studio, High Green,
Great Shelford, Cambridge, CB22 5EG
Email: publisher@januspublishing.co.uk
www.januspublishing.co.uk 020 7486 6633

Write Your Life Story
For free advice and a brochure
Phone Mike:
01869 246796
mike@boundbiographies.com

Genealogy

YOUR ANCESTORS FOUND
Retired school inspector, Cambridge history graduate, genealogist for 40 years, researches and writes your family's history. No task too big or small. Phone 01730 812232 for brochure, sample report and free estimate.

Health

«The destroyer of all ailments»

In India, they say **neem** oil is «the defeater of all ailments» – thus a great ingredient in soap. **O**ur neem soap is almost 50% neem oil pressed from seeds of the neem tree. Helpful for dry skin issues including eczema and other bothering skin problems.

Use also instead of liquid shampoo for clean healthy hair. **F**ree from artificial chemicals ☺. **N**o animal fats. Good and natural.

An excellent soap for everyone.

Also **sandalwood** soap made with a blend of real powder and oil from the sandalwood tree.

Triple milled soap with the moisturizing glycerine retained.

Neem or sandalwood soap. *True wholesome soap like no other.*

Here's your opportunity to try it. For only £16 you can order 4 generous 125g bars, including free p&p in UK. Choose any combination – 4 the same or your assortment of both soaps.

For speedy service, order at Onevillage.com – where other ideas also await you!

One Village Soap,
Charlbury, OX7 3SQ
℡ 01608 811811

onevillage.com

Old Photograph Albums. Former British Colonies Asia, Africa and Gulf up to 1960 Wanted.

Also documents manuscripts autographs letters of all periods. We can also clear books and papers of all types and are happy to travel.

Mayflyephemera@msn.com
or 07701 034472 – John Martin

Video

precious moments...
cinefilm, slides & video to dvd
CARROLLmedia 01903 725217
www.carrollmedia.co.uk

Health

arelle
Effective, quality continence care products for ladies and men

Discreet, reliable mail order service. Call 0800 389 3597 or visit www.arelle.com

---

HAPPY TUMMY NATURAL CHARCOAL CAPSULES

for • GAS • IBS • ACIDITY
• INDIGESTION • CROHN's
• ACID-REFLUX etc.

All stomach problems respond quickly!

0800 612 7496   finefettlefeed.com

Clothing & Bedding

'Underwear by Post' Since 1986

Also shirts, nightwear, socks, accessories.
Classic styles for Ladies and Gentlemen by
Hanro of Switzerland, Derek Rose, Grenouille, Mey, Pantherella, Jockey, HJ Hall, Brettles, Chilprufe, Sloggi, Triumph, Slenderella, Vedonis, Double Two, Viyella, Dents, Pyramid

Underwear by Jockey and Sloggi

Contact us for a free brochure of quality brands
Tel: 01942 674836, quoting OL
E-mail: sales@myerscough-jones.co.uk

Take a preview at www.myerscough-jones.co.uk

Underwear by Vedonis

An arch-support insole for
Diabetic, Arthritic and Painful Feet.

Stabilising heel cup
Biomechanical arch support
Non-friction, anti-blister top cover
Soft and cushioning material

'FootActive Sensi'
01963 33088
FootActive.co.uk